MW01515566

BLIND OBSESSION REBUTTAL

THE TRUTH IS NOW OR NEVER

My Peeps and True loved ones I am fuming today and the contents of this book will get racial and I will swear and for this I apologize and by no means is it a reflection of you but sometimes you have to let off some steam and I am venting because this I know is what God wants and he wants the truth to be known. If you have not read Blind Obsession please buy it and read it before proceeding with this book because this **_REBUTTAL_** and blasting is for this book and what was told to me by this **_man_**. **_I know God was protecting me on this day but I did not listen so in hindsight I got what I deserved hence in all that we do we must always listen to God and what he is showing us. Whether we want to accept it or not he does protect us from the devils and evils that lurk in the dark as well as reside around us._**

So as I get into this book I don't care what happens to me because I know God is with me and he protects me. Many will want to kill me and hurt my family and for this I leave them, my enemies in God's hands because I know God is more than capable and will deliver the blows and plots back to my enemies as well as keep my family safe from harm.

If you have read the book Blind Obsession you know what I mean and you would have gotten the over standing of this book. I make no apologies and will never make any for that book because God wanted this book to written and I am doing his work and not the work of man or men. As humans we need to see what we are doing to ourselves as well as to others. We need the truth as well as need to accept the truth because we cannot continue to live as the dead. We cannot continue to live as the dry bones of Elijah. The bible said Jesus was the first begotten of the dead and it is so correct because full comprehension will be given to those that don't know the truth and will solidify it for those that know and have the truth.

Until this day we live, eat, drink, sleep and worship as the dead. We even bow down to the dead. We need to change this. We cannot go around spreading hate and lies. Yes the media is there and they at times distort the truth but they have to account for that with God because every man is accountable for his or her own sins. This is true and right knowledge. There are two heavens.

Do we agree on this?

No, there is one you say and this is what the church and your family teaches. For many hell is here on earth as well as hell is in the spiritual domain or realm. There are two heavens and two hells but this depends on who you speak with.

No I am not going to distort what you know to be the truth because you only want to know about one heaven which is paradise but there are two paradises so continue to read and find out.

Do not throw the book out but go on and see. And stop saying I am on drugs and I don't know what I am talking about. Forget it do not get your bibles yet. Better yet if you want to get it go get it but do not open it just yet.

Stop it Sister Elaine and Sister Edna do not open it nor use it to rebuke me. Not yet anyway.

Now do you truly trust me not to deceive you?

Well I am not sure many things have been said and I've been taught about one paradise now you are saying something different. No I don't trust you.

This is what you are saying I know it because I would say the same thing if I was still in your position but know this THERE IS TWO PARADISE. I would never lie to you on this. Continue to read and tell me if I am correct. Find out the truth and do not give into the mind and just read the next sentence.

One is called Heaven for which some of us call Paradise and the other is called Hell.

Do you agree with me now?

Yes

Good because you believe this to be true but do not just believe know. Once you **_know_** you cannot be changed by anyone. Both places are beautiful and gorgeous *but in hell you will be tormented day and night. You will have no resting place and your* *spirit will be left to wonder and become a slave to the Man you gave yourself over to.*

Do you know this to be the truth?

Yes.

Then the question I pose to you now is HOW DO YOU KNOW THIS TO BE TRUE OR THE TRUTH?

My parents and pastor told me so plus the Bible, the Quran, Holy Books and Tablets state this so they cannot be a lie, these books are true and factual.

So you believe this to be the truth?

Yes.

These books cannot be wrong because they were divinely inspired.

Yes

This is your belief.

Yes

My Peeps and True Loved Ones you have read my other books do you *__believe__* this to be correct? If any of you say yes you *__believe__* I will be very angry and will tell you all off because **belief** is like the *branches and leafs of a tree* but __*KNOWLEDGE IS THE ROOT.*__

So therefore know not just believe.

Now I am sending you somewhere, do you trust me?

Yes.

Go to YouTube on your computer if the kids have it ask them to use it for five minutes or so.

Search for Madea's relationship advice, see and hear what Madea say about branches and leafs of a tree. Amazing isn't it. Keep this in your mind, never forget this because I will be using leafs, branches and roots throughout this book.

Thank you Tyler Perry for the knowledge you have bestowed upon us all.

Now search for Bob Marley's Redemption Song and listen to the lyrics. Listen when he said have no fair for atomic energy, listen when he tells you that they killed the prophets and we stand aside and look. Who comes to mind?

TELL ME SOMETHING WHAT BOOK DO WE NEED TO FULLFIL? WHAT DID HE SAY? "WON'T YOU HELP ME SING ANOTHER SONG OF FREEDOM BECAUSE ALL I EVER HAVE IS REDEMPTION SONG?

This was what God gave him. Redemption songs to teach the people and show the people but his people could not and did not comprehend. I don't even think his kids knew the scope of his righteousness. God gave him a task to do and he did it. He was given songs and he sang to educate and teach. This I know because his songs are right knowledge. ***LISTEN TO AMBUSH IN THE NIGHT. PULL IT UP AND LET IT EDUCATE YOU BECAUSE NOW YOU WILL TRULY KNOW.***

STOP IT I AM NOT TRYING TO HYPE HIM UP. I KNOW FOR A FACT THAT HE WAS A MESSENGER OF GOD, A MUSICAL MESSENGER. SO WAS MARCUS GARVEY HE WAS A MESSENGER BECAUSE HE WAS EDUCATING YOU ALL AND YOU HIS PEOPLE TURNED AGAINST HIM AS WELL AND IMPRISONED HIM BECAUSE NONE OF YOU WANTED TO HEAR THE TRUTH ABOUT HOW YOU ARE TO CONDUCT YOURSELF. HE DID EDUCATE YOU BUT ONCE AGAIN WE REFUSED HIM AND KEPT THE SLAVEMAN MENTALITY NOW WE ARE CRYING OT AND SCREAMING FOUL.

REMEMBER BOB SAID NOT MATTER HOW THEY KILL US GOD WILL CONTINUE TO SEND MESSENGERS SO THAT WE WILL LEARN AND BE FREE.

KNOW THIS WHATEVER YOU DO TO FLESH YOU CANNOT DO TO THE SPIRIT BECAUSE YOU CANNOT KILL THE SPIRIT NO ONE HAS THE AUTHORITY TO DO SO NOT EVEN GOD HIMSELF BECAUSE GOD DOES NOT KILL AND WILL NEVER KILL. GOD DOES NOT AND DO NOT DEAL IN DEATH.

THE WICKED KNOW THEIR TIME IS UP AND WILL BE UP BEFORE 2032 IF WE DO NOT

CHANGE OUR DIRTY WAYS. Do not go on a fear binge and start living in fear. Something is going to happen in 2032 but as to what no one knows. I cannot associate this with doom and gloom because I did not see doom and gloom. The time frame is too far. Maybe man will get a time extension again if we heed the warning signs of God and clean ourselves up. Or maybe the oil sands may totally dry up. Many things can happen this all depends on man and how he/she lives his life. 2032 is important to man – humanity and if humanity does not wake up then humanity will die because the earth is dying.

Please don't go there and say the bible says no man knows the hour or time. <u>True but then I am not a man but a woman and women are the true guardian's of this earth and universe not man. Our menstrual cycle reflect this. Remember this nursery rhyme "hey diddle diddle the cat and the fiddle, the cow jumped over the moon the little dog spot to see him run and the dish ran away with the spoon.</u>

What the hell do you think it meant. Men will always jump over the moon and misguide because they do not have a period so they will never be able to tell time. Men will never comprehend time nor will they comprehend the fact that our cycle changes with the moon. Men represent the cat. Remember the jingle he's a fast cat, look at the cat he's so fine. Men cannot comprehend the scope of a woman's menstrual cycle why the hell do you think they run. Run away with the spoon – they find another woman.

Far fetched and hard to believe in your book or your sense. Well I don't believe I know.

Ask your husband if he comprehends the scope of your menstrual cycle. Does he know what you have to go through every twenty eight days? Ladies I know the cycle can come every twenty seven or thirty days. It changes but the true rotation is twenty eight give or take a day depending on the rotation of the earth with respect to the moon.

Mr. and Ms. Scientist this is my logic so please do not go off. You can give perfect logic and explanation so please correct me where I am incorrect and please do not blast me because the scope of your scientific knowledge is far beyond mine, this is why God made you a Scientists and certainly not me.

Go ahead ask your hubby or boyfriend what he knows. I bet if he is not a doctor he will not be able to tell you and no matter if he is a doctor, all he would be able to give you is text book answers, what he was taught in school.

Mr. Doctor I am not trying to knock you but before you learnt this some of you did not truly know. Be truly honest with me.

Now My Peeps and True Loved Ones take a look at your calendar. What is the truest month?

If you said February take a bow.

Forget about the leap year because that comes every four years.

So no matter how much we try to hide the truth God will lead you to the truth somehow.

Yes I know many of you know this.

I know many of you know that there are 13 months to a year but because the Babylonians and their evil empire fear the number 13 they deemed it to be bad luck therefore changing the yearly calendar to reflect 12 instead of 13. They thought they could change time but no one can change time because time is ingrained in us. The truth of 13 must come out in the physical because 13 is in time and is represented by time – God. 13 cannot be broken down but 12 can be broken down because 12 represent 4 and 12 represents 3 in their book but do not be deceived by this. 12 represent ½ of 24 which are the 24 hours of sin. The 24 also represent the 24 sons born unto evil at various periods in time which are the 12 sons of Ishmael and the 12 sons of Canaan and yes this is why the bible talks about the 24 elders in Revelations. Some buildings even exclude 13 which is ludicrous. Why not just take it out of the numerical chart all together. This so does not make sense because when a normal person counts the floors they count thirteen.

Weird

God gave us 364 days to work and do our labour but on the 365th day we are to give him thanks and praise.

Ben 364 divided by 28 equals 13 exactly, no remainders no anything. That one day that is left is for God himself. You are to praise him and give him true thanks for all that he has done for you. The 13th month which is December is a holy month. It also feels holy too.

Stop Ben God has done a lot for you. You have life, you have hope but instead of having hope have faith. Trust God, not just say it truly trust God to see you through. I did and here I am talking to you.

It will not be easy, shit it is friging hard. Sometimes you want to give up, wish you were dead, you want to lash out at God.

Yeah you say. You want him to feel what you feel.

So go ahead lash out at God. I am telling you to do it. God will not sin you for this. Trust me on it. Lash out at him. Sit in your bed, in your chair and think of him and tell him how you feel. Let God comprehend. Let him know what you are going through.

No I can't you're saying because pastor said it is wrong. You have to respect God. He is the maker of all. You can't get angry at God but you can. You are not disrespecting God because you are going to him in truth.

Stop, and hear what I am telling you Ben. Lash out at God. Do not hesitate. If you feel he's unfair tell him he's unfair, if you are feeling pain tell him, whatever emotion you feel let God know. Tell him he's a liar, a cheat, he's no good because this is the way you feel. Come on sit in your bed, chair, around the kitchen table, think of him and in your mind, tell him and let the emotion flow. Trust me

God will not sin you for this. I would never deceive or lie to you because this I KNOW.

You know why Ben?

Baby I know you are hurting as well as crying.

I am crying for you, I feel your pain too and I have asked God to bless you and show you the way. Dry your tears and smile. For all of you in Ben's situation I ask God to bless you all as well as show you the way.

I was there too. Do not think that I don't know, I know. The pain is hard, trusting is hard, you lose your way, you lose your faith because no one can help you. I know it and said it but KNOW that GOD is there *and what Man cannot fix God will fix it for you. He can and will fix it for you. Give it time. Give God time.*

So Ben tell him and if you feel like lashing out lash out. Do you know why I tell you this?

No

Because you are not going to man with your troubles you are going directly to God. He is the perfect fixer and healer. This is what God need. He needs you and me, everyone to come to him with our troubles. He also need you to have faith and trust in him to fix your problems.

Guess what too when you do this what I tell you to do you are on your way. You have just made your first step towards having a true relationship with God.

Do not listen to people listen to God and what he God is telling you. Trust him to give you the answers you need because man can give you the wrong answers but God will never give you wrong answers.

As for me if I gave you wrong information I would be misleading you and would not have what.

Truly Loved God.

Hey Ben God is going to answer you and when he does, you will cry tears of JOY. Give God thanks. Do you hear me Ben? Listen to me GIVE GOD THANKS.

Sometimes for the hell of it lift your right hand in the air and for no reason at all just say Father, or God or My Boo or My True Love THANK YOU.

Come on you say and say I am weird

I mean it Ben. Say God for the hell of it, I have no reason at all, don't want or need anything in return all I want to say is THANK YOU truly thank you. Put a smile on your face. People will wonder why you are smiling or think you weird but you are not weird you are having time with God.

If you don't trust me, just try it.

Forget the I don't know; forget the doubts because you know God would rather you come to him with your problems first rather than you going to others. Trust me he will put the words of comfort in a strangers mouth, you will hear a song on the radio that soothes, someone you have never talked to for years suddenly call you out of the blue and you will light up brighter than the sun.

When you go to God with all your troubles let him know how you feel. If you are angry let him know. Tell him you are angry and this so and so is pissing you off and you can't take it anymore. Never be *fake* with God. Never ever ever ever infinitely never ever be *fake* with God because the truth never disrespect and can never disrespect. In so doing if you do something wrong let him know. Do not hide the truth. Tell him you did wrong and ask him for forgiveness. When God does forgive you try not to do it again.

Trust me when you start to have a true relationship with God the love just flows and yes you will want to call him your Boo, your sunshine. Trust me on that because I do. I am not disrespecting him just loving him even more.

So for all you haters out there forget it because a lot of you call your loved ones Apple Dumpling, My Pet, My Sugarplum.

So Ben trust me and if you don't want to it's okay. I said try it but you know what before you do, ask God if you can if you are in doubt. Ask him if you can get mad at him because you were taught by your pastors and priests and imams otherwise.

Forget the laughs homeboy. Hell no, let me spell it out for you ABSOLUTELY no way can you call God, My G, My dog, Big G, the Big God, The Big Dog, Big Fish whatever slang you use. This is plain out disrespectful and sinful do you hear me.

You cannot go to God and say Yow Big G hell to the fucking NO disrespect, disrespect, disrespect. When the emotion overflows your body mind and spirit become different. It's as if it is filled with this energy that you of yourself can't explain.

Everything wells up from the stomach to the navel. The emotion is so overwhelming that you cry sometimes. You are so in touch with God that you want to call him your Boo, your Bunnononus, My Love. The relationship is now personal, you are happy being personal with God. You are comfortable with him but never take him for granted Ben because just as how you truly love him and he truly loves you and he does punish. When I say punish I do not mean literally punish you. If he tells you to stay on his path and continue working, do it. ***Do not leave for any one because the day you leave you will fall.*** So if God said sing me a song continue to sing songs for him but do it honestly, with pure and true love and never hate. Do not tell others to hate because if you do you will regret it. God's punishment comes in if you stray. When you stray God will leave you and give you over to what or who you left him for. Meaning God will walk away from you and he does trust me on that. Therefore your fall becomes your punishment and this is why I say God punishes but know that God infinitely do not punish he would rather walk away than to punish and this is what he does like I said.

God infinitely does not punish anyone know this and keep this knowledge at all times.

When he elevates you from one status to the next, never turn your back on him, or give into the follies of the world because you will regret it. Trust me many have fallen and lost the respect of God because they fell into the traps laid out by evil. Yes there are many Delilah's out there be careful of them and that you do not become their next victim.

Do not have affairs or you will regret it because all too often we do and disrespect God. Stay true to him. It will be hard because evil is stronger than good meaning on this the physical plain it will draw you in but stay strong. ***Ask God to never let you stray but stay humble and true to him.*** Never forget that evil pulls. It's that pulling force that pulls you towards it. It's that pulling force we learnt about in basic science but with evil the pull is stronger. Yes stronger than the pull of a magnet. It is that powerful and strong.

One way to combat evil is to ask God to make everything that is evil and sinful be abominable in your sight. Yes you can ask him to make the children of sin be abominable in thy sight – meaning your sight and trust me God will do this.

Like I said evil is powerful because of the great pull it has. When you ask God for these things evil cannot control you nor can it conquer or dominate you. Evil cannot fool you when you do this.

Don't ever think evil will not continue to try. Evil will continue to try because we are living in an evil system meaning the earth is dominated by evil hence the constant fighting and abominable acts of sins we commit on a daily basis.

Don't say what's the sense of doing this? When you do this you are separating yourself from evil and trust me you won't want to live amongst them – evil. You will pray to God to find you a clean place, an island or country somewhere where you do not have deal with evil and his wicked and deceitful people. Trust me infinitely when I tell you you will yearn for this and bug God from time to time for this.

Many things will come your way women will all of a sudden see you and become interested in you but they don't truly love you. They want what you have. If you have a mate at home and he or she encourages you stick with her or him. Tell her or him not to change or live for the fame but continue to live and be true to God.

When the relationship feels like it is going downhill talk to God, hey make her take those bellying dancing classes, those hip hop classes, relaxation classes and use them in *your bedroom, do not go outside of your relationship for pleasure, it is a sin, a big no, no. Your mate is whom God has given you so respect God. If these are not appealing, take a cruise, go to Scotland, Jamaica, Russia, Spain, China, St. Vincent, The Netherlands wherever go with her and the family.* If you don't have money to do these things, go for a picnic in the back yard, on your balcony, in the living room and make it romantic. Cuddle up to her read a book with her in bed but do things the ***both*** of you enjoy.

Now that I have strayed off topic and will stray off topic to give you knowledge, know that the truth does not lie. If I give you lies I would be going against God and would not truly love you nor would I truly love God.

Yes you can blast me and say I am an idiot I'm grabbing at straws and I'm the Anti-Christ, the devil whatever but the fact is NO ONE CAN KILL THE TRUTH NOR WILL THEY BE ABLE TO KILL GOD BECAUSE GOD IS THE TRUTH AND HE RESIDE IN US ALL. SO NO MATTER THE HEATHES RAGE. GOD WILL FOREVER STAND AND EXIST. LISTEN TO THE HEATHEN BY BOB MARLEY. HE TOLD YOU.

HE IS BLESSED BECAUSE HE DID HIS JOB AND HE IS RESTING IN PEACE. I KNOW THIS. I KNOW HE IS IN THE LANDS OF HIS FORE FATHERS RESTING WITH GOD'S ANGELS UNTIL THE APPOINTED TIME. THIS I KNOW BECAUSE GOD HAS SHOWN ME AND NO ONE NOT EVEN HIS KIDS CAN TAKE THIS FROM ME ***BECAUSE KNOWLEDGE GIVEN BY GOD CANNOT BE TAKEN FROM YOU BY ANY MAN, WOMAN OR CHILD. YOU ARE SEALED WITH IT BY GOD AND NOT MAN.***

PETER TOSH I DID NOT FORGET YOU AND WILL NEVER FORGET YOU BECAUSE ***RASTAFARI IS*** AND WILL FOREVER BE. I KNOW YOU AND THE POWER GIVEN TO YOU BECAUSE YOU WERE THE

MELCHEZSIDEC (not to be associated with Melchezsidec of the bible) OF OUR TIME. MANY DID NOT KNOW YOU BECAUSE YOU DID NOT COME TO BASK IN THE GLORY OF MAN BUT TO GUIDE AND HELP YOUR SON. SHOW HIM THE GLORY THAT CAN BE ATTAINED, SHOW HIM THE GLORY OF GOD, THE POWER WITHIN YOU. YOU PROTECTED BECAUSE I KNOW THE MEANING OF "CHANCES ARE" BUT WE HAVE TO CARRY ON. YOU WORE THE GARB OF HONOUR YOU GAVE TWO COLOURS AND I KNOW WHAT THE FINAL COLOUR IS. IT WAS GIVEN TO MORGAN HERITAGE BECAUSE THEY WERE ON THE RIGHT TRACK BUT LIKE OUR MOTHERS IN THE GARDEN OF EDEN WE WERE LED ASTRAY AND STILL BEING LED ASTRAY. UNTIL THEY KNOW THE FINAL COLOUR AND START WEARING IT, GOING BACK TO THEIR ROOTS THEN I WILL SAY THANK YOU FATHER THEY ARE HOME AGAIN. HOME AT LAST.

MORGAN HERITAGE YOU CANNOT SING ABOUT ONE BINGI, COMFORTER, MORE TEACHINGS, CHANT WE A GO CHANT, AFRICA HERE WE COME AND NOT REPRESENT. YOU WANT TO REPRESENT PETER TOSH REPRESENT BECAUSE HE IS SITTING AT THE HEAD OF THE TABLE, MEANING HE WAS THE HEAD AND BOB MARLEY WAS THE STUDENT, ***THE SON***. HE HAD TO GIVE THE MESSAGE. REMEMBER MOSES WAS NOT AN ELOQUENT SPEAKER AARON WAS SO AARON SPOKE FOR MOSES. HE HAD TO CARRY ON AND RASTA'S YOU

CAN DISPUTE THIS IF YOU WANT TO BUT YOU CANNOT DESTROY THE TRUTH BECAUSE ***RASTAFARI IS*** AND WILL FOREVER BE. So Morgan Heritage if you are representing wear the right colours and get back on track because you are all off. *BRING YOUTUBE UP AND WATCH PETER TOSH TEACH THE TRUTH. YOU CANNOT DISPUTE HIM AND CANNOT DISPUTE THE TRUTH. So don't represent if you cannot. Either you get back on track or continue to stay the hell off. Continue to be apart of the PAGAN DRED yes Pagan Dread, those dreadful assholes that wear the turban, eat pork, defile their queens and kings for what the dollar bill. These Pagan Dreads that wear the crown of glory and defile it each and every day.*

Jamaicans you are a bunch of fools, you are apart of the children of God. You were in the enclosed garden, the angels of God walks upon your land, the House of God is ready to descend upon your land but yet you continue to defile the land. Clean your damned self up because if you don't you will be owe so sorry because what you sow will be what you reap. ***Stop sowing the bread of sorrow because you will eat it as well as reap it. You are not going to be warned again.*** God is being patient but he can only be patient for so long. Stop the looting, the killing and raping. Stop being like the children of the outside garden and reclaim your heritage and become the children of God once again. What is happening to you now will only get worse and when it does do not halla and ball because sey unno get warning and refuse to listen. Playing stubborn, keep it up. ***Now unno will noa when ole people sey if drangcrow did noa how im backside tan im***

wouldn't swallow abay seed. So unnu betta know how unnu backside tan and know that if you don't stop and change your dirty ways ***fiya a go dey a muss muss tail and unnu tink a cool breeze.*** Stop being like the children of Judah and Israel and stop worshipping false gods and idols. ***This is why you can't be better, never going to be better if you don't repent and redeem yourselves***. What does the motto say ***"OUT OF MANY ONE PEOPLE"*** but yet you cannot represent nor can you comprehend the motto.

You are all nothing but a bunch of liars and deceivers; branches and leafs because the truth is coming out of your land, not MOTHER AFRICA. OUT OF JA MAI CA and you all distort it, refuse it. What the hell are you telling God? Are you telling him thanks but no thanks? Are you telling him Bob Marley, Peter Tosh, Marcus Garvey, Paul Bogle, Nanny, all these people means nothing. We are making it on our own. The idols we praise and worship suits you just fine.

Stop laughing Jack, you too Joe because you are included in this. Say it, so I can tell you fuck you. It does not matter if you are White, Black or Chinese you are apart of this family. So say it, come on say it damned right shut the hell up. I WILL SAY IT AGAIN AND SAY IT OVER AND OVER I do not truly love you for the colour of your skin, your hair, your eye colour because the flesh, the skin is BULLSHIT. It means nothing because it is eaten by worms when the flesh dies. The only thing that is left is the bones, the prison that houses us the spirit. The bones keep the spirit from escaping and becoming free. The bones are the true you meaning our physical prison here on earth and all of us have bones therefore none of us are different except for genetics. Your damned DNA and some other bullshit scientists throw in there to make us different. In heaven/paradise there is no damned colour. There is no race and that race, no this tribe and that tribe. None is going to go to the North, South, East or West because we are all one in the sight of God. Know this. Jamaica is a reference because God is showing you that all races can live as one if we come together as one and stop the bullshit we are carrying on with. Just read the motto "Out of Many One People." In the eyes of God we are one people – his people – his children.

TELL ME SOMETHING, EACH AND EVERY ONE OF YOU WHICH HEAVEN, WHICH PARADISE ARE YOU GOING TO GO TO? COME ON TELL ME. GOD'S PARADISE. DO YOU EVEN KNOW WHERE PARADISE OR HEAVEN IS?

In heaven

Where is it?

Where is heaven?

With God

Where is God?

Come on answer and don't give me no or some bullshit answer like God is everywhere. Plain out truth is none of you know. I don't even know where heaven is but I know where God is.

God resides in me and you. He is TRUE LOVE, the true love inside of you that has put down hate, vanity, destruction and lies. TRUE LOVE does not hurt nor does it kill. I do not hate anyone and if I come off as being racial and or racist My Peeps and True Loved Ones accept my deepest and humblest apologies. I do not mean to.

So if you are a part of God's roots stay truthful to God. Stay righteous. Don't let me or anyone knock you off because that is just not right. It is a sin and it is not fair to God. The road is rough but stay on it. I don't care how hard it gets stay on the path of God. If I am lying to you God will show you. ***Trust me he will tell you and if God or his angels don't tell you when I am lying trust me I will be pissed.***

You all know me. I am not here to steal souls or throw people off God's true path. I will never do that because I've lived through most of my life in pain and suffering and now I know the truth and no one not even you My Peeps and True Loved Ones will throw me off. You will rock me and make me cry but ***when you make me cry woe be unto you. If you hurt me woe be unto you because your sorrows will be greatly multiplied. I know this because I have seen it that is why I leave my enemies to God.***

It is not to say if I am hurting you you can't tell me I am hurting you. You can. Like I've said this is a family, a true family, God's family, the chosen that your bible talks about.

Know this ***God only chooses a few to speak for him***. That is why it is said, "Many are called but the chosen are few." And by no means think that God cannot speak for himself because he can and do speak. So you can come with your Bibles, Qurans, Holy Water, Holy Books, Holy Text but they mean nothing because they ***are words of MEN and not WORDS OF GOD.***

When God is teaching you there is not doubt in his words, no beliefs or tales just knowledge. God does not use books of men to teach or mislead you he himself will teach you and show you the way. He puts the words in your mouth too and this is not done in the physical it is done in the spiritual realm beforehand. I hope I have explained this correctly and not confuse you. If I have let me know. You cannot just write and say you are divinely inspired that is bullshit. You cannot do for God unless God tells you to do for him and it is not all of us God tell to do.

What God gives you it is well given and no one can take it unless you give it up. You of yourself leave the fold of God and that is what the children of God did. They saw the men that resided outside the enclosed garden and because there skin was not as fair as theirs but darker than theirs they fell inlove and lay with them, had children with them.

*I know some of you are saying bullshit you are a liar, I hate you this is not true. Read genesis. Who were the people of Nod and where the hell did they come from? You are all intelligent beings use your damned common sense. Writers write and for the sake of writing. We grip you and we will confuse the hell out of you or use words and text to make you believe. **I repeat believe** and like a damned fool we* *believe. Yes I am included in this too but like I've said when God teaches you there is no lies, no doubt; no deception. All you will find is the truth so I cannot hate you for the way you look but I will hate you for the lies you tell as well as the hurt you inflict because **lies hurt.***

I know I am not supposed to hate. But I hate lies that people tell. I know My Peeps leave it to God and let God handle it but it does hurt especially listening to people say they love God and are leafs and branches in his life, killing God and not knowing that they are killing themselves. It is not to say I have not lied to save my ass, I have. Like you I do things that is not of God and yes I regret it and tell God to help me to walk in his truth. I ask him to take lying from my lips. Hey I didn`t just get here, this does not happen overnight it takes time. So to say yes I am going to fully tell the truth from this day forward good luck because it is not gonna happen instantaneously. Trust me on that.

In this family, there is no suffering or pain. If you want to hurt me then you would not have truly loved me. I will lose many over the course of time but you know what GOD IS WEEDING OUT THE BRANCHES AND THE LEAFS AND LEAVING THE ROOTS – HIS PEOPLE. GOD'S PEOPLE MUST GROW FROM THE ROOTS UP BECAUSE HE GOD HAS PLANTED THE SEEDS ALREADY. HIS SEEDS ARE GOOD AND PURE AND IT IS OUT OF THIS PURITY THAT WE MUST GROW.

So Joe, Brad and Frank, yes you Yaniska from Russia, LaToya you too, Mary, Ste as in Stefanie if you want to exclude yourself I cannot stop you. But I truly love you. Yes Joe and Tyler from Texas I see you waving your hands, hugs and kisses. Hey if I ever get to Texas for a day we so have to go fishing if not sit with our feet in the water and you had better tell me about how your farm is doing and what you are doing for God. Sarah Jane you can show me how to make a delicious apple fritter or pie. Is this a date guys. Yes. Good. Remember all organic and you all bess be happy to see me. Sarah Jane I know the guy down the road likes you but hubby is it. We will so talk.

Back on track, I don't know where our final home is. I have seen the Crystal City this beautiful city made of pure crystals. I have seen what heaven and hell looks like but God never showed me where his home is meaning the plain where he resides. One day he will. One day I know he will show me where his home is – yes his spiritual plain. When he grants me this privilege because it is a privilege I hope he gives me the permission to tell you.

Jamaica you are the only nation that was born under God and the lot of you are raping and killing each other, as well as disrespecting the name of God. Not one of you know the meaning of Jamaica because if you all did the bullshit that you are carrying on with you would no longer do it. Before I go on and tell you about the meaning and importance of your name let me tell you something "HELL IS FULL OF BLACK PEOPLE" right now as a modify this book and write these lines I am telling you that "HELL IS FULL OF BLACK PEOPLE". If you don't know now you know and trust me I did not rescue any of you I just walked out because we gave ourselves over to evil and refuse to put away evil things. Remember I told God I would close my mouth – shut it up if I saw his angels again, no that was in another book where I said I would close my mouth so no you cannot remember because this book was written long before that book and I am modifying this book because it contained mistakes – errors and no matter how I try not to correct them I have to. Yes you will find mistakes but those are the ones I cannot see or find so please help me to correct my mistakes. And yes I infinitely truly thank you my family – my true family. Yes Jamaica I was given another opportunity to save you but I shut my mouth I just walked out of hell without saving any of you. Like I've said and will forever say I want Jamaica to feel it like no other because we have brought shame and disgrace to God each and every day. I am not going to take myself out of this because I too am Jamaican and like you I have caused God shame and disgrace. I am still making mistakes but over time I will become truly perfect in God's eyes. Yes I want him to look down and cry tears of joy by saying you see that nut job Michelle she is true and I truly love her that is why she has a special place in my heart. She is my physical and spiritual defended. She is no nonsense and it's either you like her or you hate her but with me I truly infinitely truly love her because she tells me like it is and she also tell you like it is. Like I said I will not cry out Judgment even though my spirit compels me to do it. Like I said I leave it to the elders di Mada dem to cry out judgment because when they do destruction cometh like a thief in the night because like I said hell is fulla black people. I can't even tell you the names on the headstones –gravestones because like I said I left. Like I've told you in my other books I refuse to piss off God and his angels because of you. Oh man you don't know the grave sins you have committed in the sight of God and now you've allowed all facets of abomination to sin to sing to you. You have artists glorifying the devil and paying homage to the devil. We have polluted the music God has given to us. We are allowing our children to listen to these artists; we are allowing our children to buy their music and clothes and this is wrong because we are giving away our blessings. We are giving them – evil our souls and this is wrong. Infinitely wrong because like I've said and will infinitely tell "THE LIFE YOU LIVE IN THE LIVING DETERMINES WHERE YOU GO IN DEATH." And infinitely yes you are giving evil the victory over God. Let me tell you something you no mek mi show unnu. If you have one of those big old time bibles find the picture of fire coming raining down on the people and how they outstretched their hands to God and God was not there to save them. When you find the picture know – infinitely know that those people are you. Now let me tell you. ***Ja means God***. ***Jamaica stands for God made me***. *You are the children of God, the ones to be taken away to foreign lands and instead of living for God, acting like God's children you defile yourselves each and every day. None of you truly love God or respect God because if you all did.* ***Ja Maica – God made me***, *Jamaica would not be in such disarray. Truly love your damned selves and represent God instead of showing the world the Pagan's you are.* Redeem your damned selves ***and repent, live for God because he did not forget about you. He kept you safe. Put away idol worship, man worship and live. Stop walking and living like the living dead.***

Rasta's you know better but yet you of yourselves have let Pagan demonize you. Let Pagan that cannot live like you, praise like you represent you.

I DON'T CARE IF YOU HATE ME, SAY I AM A CRACK POT, A DECEIVER ALL I KNOW IS GOD DOES NOT LIE AND IF I DON'T TELL IT SOMEONE ELSE WILL COME AND TELL IT.

So know and test the spirit. There is physical wickedness as well as spiritual wickedness. Spiritual wickedness reside in their paradise which we call hell, they wonder and these wondering spirits are the ones that make your life a living nightmare in the physical. They are the spiritual wickedness in high and low places that your Pastor or Preacher so talk about in church. Are we agreed? Yes. Good because now you have right knowledge the absolute truth that cannot be disputed.

Before I go on, I don't claim to be and will never claim to be a saint or a prophetess or whatever, nor do I want to be associated or given names such as these. Like I've said my books are controversial, they will cause people to hate me, call me a bitch, the Anti-Christ, a demon, Satan, the devil, an atheist, a false prophet, many will want to lynch my ass amongst other things. Rest assured again I never claimed to be and never will claim to be but one thing is for sure I TRULY LOVE GOD AND THIS CANNOT BE TAKEN FROM ME NO MATTER WHAT YOU DO TO ME. I WILL DIE TRULY LOVING AND DEFENDING GOD. I WILL DIE IN GOD'S HONOUR NOT THE HONOUR OF MAN BUT IN THE HONOUR OF GOD. SO I WILL DEFEND GOD and no I will not use books of men to do so. No that's not true because I will send you to your book of sin because that's all you know. I will let God continue to guide me so that everyone can put the pieces together and truly go back to GOD'S WAY OF LIFE.

If I have not clarified something do no be afraid to tell me. Ask God to clarify it for you because I write and sometimes you will get the meaning but my words may confuse you and it is not my intention. God will correct my mistakes because you all know *I have no editor or ghost writer nor do I want any.* You will find typos, verb confusions because I write like I speak as well as write the way the words are flowing down to me.

You my Peeps and True Loved Ones are my editor. I know Frank you are spending a lot of money but you are here with me. Teach me about sentence structure. We are a family here and I truly love my family but do not come here to hurt me, or abuse me or tell lies on me, nor try to set me up. This is not what God's family is all about. If you cannot truly love me then you have no place here and no by means no the prodigal son cannot return home. No you cannot if you leave the path of God and his fold because in truth if you are true to God you cannot leave nor will you want to leave. Yes you will get angry and tell God you want to leave and this is okay because you are angry. Trust me once you are calmed down you will say ``you know God I didn't mean what I said about leaving your fold but I was angry.`` Trust me you will get the answers you are looking for if not at that instant or during the day, the next morning you will.

Remember when Adam and Eve got kicked out of the garden did Got let them back in. No. When the door of the Ark was closed what did the people do when the water (s) came. Could Noah open the door and let them in after God had sealed it. No. Sodom and Gomorrah how many were saved even though Abraham tested God and begged for the people. The Red Sea how many of Pharaoh's men were saved? Mu and Atlantis where is that civilization today? Do you see where I am going with this? Do not be like these people. Know the truth and live for God because no one can save you but you yourself. No one can save me but me myself.

No Jamaica I am not boosting you up but know this no matter all that man do to distort the truth God will leave the truth where he wants it to be so that the ones to tell the truth are reminded and all the doors that were sealed will now be open. So for all that say Jesus can and he will save me on the final day. The Day of Judgment.

I am telling you this Jesus will not and cannot save you on the final day. You are accountable for your own sins. You are the one to save yourself.

- Oh close your mouth and stop saying you rebuke me in the name of Jesus.
- Stop saying I am Satan and Lucifer incarnated.
- Stop it you cannot pray for me because *I know no good prayer can come* from the mind and mouth of filthy and deceitful people

- No my soul don't need saving because it is intact. God has my life because I am married to him God who is life- I truly gave my life to God and anyone that truly gives their life to God – Life they are married to Life - God. This I infinitely know and you can't change this knowledge
- Do not call a bitch either
- No my soul will not burn in hell either because there is no fire in hell not the fire you know of anyway. Hell fire is different from the fire of the sun. It is also different from the fire you are accustomed to.
- How dare you
- You are the evil one
- The false prophet
- The Anti-Christ
- A liar and deceiver

I know them all been called the devil too.

Continue

Finished

Not yet
{

Keep venting I am giving you time. The brackets represent time.

}

Done now

Yes

Good

Now think and truly think without prejudice. Forget about what preachers and imams and rabbis have taught you. Use your own common sense. I am not down playing your intelligence. I've told you when God educates you you are well educated.

PLEASE STOP BECAUSE I AM NOT SAYING I AM GOD BECAUSE I KNOW YOU HATERS WILL USE THIS TO TRY AND SCREW ME *BECAUSE ALL YOU HAVE IS BOOK SENSE AND NOT GOD SENSE.*

YOU CAN RECITE THE BIBLE AND HOLY BOOKS FROM HERE TO THE END OF ETERNITY AND ETERNITY HAVE NO END PEOPLE BUT NONE HAVE YET TO SAVE THE LOT OF YOU.

CHECK FROM THE BEGINNING UNTIL NOW.

FORGET IT BECAUSE I KNOW THE BIBLE WAS WRITTEN TO KEEP US IGNORANT AND ENSLAVED IN MENTAL, PHYSICAL AND SPIRITUAL BONDAGE FOR ALL ETERNITY.

Say it go on say it I can wait.

Say it I have just blasphemed.

Now close your mouth.

Did Moses use books to teach?

32

Did any of God's messengers use books of men to teach?

God told them what to say. Put the words in their mouths meaning God showed them what to do. What to eat; wear and drink including whom to marry. If you don't believe that's your problem because all you have are beliefs. Know and set yourself free. Read your damned bible and get full comprehension of it, full comprehension of the greatest lie that was ever told and the biggest and greatest book of lies that was ever written hence it is known as the book of sin in the spiritual world and it is because it is filled with lies – sin hence we die for it – die for sin and die in sin.

- Once God's door is closed you cannot get in.
- The door is sealed and will stay sealed and if you read the story of Noah you would know this
- You will never get in no matter how hard you try because you rejected God – you rejected life
- Forget it Mama and Granny can't either (save you that is)
- No not even daddy
- No one will
- Remember Noah's Ark of your bible
- Peter Tosh and Bob Marley told you, showed you
- Marcus Garvey educated you
- But yet we are still holding on to lies
- Expecting lies to save us

- You have to repent and redeem yourself in the physical and the spiritual
- You have to take back your souls
- If you don't live right, talk right, walk right in the physical you cannot live right, talk right, walk right in the afterlife or spiritual world
- You have to accept the truth in the physical and if you don't that's it
- God is not just Male he is Female as well
- Heaven
- Paradise is a holy place
- It is not filthy
- Nor is it dirty
- And if you are filthy you cannot get there

Stop gasping when I said God is both Male and Female because he is. He is also nature, the air we breathe, the water we drink but yet pollute. God is the breath of Life and no one can dispute this. Go ahead and try and I will point you directly to Revelations in your bible.

Pastor's stop it because the Psalms you so preciously read tells you this. My Peeps read Psalms 48 verse 3. I will not quote the verse because I want you to read it yourself. And any English Scholar can dispute this and say I am reading it out of context. My son did. So that verse can be debated.

I am not distorting your belief and will never distort it. For some it will mean nothing and others will say it is a typo to justify their belief or come up with something to say otherwise. But know for a fact that

God is both. Females are XX Males are XY. Females are the dominant force from a physical and spiritual perspective because we cannot change and never will change but Males can change. They are a part of us and this have to do with evil.

Males stop gasping because we are three and you are one so in this sense females are the dominant force and as you read further you will get full comprehension because this has to do with the spiritual world – evil. This is also where you get 3 in 1 – the Trinity.

XX   XY   Cool so far now look
XXX   Y   Get it
No

XX   XY
Take the X from the XY

Now you have XXX and Y

There will always be 3X to 1Y or 3XY simplified and this is not based on good but based on evil.

Yes it's mathematics because mathematics plays a significant role in creation as the higher heads call it the science of creation.

This is what you call the trinity and this is why you say God is three in one. Trinity explained. Simple isn't it and so is God. But God is not three in one, could never be and never will be. He is not alone nor will he ever be alone. <u>The God you were taught to worship and give homage to is alone.</u> He *is the 3 in 1 but everyone knows you cannot have 3 in 1 you can only have triplets. So therefore the triplets – trinity – 3 in one refer to the 3 daughters of Eve – yes sin. Death – the god of death or Satan as you call him – the god that you bow down to requires as well as need worship and praise to feed his narcissistic nature. The true and living God does not because he is not dead. He is alive and will forever be alive. Now we know this to be fact right.*

To take it further there are four plains that man know of based on what we have been taught.

NO

TWO

There is FOUR

The four are as we know it in simple terms are:

Earth   physical
Heaven/Hell   spiritual   both   these plains are side by side and you can see from one to the other but in this realm those that are in hell cannot cross over to heaven –heaven is a resting place, a place of peace and the inhabitants of heaven cannot cross over to hell in this realm while in this resting state. (This can be debated but I will explain and clarify later once you have higher learning.)

Are we agreed?

Yes

Good now you have right knowledge and the truth. This truth cannot change.

Heaven is a place where there is no war, hatred, crime, or pollutants. Know this to be true because it is true.

In hell there is fighting, war, hatred, sin, abomination of sins so get rid of beliefs because beliefs are like the leafs and branches of a tree. They blow away and whither but the root can never go away. You can uproot it but once you replant it the roots will grow.

You have the two that preachers teach you in church. The other two are:

The realm of the angels – this is number 3
The realm of God – this is number 4

The first three are your XXX
Number four is your Y

Therefore these are your 4 and this is how it is represented by Man but there is significantly more. Representing the planes in this text is infinitely incorrect. It is not right but wrong. The reference above is to open your eyes based on what you have been taught in Islam and in some cases Christianity. Now sit back and relax for solid comprehension. If I have confused you I do apologize it is not my intention.

For you that know and those of you that are using the 4 analogy based on what you have been taught

I will also confirm the four also represent 4 races, four rivers, four corners of the universe. This is the four that you know of the XXXY (3XY) and the races and I will tell you that this correlation to the square is wrong. Infinitely incorrect and you cannot correlate the square in this way.

Like I've said and will say the truth must not be known because if it is known then evil will die. Truth is the beginning of the death of evil – negative energy and forces that surrounds you and your family.

Truth is the beginning of the end of lies and the demons that torment you at night

Truth is the beginning of the end for all evil domains on land as well as in the spiritual realm.

Know this to be the infinite truth. The 3xy analogy has nothing to do with God and the domain of God it has to do with the devil and his dwelling in the spiritual realm.

3XY represent the three (3) females of sin in the spiritual world and the Y represents their father who we call the devil. Satan as you call him had three (3) females meaning Satan had three (3) daughters but the bible represents them as being good. These females are your father, son and holy ghost analogy in Christianity and this I will clarify later as I move forward. This is your father and mother analogy also and yes I will clarify this later maybe not in this book but in another book if I don't get to the clarification within this book. I will also explain how Cain fits into this analogy as well. Each female has a 6 on their forehead as this is why the bible uses 666. 666 represents the three females and this is why we say evil has six thousand six hundred and six years to do evil but this is a lie, an infinite lie. Each one has 6 thousand years to do damage upon the land hence they have 18000 thousand years in total and that is just three sides of the square. Satan himself also have 6 thousand years that is a total of 24000 years hence you have your 24 hour clock, yes your 24 hour day and yes my peeps and true loved ones this is infinite and true knowledge hence they say God created things in one day which is a thousand years. Now the knowledge of the square is complete and no man or spirit can dispute this because they don't know this. You can also correlate the square to night and day as well as the Blue and White Nile.

To say God created in one day based on physical time is an infinite lie because man does not know the difference between spiritual time and physical time. Spiritual time varies and this variation you need to know. You need to know how to tell spiritual time and this is very complex. It is not easy to tell.

Preachers stop fuming. Like I've said and will forever state when God educate you, educate his people it is never wrong and can never be wrong.

We cannot under any circumstances use the knowledge of God to deceive and spread lies. This is not fair to people and it is so not fair to God. He does hurt, feel pain. He is someone. This beautiful being that is giving you true love and all you are saying to him is Screw You we don't need you. We don't need your knowledge; I can do it on my own.

I can do what I want, when I want and how I want. Try telling your boss this at work. I am infinitely sure he will fire your ass so why are we doing this to God. Why are we not teaching the people how to walk right, talk right, praise right, live right, love right, give thanks right. You are there to represent God, represent him. When our children get good marks in school are we not proud of them, kiss them and tell them we love them. When they become lawyers and doctors do we not hold our head up and say yes you did good. You hold your head up and brag to family and friends so why can't we make God proud, why can't we make him brag about us.

Job showed us how. Come on My Peeps and True Loved Ones make God proud put a freaking big smile on his face. Join in my happiness now and smile. Stretch your hands out like you're hugging me but do not hug me, forget them oh's and negative sighs. Hug God and kiss him on the cheek, squeeze him. Squeeze him like you would squeeze someone you truly love. Feel good doesn't it so why can't we do this from time to time to God. Why can't we hug him and kiss him. Just hug and kiss him for no reason and feel good about it. You think your life is depressing go ahead hug him and kiss him. I am not telling you anything that is wrong. God wants you to hug and kiss him.

Never forget this because it was given to me in my vision "FOR GOD SO LOVE US HE IS

WORTHY TO BE PRAISED." How it was given to me is I saw it being written on a school wall.

This song "WHAT MAN CANNOT FIX GOD WILL FIX IT FOR YOU" I was singing in another vision.

Trust in those words because if it was not so God would not have given it to me. I know those words to be true and faithful. I've been tested and tried in my life but God was there for me. Faith heals and move mountains and God is Faith and the mountains are your enemies that are trying to hurt you in this sense. They are the mudslides and rocks that come crashing down off the top to crush and kill you.

Never give up on God no matter the storm. I know this now because once I did not know. I gave up on him, cursed him for him to kill me because of what I was going through but God saved me and taught me about him and his abundance of truth – true love. He is still teaching me. So take it from me never give up.

Mr. Pastor I know how you ar, you will try to turn the words above to discredit me by saying she cursed God is this the type of person My Peeps and True Loved Ones as well as people are listening to. Don't even try it because God knows what you will do and are going to do before you try. Hence God gave me knowledge to put it in this book because God knows you and now I know all of you. I know how wicked and deceitful the lots of you are.

Been there done that Beth, even said there is no God. God is unfair but no one on the face of this planet is as fair and just as God. Don't even look at me because I am like you. Faith rocked, death called, been persecuted, been called the devil from I was small until now and many of you are calling me the devil now but no matter. If God which is the truth is the devil then baby I am in good company and I am blessed and highly favoured as well as truthfully loved.

I've told you a dirty pastor cannot baptize you and you be clean. Many of us are dirty and filthy because we make dirty and filthy people baptize and preach to us.

If the head is dirty the body cannot be clean. You have to clean yourself up. Make yourself clean and that is through redemption and repentance. This was what John the Baptist tried to tell you and today you are still not listening. ***Negative energy is greater and more powerful than positive energy. Negative energy has a greater pull.***

Now you are just false. Now I know you are the Anti-Christ and a demon. You are lying.

Okay prove me wrong. Bring your bibles now, bring your Pure Pages, bring the Suhuf, bring your Quran, bring your Torah and prove me wrong. Blast me, curse me, throw this book away but prove me wrong. Shred it or burn it whichever pleases you.

Was it not negative forces that caused us to be kicked out of the Garden of Eden?

When your child does wrong is it not negative influences that turn them?

Is it not negative influences and forces that have thrown this world, meaning the people of this planet into chaos?

Is it not evil forces that is causing us to hate based on religion, skin colour, race, ethnicity, self beauty, sexual preferences, vanity? So prove me wrong. Look at the world today what are we still doing? Are we still not living like the children of Sodom and Gomorrah, the children of Israel and Judah?

If you are clean do not eat, drink or commune with filthy people you will become dirty and filthy like them. Now you can open your bibles. Go to Psalms One (1) and read what it said. Let it tell you how to live. Some of us say we know this. Then the question I pose to you is why are you still communing with dirty and filthy people? Why aren't you living by Psalms 1?

Like I've said you can hate me, rebuke me, chastise me, do to me like the true messengers of God that came before me but rest assure and know this YOUR TIME IS ALMOST UP. None will beg for you. Time and time again God has shown you and like ignorant fools you choose to disobey and follow after idols, follow after false worship, false praise, false love, false giving and false everything.

Listen to Time Will Tell by Bob Marley. God will never send a false messenger or false people to preach and tell you of him – tell you the truth. If

he did God would not have truly loved and cared about you. He would be a damned liar and I know God is not a liar.

Your pastors and imams, priests and bishops were ordained. They were ordained by MAN and not GOD. Some bought their ordination because they went to Theology schools to lie and deceive. Some got ordained by bishops. If they were all ordained by God why is the world in the state of disarray it is in?

Let no one tell you it had to be so because it did not have to be this way. If we only listen to God then the world would be better. He would show each and every individual what to do but because of doubt and fear inflicted upon us by Men Of God as you call them we are being <u>led to the slaughter house believing their lies to be the truth</u>.

TRUE LOVE does not lie nor does it deceive. If you are ordained by God you will be living right, talking right, walking right. The Children of God would be rushing to your church not wanting to leave. Women would not be around pulpits preaching in pants and disrespecting the Omnipotent One. Women would wear head coverings in church, not hats but head coverings. We would cover our heads, men would wear long garbs over there pants so that when they sit in the house of God their Private Parts would not be showing in their pants. Women would wear the appropriate dress.

Yes render your hearts and not your garment some of you are saying. Screw you. When you go for your job interview do you not dress appropriately? Do you not respect the person that is going to conduct the interview? Before you go, do you not run to the clothing store to get the proper outfit? Do you not go to the hair salon, nail salon to be done up so you can impress the person that is going conduct the interview? When you are going to the club do you not dress appropriately?

What are you telling me?

Are you telling me that God does not deserve respect? Dress appropriate for God and not man. When Peter Tosh sang Rastafari Is did he disrespect God? No he did not disrespect God because he was dressed like the angels of God with the exception of a head gear and one colour was missing but that colour was not for him to give.

I am not in any way turning you from your religion and I will never do that. **I will never change you because you cannot change people.** *God will never change you. In order to have change you need to want change. You have to want and need to change yourself.* **If anyone say's God will change you tell them I say they are a damned liar. God does not change anyone, you have to need this change and change yourself. God cannot go against his laws to accommodate or please you.** *From you accept change God will guide you and show you how to keep on his path in the physical realm but the spiritual is different and you need to know the difference between the two.*

And perish the thought of God punishing your children because God punish no one. Like I said he walks away from you so that sin will have his way with you. As for your children "the sins of the fathers and mothers" is all I have to say.

Is there changes, or can we change?

Yes, in the spiritual realm you will be changed, be operated upon.

My Peeps and True Loved Ones I can only describe it as an operation because this is how I saw it. I was taken to a different land in the spiritual this was a land where the people were getting ready to do battle and before I could go into the land I had to be operated on, changed. The land was dry and desolate and you could see the blood on the people, the determination in their faces as they got ready to fight. Get ready for war.

I cannot say it is hell but in retrospect it had to be and God's Angels had to change you to protect you so that they don't kill you. This was a land of war. A land of battle but funny none knew what they were fighting for. I didn't ask all I saw were people including women getting ready for battle. I saw them. I was changed not to look like them but changed to be protected so that they could not tough me, kill me because I was a stranger in their land.

And people do not call me Cain because I know you will use Cain as an example and say I am the murderer. I am Cain incarnated. So please do not go there.

Like I said I will not change you from your religion nor can I change you. What I am saying is let the religion be about God and not the teachings of men. Take the damned collection plates out of church and teach and preach about God and God only. Show the people how to attain the truth of God which is in them. The light and spark within you is God – the true and living God and you need to cultivate and harvest this light so it will forever shines within you.

Yes here we go the pastors are in uproar. Too damned bad, take the damned collection plates out of church. The inside of the church was meant for God. People why do you think the first thing they said Jesus did was to go into the churches, synagogues so let me use the right term and be in your terms politically correct and beat there asses because they are disrespecting God. And take the fucking ATM Machines out of your churches. What the fuck are you telling me? Are you telling me you are not about God but about Mammon the Money, The Beast and you can't dispute it nor deny it.

God does not want people's money he wants their true love. He wants us to be his roots. What the hell does God need money for? You are the ones that need money to live your lifestyle of luxury. The place you preach to people is to be holy and not filthy. By letting people drop money in collection plates you are making them dirty and filthy. You are defiling them and more importantly defiling God and his holy grounds and this is why I say to you if the head is filthy how can the body be clean.

Greedy pastors you cannot buy God. What you are telling the people, they can buy God and they are buying God. God is not a supermarket or a grocery store people. You cannot buy him and never will buy him.

You can buy death but absolutely no one can buy Life.

Life is not a toy it is sacred and true. Death is not true because no one have to die to see God.

We die to see death – hell and this is why you tell people they have to be washed in the blood of the lamb. Simply put you are telling people to further dirty themselves because all of you know that God does not deal in nastiness – filth. God is not a Obeah worker nor is he a seer man or woman that deals with the dead.

Death deals with the dead – evil and wicked people that have died and yes the innocent souls you have taken with your bullshit and lies. These are the people who death – your witches and so forth deal in.

Good cannot die and I've told you this. Evil is the one to die and it is evil that has humanity – every race on the face of the planet bowing down to him.

There is no cost associated with God but with evil there is a cost and the cost is your soul and spirit in the end.

Further, take your damned shoes off too. When you go into your house do you not respect it by taking your damned shoes off?

Do you pray and worship in your shoes when you are at home?

All of you give your house more respect than you do God. If you can't go barefoot wear socks, knit socks shoes for your feet to keep them warm. But do not wear your filthy shoes that you wear on the road that people piss, dogs shit, and people spit upon and go into God's Holy Temple. Come on now do you really think that God is in these churches? Please. It is only a foolish man thinks this way. So clean your damned self up and live for God the best way you can.

Do you not sing Moses, Moses take off thy shoes cause the place you are standing on is holy ground in your churches?

So why is Moses not taking off his shoes?

Why are you praying on filthy grounds?

Tell me truly come on tell why you're mocking God?

Come on now who are we fooling. And I do not exclude myself out of this because I use to go to church and wear my shoes in church. Sometimes I would take it off and trust me it felt so good so all chances I got I took them off.

Deacon Brown and Sister Wright, yes you too Sister Sylvia I see you because you are not fooling God. God see's your thoughts and this gives you no right to sprinkle powder, goozu water, Florida water, oila kip dung, oila tun back, oila a diss and that in your brothers and sisters shoes. Nor does it give you the right to go write your brothers and sisters name on pork or meat wrap it up in parchment paper and put it under rock stone to keep them down. Nor does it give you the right to write your bothers and sisters name on parchment paper and wear it in your shoes to keep them down. Nor does it mean you must go to the obeah man to work obeah to keep your brothers and sisters down. Nor does it give you the right to give them your nastiness in water to drink to kill them. Nasty and defiling sinners. Walking and defiling abomination of sin. Unnu naasi and stink, unnu a walking cesspool of abomination and condemnation but yet unnu a gaa church and worship God. Somea unnu roune pulpit a preach and when unnu done unnu go roune a backroom ana work obeah, black magic and the sorts. Anno God unnu a serve and worship a di devil because im sit at the head of the church. None a unnu no noa sey the church was once a casino and a whore house. Churches were bath houses, the den for filthy and perverted men in the past. Your bible tells you this but yet you keep going in them. Yu caane fine God inna whore house. Yu caane fine God inna di den of sinful and deceitful men come on now but don't worry God knows your thoughts and works that is why IN THE NAME OF GOD I CAST YOU ALL IN THE PITS OF HELL. IN THE NAME OF GOD I REBUKE YOU ALL TO FALL IN YOUR OWN NETS AND BE PERMANTENTLY TURNED BACKWARDS IN YOUR OWN ABOMINATIONS OF SIN BOTH IN THE SPIRITUAL AND PHYSICAL REALM.

IN THE NAME OF GOD LEAVE GOD'S CHILDREN ALONE.

BE GONE IN THE NAME OF GOD YOU CONIVING AND DECEITFUL DEMONS.

ALLELUJAH IN THE NAME OF GOD I REBUKE YOU ALL AND GIVE YOU OVER TO YOUR OWN CONDEMNATION. IN THE NAME OF GOD I BOUND YOU ALL TO YOUR SPIRITUAL AND PHYSICAL HELL. ALLELUJAH MY GOD, TRUE LOVE LET THY WILL BE DONE IN EARTH, IN HEAVEN – THE SPIRITUAL REALM. LET THY WILL THY TRUE AND GOOD WILL BE DONE GOD AND CHASE THE DEMONS OUT OF YOUR HOUSEHOLD. ALLELUJAH FATHER LET THY WILL BE DONE NOW. AMEN. LET THE ANGELS SAY AMEN LET THY WILL BE DONE GOD LET ALL THY WILL BE DONE. ALLELUJAH LET THY WILL BE DONE BECAUSE YOU ARE THE BREATH OF LIFE. YOU ARE LIFE AND IT IS YOU, YOUR LIGHT AND LIFE THAT WILL SAVE HUMANITY IN THIS WORLD.

Sister Paulette stop carrying news. Who the hell needs it? Kibba Yu Mouth before God closes it permanently for you. Chat too damn much. Pastor Blake, Sister Pat the voodoo shit does not work with God so stop. The invoking the death shit does not work either. What God has given me, Sister Ann-Marie, Sister Bev, Baby Andrew, and Little Tommy is for us and not for you. If you were clean and not filthy God would give you your portion but no you want what God has given to us, fighting us down for it. Man did not give it to us God did so you can't have it. Live right and talk right, walk right and praise right, stay on the right track and God will give you your portion. Damn fool.

Nuff a unno a damn big head bud. When you try taking what's mine do you truly believe God is going to let you have it. Come on think. It's mine and no one can take it. Learn this and stop stooping and wallowing in filth like the big ole dutty pig dem inna pig pen.

Know that God will never let you take what's mine because the destruction and pit you set for me and your sister's trust me you will fall right in it because God will protect us and favour us more over you. God knows you and your works why the hell do you think you can't prosper. Stop the shit you are doing. Keeping your brothers and sisters down does not work because the physical plain is just one factor. The wickedest plain you can be on is the spiritual plain. If you live the life of the wicked trust me from the time the grave diggers put the final scoop of dirt on your home because the grave is now your home __*woe be unto you.*__

This is why many of us hear the dead crying. Don't laugh, ask a Jamaican, ask them if they have seen the dead walking? Ask them if they have heard the dead cry, even call your name? Go ahead and ask, take the old mother out of the church and ask her and if she is truthful she will tell you YES.

We hear you and see you and it is not many can hear and see now because we have perverted our way and brought things into the house of God that should have never been there; things that should never come in there.

Remember there is:

2 heavens and 2 hells
2 deaths and 2 life
There is a spiritual life and death, physical life and death, physical heaven and hell and spiritual heaven and hell but in fact there are 3 deaths.

People as it is in heaven so it is on earth.

*Pastor we know your need your tides because you are damned greedy this is why you keep telling people to give you ten percent of their earnings. Fuck you. Fuck the lot of you. It's the church that is supposed to give ten percent of their earnings to the poor. If Mother Walters cannot pay her bills you are to step in and do so. Greedy bastards raping the people of their wealth and their prosperity. (Note 1/10th represent 10%). Some churches remind you every Sunday of this by making you read it and telling idiboos like myself you are robbing God. How the fuck can a man or woman rob God? You rob us of our souls by making us worship in filthy churches, worship amongst filthy people that say they love God but yet as church is over everyone rushes out and leave poor Mother Waters to sit and wait for Wheel Trans or a taxi and the majority of you are passing her direction. **Fuck the lot of you this is not love this is hatred.** None of you can tell Mother Waters the truth because truth does not reside in any of you.*
If you do something for me you want something in return. I either have to sleep with you or do something for you. Hypocrites and Parasites no wonder Revelations say God is against the lot of you because you have all turned from him. But trust me man's vengeance is nothing compared to God's. Why do you think many of us our lives are still

messed up? Our lives are a mess and we don't know how to fix it. The only fixer and healer is God. No man can fix your problem only God can but some of us don't know this though.

We run to the shaman, voodoo priest, psychic, whatever for help instead of God and still don't know that God can and will fix everything. Now you know better so do better.

Yes Pastor fume, bishop fume because greed and money is your part and parcel. It's your nature because it is sealed with the mark of the beast 666 which is the invert of 999. You need nine hundred and ninety nine years no that's wrong you need nine thousand nine hundred and nine years to deceive and spread lies but it will only take God one year, less than a day to clean up the planet earth and set his captive which is his people free. But for those who know better it is not nine thousand nine hundred and nine years it is 666 and if you add 6 more you get 24. 24000 years was allotted to Satan and his clan to do better but instead of doing better he continued to mess up hence evil cannot change and you cannot change anyone. For those that don't know this mark (666) has a seal above and below it, it must be contained. This is your square. The square must be contained and there is a containment unit for the square but in today's society man use 666 to represent money your economy and the chaos money is causing. Man rape, murder, rob and steal for it. It kills and takes your soul. We use it to buy and sell and if you don't have it you can't buy and sell, pay your rent, car note, pay your taxes, medical bills whatever. If you don't have it you are doomed because evil made it so. Sin made it so, you made it so. Yes this is just the surface of the beast because the truth goes further and there is significantly more to this. **_Money is the man today and with it you have power to do whatever you want it to do. It gets you everything in the physical but it cannot get you life nor extend your life in the spiritual._**

It cannot and will never save you in the hereafter. You cannot use it and will never use it there.

You have a church and you say it is of God PUT your damn collection box in the office. Make a separate room for it but keep it the hell out of God's sanctuary. You have an office but yet for some of you your office cannot house this collection plate. Why? Is your office too good? You give your office more respect than you give God's sanctuary. Supply people with envelopes so they can drop the money in the box then go onwards into the church.

In this way there is no gambling being done in the sanctuary you have given for the devotion and praise of God. Praise God without interruption because as it is you are gambling and using God as a bargaining chip. You cannot use God as a bargaining chip. He does not use you as one so why the hell are you using him as one.

Think this is God, it isn't and it isn't good. We respect our wives, bank accounts, money, pets and dogs more than we respect God. We have taken him for granted and will forever take him for granted. God hurts too people. He feels pain. Let him run your lives and business because when you are dead you are dead. Bring your money to the grave outline your coffin with money. You can't enjoy it but those grave diggers sure as hell will. They will dig your ass up, throw your ass off that money and make good use of it after they are finished.

Many of you worry about your big house and yacht. Well put them in the grave with you. Literally put them in the grave with you and enjoy it down there with you. Can't can you? So think about what you are doing?

We are all worried about money and when we are dead we have no use for it. In the living we can't enjoy it because we listen to liars telling us to give up 1/10th or 10 percent of it to them and telling you and me if you don't you are robbing God. Then to add salt to the wound they make you pay for special prayers and tap water oh sorry holy water. Tell me how the hell is the water holy? Did God directly give it to them? God did not give any of you his water so how can your water be holy and blessed?

How can it be of God?

My Peeps God does not want anyone to be poor. If you are rich give what you can. If I tell you to give five dollars and you can afford it do it. Listen to me and hear what I say when I tell you that God will never steer his people wrong. When you read further you will see what I mean.

What are you doing now are you not telling us to give. We are not giving freely. You are telling us to do so what makes you any different. Tell us now don't wait until later.

*Alright, Ken you are correct but I am not telling you to give I am asking you for help you are not obligated to do so because I am not a church. My Peeps and True Loved Ones, I am asking you to support these Hospitals if you can. Once only but if you can continue to do so please do and I hope God richly reward you in the physical and spiritual for your gift. My Peeps and True Loved Ones these hospitals are in need. God I know this is what you want. **Ben I know you are struggling and don't have it to give financially but you have good, true and clean prayer so you can pray.***

*Sick Children's Hospital in Toronto and Bustamante Children Hospital in Jamaica I am asking you to send **$5.00 if you can to them.** If it is 5 pounds, 5 Euro, 5 US or Canadian please send it.*

People I know Shaggy has a foundation that supports Bustamante Children's Hospital you can deal with him if you choose to do so. He's got a song called Save A Life on the internet please look at it and see the difference he is making.

So Mr. Shaggy, Mr. Bombastic may God forever bless you and I hope his light shine upon you for the work that you are doing to help the children of Jamaica and the surrounding Caribbean. Never change maybe now we can take it further, beyond Jamaica in the true love and spirit of God. My Peeps and True Loved Ones Bustamante Children's Hospital is the only hospital of its kind in the Caribbean to help children.
If you don't have it to give do not stress yourself.

*When you have it buy $5.00 worth of food, whether canned or whatever and give it to your local homeless shelter or food bank. If you can afford a pack of diapers go for it. People buy Pampers. The reason why I say Pampers is because $1.00 from each purchase of Pampers goes towards helping young girls in Africa. Pampers put your money where your mouth is now because I am endorsing your product and asking people to continually buy your product. Add another dollar to it now and help the children in Russia. So one dollar goes to Africa and the other dollar goes to Russia. Come on accept my challenge as I dare you to make a bigger difference and lead the way. When people see you doing this which product do you think they will buy more of **and please do not raise the price**. If you have seconds, I hope you don't throw them out but donate it to places like Costa Rica, St. Vincent, Jamaica, and Haiti. I know I am asking a lot but you know what God will bless you even more. So continue to make that difference because I do love your product and yes I used it too. Smile.*

For those that are millionaires if you can afford new equipment for Bustamante Children's Hospital please call them at 876-968-0300 or 876-968-0309 or fax them at 876-929-2631 and see what equipment they need right away and try to help them. I am not forcing you just asking you nicely in the name and true love of God. Please note none of you are obligated to do this but it would be nice and yes if you can send $10.00 do so. I know I am stretching it. So mister rich man do not go overboard and say I am going to out do everyone it simply does not work and God will so

not bless you. I only asked for $5.00 and stretched it to $10.00 for people like you that can afford it.

Forget it Beverly not $50.00 but $5.00 or $10 or good and truthful prayer nothing more, nothing less. Oh yeah forget the tax receipt. This you are doing out of the goodness and generosity of your heart and more importantly you are doing it for God.

Sick Kids can do with the money My Peeps.

Address envelopes to ***Administration Office***

Here is the address for The Hospital For Sick Children or Sick Kids Hospital
555 University Avenue
Toronto, Ontario
M5G 1X8

Bustamante Children's Hospital
Arthur Wint Drive
Kingston 5
Jamaica West Indies

Special Note: For you psycho's out there that believe in sending chemical's and pipe bombs, what ever sick shit you do. Don't!!!!!!!!!!!!!! because God will not put up with it. These are children you freak. Look at them one day your children will be in the same position. Right now many of you know children that are in dire need of help. Help them and stop the nonsense you are doing because God see's you before you act. Kids from different parts of the world go to sick kids for

treatment and there is no racial divide so forget your sick act and lose the damned sick and racial yes radical mentality.

Banks can you waive your $7.00+ fee you charge for a bank draft – money order. If you can't waive it how about charging $1.99 as these people are doing something GOOD and you cannot charge them a fee for goodness it is simply ungodly.

*From time to time I will ask you for support but it will not be often My Peeps and True Loved Ones. And if someone come to you and say Michelle said to give this or that, or some lame ass use my name to solicit you tell them to **FUCK OFF**. Let no one use you by using my name or any derivate of it. You will know because God will show you. He better.*

*Also for your generous donation my next book will be free. Well not totally free because you know LULU is going to want their cost. Do not worry My Peeps and True Loved Ones God will show me the way to make it totally free. Free download from my web page but I do not have one yet. You will know when I have one. **My Peeps and True Loved Ones I am not asking for me but asking you to show God you care by giving freely, truthfully and lovingly.** Look out for free downloads from the LULU site. People I cannot start with Africa, I have to start with my own. I have to help them in Canada and Jamaica first before I can help others. Once I start from home I will stretch my hands out to other nations and when you read further you will see so please do not say I am prejudice because I am not and this can be debated. If you think I am then I* *cannot change that but in time I hope to prove you all wrong.*

So My Peeps and True Loved Ones truly, truly thank you. In the name of God by God's grace and mercy I truly thank you all.

<u>No Jane I don't want or need a foundation nor do I want or need anyone to start one for me.</u> *Don't like them nor do I <u>believe</u> in them. Every cent that I ask for should go directly to the source. With foundations you have to worry about overhead, staff, fees for this, fees for that hell no too damned complicated and stressful. I am asking you for help so every cent I get must go directly to the people – the source. Nothing should go to overhead and this cost or that cost. Do you know what I mean? <u>I am not saying not to give to organizations</u>.* **<u>Please don't stop because people need them and their support and if you stop I will not forgive you. Please continue to do because every help matters and counts.</u>** *For me I don't want none would rather you send money to these hospitals directly.*

Mr. Scientist, Chemist and Ms. Scientist and Chemist I am coming to you now. Take a good look at those children and tell them you truly love them and that you are going to develop drugs to ease their pain ease their suffering. You give them your word that you will create drugs that have fewer side effects. Develop drugs that will cure them.

Ms. and Mr. Chemist and Scientist I am not saying you are doing a bad job what I am saying is that it hurts me to see children suffer. **<u>I know you guys can do so much and are doing the best you can but</u>**

please hurry to develop safer drugs to help them.
When I go to Sick Kids and see the children it hurts me. It's not this child or that child, every nation, every nationality, people of different races and religion go there and not one is treated differently so why can't we treat each other with true love.

Seeing those kids my heart ache because I don't know how some mothers deal with the pain and anguish, the pain of seeing what their child have to go through. These children are the hero's of our time because none of us can imagine what they have to live with. So for God, truly help them. Do more to help them. People once again pull up Save a Life by Shaggy and truly see. Go down to Sick Kids Hospital and see. So how can we as nations of people say we hate each without seeing the pain and suffering we are causing each other?

Look at the kids; they are suffering so tell me why are we not saving them and making a better future for them.

People it is about life and the sacredness of life. It's about truly loving each other and coming together as one. All I can do is show you how ridiculous we are when we say we hate without knowing what we hating and without you seeing the pain you are truly causing.

Tell me something people, if we truly love God so much, tell me, truly tell me why do we hate each other. Why can't we see beyond race and colour and truly live for God and live in peace with each other.

*So Joe do not give away your riches that is simply stupid and when I see you I will tell you you are a fucking idiot and big head bud and I will tell your wife she had a right to leave your ignorant ass. You and your wife worked too damn hard to achieve it to now lose it because some greedy Cyclops tells you to give it all to him. **Please. I know the story and a child of God would never tell you to give all you have to the poor. Leave you penniless while your family go hungry. Please that was added by greedy clergymen to rob your ass.** Wasn't Solomon and David rich, was not Abraham and the profits oh sorry prophets of old rich. Did God tell any of them to give up their wealth?*

In the interim do not use your wealth to spread hate, commit crimes and hurt others. Use it to help your family and others and truly love doing it. But do not give all because when you give all what about tomorrow. Do you want to be begging in the streets? Think.

Strayed again I know. Now after all that the reasoning behind this book.

I was told to write *a book*. *__A book__*, not many books and trust me I have written many and no it was not a man in the physical that told me to write the book it was God and trust me I was like Jonah and tried to evade it. I tried not to write it but I could not get away from it. Could not escape and after speaking to a Pastor friend of mine he said do it. He said God told you to do it. Do it. Suffice it to say the book I originally wrote, I lost my cruzer with the completed manuscript on it. It also had the original version of Jamaican Tsunami on it. Oh well such is life. But cuddle up and remember you are apart of God's true family and you need to know that God truly loves you.

Know that my swearing and anger is not towards you and by no means reflect you. If you don't want to go further with the book by all means close it because like I said it will get racial, prejudicial and I will continue to swear. If you proceed I did caution you because I truly love you guys. I may lose a lot of you but this My Peeps and True Loved Ones this will be your test to see if you truly love and care about me as well as what I have been telling you. I will know if you TRULY love God. I am not going to endorse my other line here because my venting has to do with Blind Obsession. The truth above has to do with below and below was written before above. Confused? Below was written first. Now you are going to read below. Are we true and on the same page now?

Yes.

Excellent.

On December 08, 2010 I did the flyer for Blind Obsession and I said to the gentleman Muslims are going to want to lynch my ass after they read the book because they have a peaceful way of life and they are distorting it. They are letting the world see them in a destructive light; making the world hate them because they are distorting a beautiful way of life. He asked me what does it mean to be a Muslim and I said a Muslim *to me* means one of peace. He said no I don't know what it means to be Muslim. He asked have you read the Quran and I said no,

not from back to front but what I studied it would reference passages in the Quran and he said I know nothing about Islam and that I had no right to write about Muslims/Islam because I have not read the Quran. ***He said I was just like the man that wanted to burn the Quran I am no different from him.*** Man tears came to my eyes and my faith was shot right there. It was shot to hell. I am a person that loves everyone, truly do, and respect your religion, but I never expected that from a Muslim. After crying to God and praying, I know, truly know now that God is with me because he answered my prayer and gave me food to eat. Also there was an older Christian lady in the store and she gave me words of encouragement when he was out of ear shot. ***She said you said your peace leave the rest to God and I did.***

I know now and truly know that religion and God will never be one. I thought about Jesus from what I read in the bible and how God sent him to preach to his own and his own refused him. His own set him up, tried to kill him, persecute him well what about me. ***But now I know the truth of why his people refused him and this I will clear up in another book***. In all the years of my life I find men and women will kill you for RELIGION, THEIR PROFITS - PROPHETS, ***MEN THEY BELIEVE IN*** but none will or can kill you for God – the True and Living God.

My Peeps and True Loved ones no one can kill you for God because this is not what God wants besides no one knows God nor do they ***know what he God looks like***. (My Peeps and True Loved Ones close your mouth as I am seeing if the others know).

No one knows how to represent God and do for God. *All that we do we do for self and self gratification and if we say we are going to help our fellow sister or brother, even donate we want something in return for our efforts.* We want a tax receipt or our sister and brother to do something in return for your efforts. Yes I am generalizing but take a look around. If you donate do you ever say its okay I don't need a tax receipt. Try not taking one for a change. Donate $10.00 and before the person can ask you if you want a tax receipt tell him or her no you don't need one. *If he or she say it's the norm, insist on not having one or when you get a donation card in the mail and you donate write on it I do not need a tax receipt so please don't send me one. How many of us can do that? Not all so hey I rest my case. We do to get something in return. A place in paradise, approval from friends and family but never do we say God I am looking for approval from you. You are whom I am living for. You are whom I am doing this for. My mother and father is not alive and God I want to do something for them I am going to donate $10.00 in their name to their favorite charity, the local food bank, homeless shelter and not want anything in return. I will not expect you to bless me because this donation is your blessing to me. Bet you never looked at it like that before hey.*

Onwards we go. God has a funny way of working in my life and no matter the storm and heartache, no matter how many friends I lose, this include you too my Peeps and True Loved Ones no one can take God from me. Not you. No one. The only way for me to lose God is for me to displease him and trust me I aim on continuing to educate truthfully with what he is teaching me.

No man, no books, no Imam, Priest, Preacher whatever can tell you about God because they know not God and I stand by my statement because if they did the world would not be scheduled to be destroyed and no it is not 2012. Many things will have to come to pass first. Meaning the people of the whole world will get their final warning and if they don't accept the warning and change their lives then that's it you will die. If you don't listen now and like I have told Jamaica if they don't listen and live up to the name that they were born under as well as live under they will be destroyed. Haiti is just a testament because it was scheduled to be destroyed and the Tsunami that hit them was to have destroyed them but someone stood up for them and if they don't change I know the next time around they will be no more. You don't have to take my word for it because the war is brewing. It is brewing in the spiritual world then it will come to the physical world. It has to take shape in the spiritual before it comes here and it is coming. When is another story because this planet is scheduled to be destroyed before 2032 meaning something major is going to happen between 2012 and 2032 but what it is I do not know.

There is no more time extension for man because we are doing that which is not of God. We praise men and prophets and not God. We don't see God and will never see God under the present condition of this earth. The only way man can get a time extension is if they start living right and do that which is right in the sight of God. Either we repent and stop living for the devil/evil or that's it for man. The environment is in chaos and no one wants to clean it up. We have two decades to do something positive to change our destructive path and we had better start now if we want to see 2132 and beyond.

Religion cannot save you because in Paradise there is no such thing as religion. In the spiritual realm there is no such thing as religion. There is no section for Muslims, Christians, Jews, Gentiles, Buddhists, Naturalists; you name it there is no section so stop being deceived.

Stop living a life of a lie.

Like I have told you time and time again no one can teach you about God apart from God himself because when God educates you you're well educated and your education is solid. The knowledge he is giving you cannot be broken. When negative people come to you and try to break you, you cannot be broken because God has placed his seal around you. That knowledge is sealed so that when this person gives you a hint of the truth in their religion you will not be moved, or go with them because God's knowledge is factual. It is correct. Right knowledge, right education, true and perfect love and peace.

I was broken yesterday. December 08, 2010. So broken was my faith as well as all that I *believed* in. Man was I rocked. All that I was taught about Islam and the Muslim world became naught for me but because God truly loved me he showed me the way, the true way and the books this man gave me my mind said throw them out. Do not read them, my spirit kept on nagging me and I listened to my spirit and threw the books out and I feel so much better because if it is one thing that ***GOD HAS TAUGHT ME IS THAT MAN CANNOT EDUCATE ME ABOUT HIM. NO BOOKS OF MEN CAN EDUCATE ME ABOUT HIM BECAUSE HE IS THE TRUE LOVE IN ME AND HE IS THE ONE EDUCATING ME. GOD IS WITHIN ME AND HE HAS SHOWN ME HIS TRUE LANGUAGE. SEALED ME WITH HIS SEAL SO NO MATTER HOW MUCH MY FAITH IS ROCKED BY EVIL AND WICKED PEOPLE THEY CAN'T TAKE MY GOD, THE TRUE GOD AND SUSTAINER FROM ME BECAUSE I AM APART OF HIM AND HE IS APART OF ME MEANING HE IS THE TRUE LOVE WITHIN ME AND THE TRUE LOVE WE HAVE FOR EACH OTHER.***

My Peeps and True Loved Ones you need to know this. I will forever tell you TRUE LOVE never hurt, it heals and protects and this is God.

Man kill but God never killed anyone. Yes the bible said God told his prophet to kill every man woman and child but come on now who are you kidding.

If God created everything out of true love and requires every life back at the end of its cycle why would God tell his profits – prophets to kill.

God has given you life why would he turn around and take it, he's not evil and he's certainly not death.

Like I've said God does not deal in the death nor does he mingle with filth.

God is clean and true, he cannot lie.

GOD DOES NOT KILL AND NEVER WILL KILL BECAUSE IF HE DOES, IF HE DI, HE WOULD BE A LIAR. HE WOULD NOT BE A GOD OF LOVE TRUE LOVE.

I stand by my words and will not retract them and if God was to say Michelle kill I would tell him to Fuck Off and say he is a damned Liar a fucking liar that does not live by his word. I would tell him to go fuck himself he's not God. Yes go ahead and GASP. *Man kill, God does not kill nor does he steal, rape and take other people's land. You need to know this.*

So for you Mister Muslim man when I asked you if God kills you said yes. Well I am telling you to *FUCK OFF, FUCK OFF, FUCK OFF, FUCK THE HELL OFF MOTHERFUCKER BECAUSE MY GOD, THE SUSTAINER AND CREATOR OF THIS WORLD, THE GOD OF TRUTH – THE TRUE AND LIVING GOD NEVER KILLED ANYONE AND NO BOOK THAT IS WRITTEN BY MEN CAN CONVINCE ME OTHERWISE. TAKE YOUR FUCKING LIES AND EAT SHIT BECAUSE GOD IS NOT A MURDER NOR IS HE A KILLER LIKE YOU.*

You are raping and killing people's souls with your lies and condemnation. Telling me that God kills I know better asshole because God's people are *BLESSED AND MORE THAN HIGHLY FAVOURED BY HIM. GOD EDUCATES US ABOUT THE TRUE LOVE OF HIM. SHOWED*

US HIS LANGUAGE, SHOWED US PARADISE AND HELL AND YES PROTECT US.

You can never educate me with your lies because I am created by God. For some of you who believe the ethers and say the ether has to do with hair. Let me put it in your context then because this is what you believe to know. No I refuse to go there because the people of the garden when God took me back in time was not just black they were white and we existed in peace, as one, on one accord with God. So you can keep saying 9th ether and 6th ether it was not so. None of you 9th ether haired people as you call yourselves have it. Look at Bob Marley, Peter Tosh; look at the Jamaican Rastaman's crown of Glory atop his head. This was how I saw the three angels of God and each time I see them I see this Lox upon their head. I also see the colours of God and none of you can wear the colour, will ever wear the colour of God because it was never given to any of you.

My Peeps and True Loved Ones stop fuming and call me prejudice. You wear the crown of Glory too. Take a look at Alborosie so don't tell me shit about you don't have hair like this.

So for all you haters that use the ether as your bargaining chip go fuck yourselves because the lot of you know better. Fuck all of you because the 9th ether have to do with the gases of the world and the 999 years you want so you can continue to lie and deceive. Yes this is why you invert the six and turn it into a nine. As for you blacks and whites stop listening to liars that use books written by men to deceive and pit one race against the next.

Pit one religion against the next.

Come on people where is this of God? Look at the damned world today who the fuck is killing each other, fighting against each other. It certainly ain't God. In the past the bible said God told those people to kill, take land, why the hell is he not doing it today.

Some preachers go as far as telling people they cannot see God and they know better. People read Job 42 verse 5 and come tell me otherwise because Job saw God and lived.

When Adam and Eve was in the Garden of Eden did they not talk directly with God and see God?

So Mr. Muslim man back to you and let me educate you now. We deceived and condemned ourselves to hell and death by lying with your condemned asses when we should not have. God told us specifically not to lie with you – your race but nooooooo we did not listen. Now look at us today, confused and without a home – the abode of God. Your race resided in the land of Nod – the North- you were the murder's yes the sinful beings outside the Garden of Eden. Yes the keepers of the death that's why you invoke the dead and have people praying to the dead – your dead God <u>now you are taking our birthright, that was given to us</u> and using it against us. Well mother fuckers I evict all of you out of God's garden of peace. We don't want you here you are not accepted nor welcomed and never will be accepted and welcomed here because none of you can wear the hair of God's angels, God's crown of Glory, or *wear the colours that he has given unto the children of God. His good people the rightful and true Jews. So go fuck yourself because the lots of you wanna be and no matter how you all say Allah it means nothing in the sight of God because you're all thieves. None of you know what Allah means so because you don't know none of you are counted. You and your fucking race is a condemnation and an abomination of sin – a fucking curse. You're the fucking cursed race bitch. The only thing you have is looks hence Satan your father was a pretty – the prettiest angel amongst the dead. He was fucking vain hence you'll think you're pretty but the lots of you are fucking ugly like Satan. No truth reside in the lots of you because you're all liars and deceivers, warmongers and thieves.(Yes people here you can say I am being racist and you have all reason now to call me racist based on my tirade.)*

None of you can speak God's true language because it was not given unto you. <u>It was given unto God's people and God's true language is not spoken, will never be spoken by man because it is written.</u>

<u>*Move yourselves because Bob Marley was right. He specifically told us in Time Will Tell that God will never give the power to a BALD HEAD AND YOU'RE ALL BALD HEADS. WANNA BE'S THAT TOOK OUR GLORY AND NOW SAYING IT IS YOURS. LISTEN TO THE SONG BECAUSE I DEDICATE IT TO ALL YOU DECEITFUL DEMONS THAT WANT TO TAKE THE PLACE OF GOD'S RIGHFUL PEOPLE. REMEMBER YOU CANNOT TELL ME I KNOW*</u>

NOTHING OF PEACE BECAUSE I WAS BORN UNDER GOD'S BANNER, I HOUSE ONE OF HIS NAMES IN MINE, I HAVE HIS SEAL, I HAVE THE HAIR, WHICH IS HIS CROWN OF GLORY. I KNOW HIS COLOURS FOR WHICH YOU CANNOT AND WILL NEVER WEAR. I HAVE HIS LANGUAGE BECAUSE HE SEALED IT IN MY HANDS SO WHEN YOU TELL ME I KNOW NOTHING OF ISLAM FUCK YOU. I KNOW WHAT ISLAM IS IT IS A BREAK OFF OF CATHOLICISM, GIVEN TO JESUS BY YOU TO DECEIVE GOD'S PEOPLE THE TRUE JEWS.

THE CHILDREN OF GOD ARE THE ORIGINAL INHABITANTS OF THE GARDEN OF EDEN AND BECAUSE WE HEARD YOUR DEAD CRIES, SWEET LIES, WE HAD MERCY UPON YOUR CONDEMNED ASSES AND LET YOU IN.

WE WENT AGAINST GOD. WE WERE THE ORIGINAL AND STILL ARE THE ORIGINAL CHILDREN OF GOD. DID YOU WATCH THE MOVIE 10 000 BC IT CERTAINLY WAS NOT MY PEOPLE DECEIVING BUT YOURS. SO TELL ME WHO IS MORE ENTITLED TO BE CALLED ONE OF PEACE, CERTAINLY NOT YOU, BECAUSE NONE OF YOU WILL EVER BE CALLED EL ELYON, A CHILD OF GOD. I DON'T WANNA BE BECAUSE I KNOW I AM. I KNOW THE GOD IN ME. THE TRUE LOVE IN ME SO STEP BACK AND GET OUT, GET THE FUCK OUT. IN THE NAME OF GOD, MY TRUE LOVE AND SUSTAINER GET OUT, GET OUT, GET OUT, GET OUT. YOU AND YOUR

KIND ARE EVICTED PERMANENTLY FROM THE PHYSICAL PLAIN AND THE SPIRITUAL PLAIN. KEEP YOUR FUCKING CONDEMNATION TO YOURSELVES BECAUSE NONE OF YOU WILL GAIN ACCESS TO GOD'S ABODE – KINGDOM NO MATTER HOW YOU MARRY INTO OUR RACE WITH YOUR LIES AND DECEIT BITCH. EVERYONE MUST BE CLEAN AND NOT DIRTY AND BECAUSE YOU WERE BORN INTO LIES – PHYSICAL AND SPIRITUAL LIES YOU WILL NEVER GET IN IF YOU DON'T REPENT AND CLEAN UP YOUR DIRTY, SINFUL AND CONDEMNED WAYS.

OH YA AND FORGET THE SEPTRE BECAUSE YOU DON'T HAVE IT AND NEVER WILL HAVE IT. NO ONE IN THE ISLAMIC WORLD HAVE IT BITCH BECAUSE IT WAS TAKEN AWAY. IT HAS BEEN PASSED ON AND THIS CANNOT BE DISBUTED BECAUSE I KNOW I SAW IT. THIS IS RIGHT KNOWLEDGE AND YOU NOR YOUR BOOKS OR IMAMS CAN AND WILL EVER BE ABLE TO DISPUTE THIS.

DON'T FORGET BILAAL THE ONE THAT HAD THE SEPTRE ACCORDING TO ISLAMIC STORIES TOLD BY YOU NEVER HAD IT. THE SEPTRE HE HAD WAS NOT OF THE TRUE AND LIVING GOD THIS I KNOW, YES HE CALLED THE HADAN FOR PRAYER BUT FOR ALL OF YOU THAT THINK HE WAS A PALE ARAB HE WAS BLACK A BLACK MAN. DISPUTE THAT AND YOU CAN'T BECAUSE GOD SHOWED ME HIM AS A BLACK MAN

ROBED IN WHITE WITH A TAGIA ON HIS HEAD.

Better yet keep Islam because the children of God don't want it nor do we need it. You stole our peaceful way of life and made it yours by calling it Is Lam. You changed it to suit you, made it dirty. So keep your dirty land I know you gave that to Jesus that is why he said Peace be Unto You. Your kind indoctrinated him into Islam, which is your land but I know the full truth about the story of Jesus. Remember you can fool some of the people sometimes but you cannot fool all the people all the time. Keep Islam because we are not for Islam but for God's true land, his truth his true love. We are no longer your fucking lambs going to the slaughter house. We are not your lambs hence Islam. You can't slaughter us anymore with your bag of lies and deceit. We will no longer kill and defile God for you because we have the truth and always had it. You don't.

We don't need Islam because it pollutes, it stinks to the core and have no part and parcel with God. This I know because once you come into our land with Islam we are enslaved, women are subservient to you, they have to sit at the back of your Mosque's when they are on their period, they have no say or religious rights, they have to do as you say, walk behind you. Some even sleep in separate rooms because that is all Islam does. It enslaves and beat. Islam has no heart nor does have true love. Men under your Islamic code beat women if they don't adhere to you. Islam enslave mentally and physically, rapes you of your soul and dignity, it pits race against race, wage war with other nations that do not accept you, accepts your words. So fuck the lot of you with your dirty religion because not one of you represents God – the TRUE and LIVING GOD. You all represent Satan because death is your God. Death is whom the lots of you have to kill for hence you say God kills because your God is death - dead, a viper – a murderer – Satan himself. Further, that's why you prostrate to the ground and pray to the dead – your dead god that wallows in shit because we dump our shit and all manner of waste on him – in the ground. Your God stinks worse than shit itself and once again that's why we flush our shit and piss on him. Fuck you and all your Islamic kingdoms because you're all Satan's Minions – Satan's goons – his people that he is going to screw over once his time is up and his time is almost up.

As for you black people that have given themselves over to Islam and the Islamic bullshit you have been fed trust me if you think this is hell wait until you are dead because trust me you will have more than hell to pay in the grave. God gave us life but noooooooooo it wasn't good enough, well feel it in the end because when death has and have you there is no letting go so stop fucking around with your soul and spirit.

There are 2 Gods

The God of Death and the God of Life

With God – the God of Life there is no death. You cannot die to see him because you see a part of him each and every day in nature, the air, the food we eat but yet each and every day we kill life by polluting and destroying all that he has given us to maintain and sustain our lives.

Onwards I go

Remember Mr. Muslim Man, my people were in Egypt long before you came but you enslaved them, made them accept your false worship. Your people stole their land which is in Africa and this is why you tell the world we were slaves. I know the truth asshole do you?

Well let me tell you something, God who is the truth does not enslave, nor does he beat, nor does he pit one nation against the next, nor does he enslave, nor does he walk into another man's land and take what is not given unto him. Islam does. Read your damned Quran properly. God's people, the children of God does not want your polluted land, your polluted religion because religion distort, deceive, murder, rape and steal and this is not what the true and living God is all about. The true and living God is proud and have a lot of ambition and integrity, your God does not. Your God cannot and could infinitely never ever walk in my God's shoe because your God is not clean enough. Your God is not gorgeous enough – he's too ugly because your God is the waste that humans pass each and every day – hence we dump it on your God.

My Peeps and True Loved Ones ISLAM ENSLAVES SPIRITUALLY AND MENTALLY. KNOW THIS. KNOW GOD. KNOW WHO THE TRUE AND LIVING IS BECAUSE LIKE I SAID

THERE ARE 2 GODS, THE GOD OF DEATH AND THE GOD OF LIFE. DO NOT BELIEVE THIS KNOW THIS. ISLAM IS NOT FOR GOD AND WILL NEVER HAVE ANY PART AND PARCEL WITH GOD. ISLAMIC WORSHP HAVE NOTHING TO DO WITH LIFE IT HAS TO DO WITH SPIRITUAL DEATH – THE DEATH OF THE SPIRIT. IT IS SPIRITUAL PRISION. ISLAM WAS WHAT GOD WAS PROTECTING US FROM AND I WILL EXPLAIN FURTHER ON IN THIS BOOK. SO MR. MUSLIM MAN FUCK YOU BECAUSE ISLAM IS A SPIRITUAL PRISON. I KNOW THIS AND NO ONE THAT IS BORN UNDER THE ISLAMIC BANNER WILL REACH PARADISE OR GOD'S ABODE. NONE, NOT ONE OF YOU WILL REACH THERE BECAUSE ISLAMIC IS THE PRACTICE AND WORSHIP OF SATAN - DEATH.

DISPUTE ME AND TELL ME I AM SPREADING HATE ALL YOU WANT BUT I GIVE YOU FACTS AND THE TRUTH. DO NOT ACCEPT ISLAM.

My mother did and I did but I begged God for forgiveness. My mother is buried as a Muslim and trust me if I could dig her bones up and move it I would but I have to let it remain.

How Islam catches you especially us backsliding demons, yes black people. It gives you a bit of the truth and from there it hooks you. You are hooked and it will pit you against your family. It will cause you to hate, Whites, Chinese, and your Family.

This I know because I was there but repented of my sins because I did not know.

Yes you Muslims will call me Kafir and mark me for death but guess what I do not care because God showed me your religion. Showed me that it enslaves spiritually and trust me infinitely when I tell you that you will be imprisoned. Trust me I know as well as know the containment that is going to house your spirit.

This is how God showed me Islam. In my sleep this lady came to me, it's not the first time I am seeing this lady, I have seen her before in a different instance and she said to me "WHY IS MY MOTHER IN PRISON?" I said my mother isn't in prison and before I could elaborate further she disappeared. Man I woke up and I cried, because I thought something was wrong with my brother, so I called him and cried. Nothing had happened to him and until this day he's okay.
You see <u>My Mother is buried the Islamic way.</u>

Before I got the first visit above my first encounter was this one.

It was Ramadan season in the physical and I dreamt Sodom Hussein. Three days, yes people three days after he passed on I dreamt him and this is how I saw him. He did not speak to me. I saw him clothed in Black, standing at the inside of a fence with a bullet wound in his head looking out. He was enclosed, could not come over the fence nor go through it. You know those prison fences. That was what surrounded him.

You Muslims and Iraqi's can dispute this all you want but this is what I saw. He was in prison in the spiritual world and none of you can take this from me because this was how I saw him. His spirit trusted me, found me and made me see it. He did not show any of you in the Islamic world he showed me. This is what his spirit showed me and I will not take it back. If I did I would be a liar and a deceiver. If you want to dispute it and mark me for death then so be it because death is all you know. Everything for the Muslim or Islamic nation is death. I am going to kill for this or that because <u>none of you can accept the truth.</u> Islam is physical and spiritual bondage. It is hell and from you die in it, continue to live in it you are bound for hell. You will be imprisoned in it for all eternity. You will be tested and tried and if you do not know the right answers you will be doomed. <u>(This test phase is for those good people who converted to Islam like my mother. If you are born in it you are doomed because there is no first or second resurrection or judgment. There is no resurrection of the dead because the life you live in the physical determines where you go in the spiritual.</u> Once you die that's it for you. You are dead if you die dirty and filthy. This is what was shown to me and yes you Christians can say I am spreading hate all you want but this is what I saw. This was what was shown to me. As for you Christians you have followed Jesus unto hell and to say I do not know what will happen to you is an error on my part because you have to go through a different tribulation which is not included in the second resurrection because there is no resurrection of the dead. Know the truth and reclaim your life.

So yes I know Islam bounds you spiritually and physically and you can never have any part or parcel with God if you are wicked. Only a clean Muslim those that have converted can go through but they cannot go through without being tested. They will be tested and tried and if they cannot answer correctly they will be given one chance to call upon someone in the living that they trust for help to the answer that which they do not know. Once they get it right they will be changed operated upon so that they can pass over to the next life or phase which you call and I call heaven. Here they will rest in peace until the Day of Judgment or the day of reckoning as I would like to call it in the physical world because there is no day of reckoning or judgment in the spiritual world. If you die dirty you cannot cross over to heaven. If you don't accept God and live for God truthfully in the living you cannot accept him in the grave. If you do not live your life in truth meaning if you live your life in lies and deceit – hate you will be tested you will go directly to hell and this is if you cannot answer correctly. You have to do the bidding that is outlined for you by Sin – death until the appointed time when your spirit must die. There is no resurrection of the dead and I wish the church would stop telling people that the dead will be resurrected. I too had thought so but there is none because I have seen the dead and hell and I yet to see the resurrection. For those good people that have answered correctly they made it. Trust me infinitely they made it. You made it. It is not to say that you cannot go through judgment in the living, you can and this is for those who God has chosen. You have to live it and be tested like Job. You have to lead the people like Moses but you cannot stray or be ignorant like me and yes Moses. You have to lose it all in order to gain it all meaning walk with God in his light – his integrity. Trust me this is extremely hard and you won't want to do it. Come on who wants to. Do you think educating people about God is easy? Look at the failure rate from the beginning until now. Everyone in Noah's time perished. I would be a fool to say it will be easy today and that everyone will turn to God. It would be good, excellent to think this way but in reality many will still continue to do wrong. Do what they please because they are depending on one man that will save them from their sins. They will continue to go down the wrong road only to find out when it's too late that they were following after SIN their Social Insurance Number. Yes your Social Security Number for those in other lands.

Yes we all have a number, there is no hidden agenda, he made it so but the soul is another domain and this is what sin wants and for billions of us sin has us because we are still lusting, committing adultery, still committing murders, still doing whatever WILL tells us to do. We don't think of God because the God that you have been taught to believe in is not the true God and none of you can see this but I hope as you continue to read you will find the True and Living God who is named Allelujah and not Allah. Yes Allah is taken from the root Allelujah.

The third dream of Islam is given below.

AS FOR YOU DR. YORK I KNOW WHO YOU ARE. I KNOW YOUR AGENDA AND IT HAS TO

STOP. YOU SHOULD BE ASHAMED AND DISGUSTED OF YOURSELF FOR MISLEADING THE PEOPLE AND NOT TELLING THEM THE FULL TRUTH.

YOU SAY YOU ARE OF GOD AND HAVE BOOKS, READ ALL THE RIGHT BOOKS BUT YET DO NOT HAVE RIGHT KNOWLEDGE.

TELL THE TRUTH. TELL THE PEOPLE YOU ARE OF BABYLONIAN DECENT BECAUSE YOU SPEAK THE LANGUAGE OF THE BABYLONIANS.

WOE BE UNTO YOU BECAUSE YOUR HELL IS AND WILL BE A GRAVE ONE BECAUSE WHEN GOD TELL YOU TO DO SOMETHING DO IT CORRECTLY AND WITHOUT A SHADOW OF A DOUBT. DO IT HONESTLY WITH THE FULL TRUTH.

DO NOT LIE TO THE PEOPLE AND SAY YOU ARE AN INCARNATE OF GOD'S ANGELS BECAUSE YOU ARE INFINITELY NOT.

- *NO ONE CAN NAME THE ANGELS OF GOD*
- *NO ONE INFINITELY NO ONE NOT EVEN ME*
- *AND NO HUMAN ON THE FACE OF THIS PLANET CAN BE AN INCARNATE OF GOD'S ANGELS BECAUSE WE ARE FILTHY AND THE ANGELS OF GOD ARE CLEAN. YOU CAN'T EVEN TOUCH THEM LEST*

THEY BECOME DIRTY – UNCLEAN SO STOP MISLEADING AND MISGUIDING PEOPLE. STOP POSING UP AND BOOSTING UP YOURSELF BECAUSE YOU ARE SO NOT OF GOD.

THE ONLY WAY YOU CAN HOUSE A SPIRIT IS IF YOU GIVE YOURSELF OVER TO UNCLEAN SPIRITS – MEANING SELL YOUR SOUL TO THE DEVIL – EVIL. WHEN YOU DO THIS EVIL COMES IN – POSSESS YOU. THIS IS WHAT YOU DID HENCE YOU SPREAD LIES AND DECEIVE PEOPLE WITH YOUR ISLAMIC BULLSHIT. YOU TELL LIES ON THE TRUE AND LIVING GOD HENCE YOU WILL HAVE HELL TO PAY WHEN I'M DONE WITH YOU.

TELL THE PEOPLE THE FULL TRUTH IT IS UP TO THEM TO ACCEPT OR REJECT IT. HOW DARE YOU USE GOD FOR YOUR OWN PERSONAL JIHAD. IT'S NOT GOING TO WORK BECAUSE GOD WILL RAISE UP THE BLACKS OF THE WEST AND SHOW THEM THE FULL TRUTH AND TRUST ME WHEN THEY DO THEY WILL TURN FROM YOU AND YOUR LIES.
YOU KNOW WHO THE COMFORTER IS.

YOU KNOW WHO MARY IS SO WHY HIDE THE TRUTH OF HER BECAUSE SHE IS THE TRUTH AND TAUGHT THE TRUTH. IF YOU ARE OF GOD YOU SHOULD KNOW THIS AND NO BOOK OF A HIGHER ORDER CAN TELL YOU THIS BECAUSE GOD WOULD HAVE TOLD YOU, EDUCATED YOU ON THIS.

STOP QUOTING BOOKS OF MEN BECAUSE THERE IS ONLY ONE BOOK AND THAT IS GOD'S BOOK. IT IS A SMALL BOOK THAT SAYS HOLY BIBLE AND MY PEEPS AND TRUE LOVED ONES IT IS NOT THE BIBLE AS YOU KNOW IT.

This we cannot comprehend. True love has nothing to do with hate, colour of skin or eyes. Stop telling people that God is going to judge the guilty blue eyed. Stop it because none of us are pure, none. No not even the Ethiopians, and yes the Sudanese, none, we are all of mixed lineage. You should know this.

Stop telling them that Arabic is pure and so is Aramaic because it is not. NONE OF THE LANGUAGE UPON THE FACE OF THE LAND – THIS PLANET IS FROM GOD. YOU CLAIM TO BE ONE OF THE TWENTY FOUR ELDER'S INCARNATE BUT YET YOU DON'T KNOW THIS.

SANDSCRIPT, YES PEOPLE SANDSCRIPT IS THE ORGINAL LANGUAGE SIN - MAN AS WE KNOW IT. NOT HEBREW, NOT ARABIC OR ARAMAIC, BUT SANDSCRIPT. EVERY KNOWN AND WRITTEN LANGAUGE OF MAN CAME FROM THIS TONGUE SO DR. YORK TEACH RIGHT, READ RIGHT, WALK RIGHT, PRAISE YOUR NAME GOD PRAISE YOUR NAME PRAISE YOUR NAME PRAISE YOUR NAME FATHER PRAISE YOUR NAME. ALLELUJAH, ALLELUJAH, ALLELUJAH, ALLELUJAH, THANK YOU FATHER THANK YOU. LET YOUR WILL BE DONE WITH THIS

BLIND OBSESSION REBUTTAL THE TRUTH IS NOW OR NEVER

MAN. ALLELUJAH, ALLELUJAH, ALLELUJAH, LET THY TRUE AND RIGHTEOUS WILL BE DONE FATHER, PRAISE YOU HOLY NAME, PRAISE YOUR HOLY NAME, ALLELUJAH, ALLELUJAH YES GOD, YES GOD THY WILL IS NOW DONE. AMEN. CONDEMNATION IS NOW IN YOUR HANDS DR. YORK. CONDEMNATION IS NOW UPON YOU AND IN YOUR HANDS.

Dr. York you claim to be one of the twenty and four elders but yet your home is in disarray. (I am going to leave you now but I will be coming back to you).

George I am coming to you. Yes you George Clooney I am coming to you. Yes you say you are a humanitarian and that you want to help the people of Sudan. Please let it be about the people of Sudan and not some hidden agenda. If you love the people of Sudan**, *truly love them, then let your efforts be about them*** because what you do not see ***God sees.***

So George if you truly love them and you are truly doing God's work and want and need what is best for these people let it truly be about them because as it is something stinks about your agenda and the people you are working with.

Do not tarnish or soil your reputation with others without knowing the full truth you are too good for that. If your heart is in the right place let it stay in the right place.

My Peeps and True Loved Ones I don't know but something does not sit right with me Allelujah,

Allelujah, Allelujah, glory be to God but something does not sit right and I have to open my mouth. George Clooney please do right by the people of Sudan.

When I look at you I read something different in your face, hey and I could be wrong but in the face of your colleague I read something else. I read a different agenda. Yes you are an actor and you can play any role you chose and maybe the face I see is a front who knows but once again ***if you are sincere and true about your efforts and what you want to do in Sudan, let it be about the people and truly helping them and nothing else.***

As I sit and watch, as well as listen I find nothing genuine in what your colleague and you are doing. Mainly in your colleague and his agenda is not about the people of Sudan. His agenda is different and therefore your agenda cannot be different from his and neither of you are fooling Africans.

None of you care about the blacks of Sudan. Yes you can say I am racist my Peeps and that he is trying and you don't see black people trying to help there own so don't bash George and his colleagues efforts for trying.

Go ahead you have all right to and you can tell me off too. But my peeps I am telling you how I feel and this is why I said to George ***if you care about Sudan and the Sudanese people let it be about them, helping them and nothing else.***

George if you care about the people of Sudan so much, why are you setting up Satellites to watch over the country. ***The way I look at it is you are spying on the people***.

Nothing that you or you colleague say will be able to justify this. ***You are spying*** and my Peeps get mad if you want to.

George who gave you the authority to do this? Who are you to do this? Forget the genocide for a minute here. Can any member of a African nation whether white, black, or Chinese come to you and say America has done this this and this and we are going to set up a satellite to watch them or watch you.

If I wanted to set up a satellite and watch you can I do so without the law intervening and arresting my ass?

Who the hell do you think you are setting up a spy camp in Africa?

Neither you nor your colleague care about Sudan and its people, the agenda is ***OIL*** and we know it because your colleague keep stressing on it.
The OIL in the South is your only motive and we the people of the West know it because the pitting is done.

North and south separating and once the South separate from the North all hell will break lose.

What will stop foreign investors from going into the South and swindling the people out of what rightfully belongs to them?

What is the political agenda or the underlying political motive on your part as well as your colleague? Yes I am questioning your integrity as well as his.

God see's and knows and trust me what man is planning he's wiping out.

George if you know you are not for the Sudanese people stay the FUCK out of Sudan because we don't need it. Too much has happened over the centuries and frankly Africans don't need someone to come into their land and bullshit them anymore.

Sudanese people you can tell my ass off and tell me to shut up and mind my own damned business because I am not Sudanese, nor represent you. You can tell me don't speak for you because you can speak for own damned selves and look after your affairs by yourself. What is happening in your homeland does not concern me so stay the Fuck out of your affairs because I am not Sudanese.

George, I thank you, truly thank you for your efforts but if it is not genuine take your help some place else. ***We as Africans have done a poor job of helping ourselves and looking after ourselves and frankly I am tired of different nations raping us.***

It is not about the colour scheme people it is about life and human dignity.

Do not throw us a bone and expect us to eat it. We are not dogs, we are human beings that have lost our way because we let people that did not care

__about us, people that do not care about Africa on a whole pit us against each other and made us hate each other. No one has or have the best interest of Africa or Africans at heart not even our own people because if we did we would not be fighting and killing each other. We would respect and help each other instead of disgracing ourselves.__

Do not say you are throwing a lifeline to Sudan and then stab them in the back. I don't care what your motives are as well as the other gentleman's motive but it just does not sit right and it stinks to the core.

__I do not speak for the Sudanese people__ I'm just telling you how I feel from what I see. If the world, international nations had truly cared about the genocide in Sudan or in any part of Africa they would have truly done something positive to help them long ago. *But instead like scavengers you're all waiting for war to break out then you go to the people and tell them if you want our help you have to give us your oil, your riches. Fuck the lot of you.* God sees this and this is why very shortly many of you will pay including those greedy Arabs. The oils of Africa will be taken away but I don't know when and when it does get taken what are you going to do? You cannot rape people of their prosperity and dignity and you the American's need to know this. You were once linked to Africa. You cannot kill your own family and take what's there's and this is why you are being punished today because you refuse to listen and truly help your own people.

As for you Sudan, Allelujah
Sudan

Sudan
Sudan

The bullshit has to stop. Take a look at yourselves.
Take a good look at yourselves.
What did God turn the lot of you over to?
Tell me (Yes I am yelling)

Tell me what has God turned the lot of you over to?

How the FUCK can a MUSLIM AND CHRISTIAN SAY THEY LOVE GOD AND IS GOING TO PARADISE WHEN BLOOD IS ON YOUR HANDS?

How is your actions justified?

How is this of God?

Half is Muslim, half is Christian and the lot of you are no damned different. Killing each other for a piece of land and religion then have the idosity to turn around and say you have God. Respect your damned self. I was going to say black beauty but then the lot of you are not pure bred – meaning pure black you're a mixture of black and Babylonian and none can dispute this or I will definitely come there if God permits me to and point out the hair, the culture and defiling of body – body art - henna.

Rest assured when the West is ready you will be living like those in Iraq and Afghanistan. Food for oil will come to you and what are you going to do?

How the fuck can you have God and doing what you are doing, fighting amongst yourselves because of Religion? Dumb asses. ***Look at you like fucking scavengers begging for bread.*** Stop killing your people. Stop letting the devil or Shaaytan as you would say destroy you. ***Do not separate your country because if you do when war starts neither side can blame each other because both of you would have let the devil win.*** No I should edit this. If you do separate let it be good separating from evil. Give evil his portion but keep God's side – God's people clean and holy. God's people must not mingle with evil's people. God's people must live as Psalms 1 of your bible and the only way to do this is by separating yourself from evil. As it is right now both sides have turned from God and now you are feeling the pains of it. It will get worse. Do not follow the Ethiopians, and sell your souls, it is not worth it. ***Find a common goal which is God and live for God. Turn back to him and let him fix the problems between North and South because man cannot fix it. Man as it is have their own agenda and it is not to truly help you but take what you have and leave you and your people to die, continue to die while your land lay in ruin – a wasteland.***

Hate my ass I don't care.

Islam and Christianity is the same thing you dumb fucks.

Yes I am mad.

Practice what you preach and stop fighting amongst one another.

93

Tell me something how the hell can a man fight for God?

Tell me, come on tell me. How the hell can a man fight for God?

Does God – the True and Living God fight against you, so why are you fighting him?

Why are you destroying Life?

Why are you killing the True and Living God?

You can't use religion to fight for God because with God there is no religion. All the North and South are doing is raping each other of their dignity and self respect as well as raping each other of your souls . Look at what you are showing the blacks of the west. You are being portrayed as barbarians that can't look after your own and all of Africa is pleased with this.

Tell me something is this what black people have become?

Is this – the religious fighting and slaughter our legacy – our heritage and future?

We were once proud kings and queens now look at us. Look at us. Branded and caste lower than dogs. Why?

Come on tell me why.

Let me tell the lots of you something Islam and Christianity does not represent God they represent the devil – evil. Neither religion represents the black race because God gave us none. If God gave us religion which religion is God?

Which religion represents God and which religion is God? Come on tell me because I would so like to know.

Look at you, look at all of Africa acting like damn fools, no wonder you are all this way, left in confusion to wonder in the wilderness of death and despair for all eternity.

If you all truly love God the lot of you would respect him and live for life and not death. You would all put away your pagan worship and practice and live the right and proper way.

None of you, not one of you have an ounce of respect for the Mother Land. None of you respect yourself or have any self respect because if you did none of you would be fighting and killing for land and religion. Nubia is too good a name for the lot of you. Africa is too good a name for the lot of you. DEAD LAND BETTER SUITS THE LOT OF YOU BECAUSE YOU ARE LIKE UNTO THE WALKING DEAD HENCE YOU PRACTICE THE ISLAMIC AND CHRISTIAN WAY – THE PAGAN WAY OF LIFE.

__All of you are disrespecting Africa, a place where the God's Garden once situated.__

__You're not all Pagan some are pure blood – pure black.__

God blessed the lot of you and look at you but it is only a matter of time before God really turns back the hands of time on your asses and all the **_oil_** that man is fighting you down for, all the diamonds and gold will be all gone.

It is Revelations time people what are you going to do?

The lot of you taking up Religion of Men.

Something that God did not give to you, you are killing each other for.

God never gave you religion; you are apart of God's ancestral home but yet none of you can see it. None of you can be proud of it. None of you can respect it. You all have turned from it.

No body cares anymore because the world is tired.

Go ahead the whole fucking lot of you can kill yourselves because you are all a disgrace to humanity. A disgrace to God and the beautiful land – home he has given to you. **_Look at you beautiful people_** whoring for the devil. Hence the lot of you bow down and praise Satan with religion.

Who the hell do you think gave his people religion? The devil did so he can fool you and take your soul – spirit to hell with him.

This is all a trap and it worked. He fooled Eve and Eve gave up everything including her life for Satan and look where she is now.

She's locked out of God's kingdom because of her act of sin. She lost her life because of him and this is why we are the way we are today. Satan – Evil needed a pansy and he got one and man he screwed her good.

We were no longer free. We became slaves to sin because Satan did not tell Eve the full truth. He omitted the part that once she let him in his race would dominate the world. They would be free to pollute every land there is on the face of the planet and when he they did so the True and Living God would have to flee – leave. He could never come back into this planet because the land – this planet – this earth was now dirty – filthy.

Do you think the devil likes you or even care about you?

Look at what he has made your land into and the lot of you are pleased with this – happy to know that all African lands have been raped of its riches and dignity.

Come on now take a look at all the African lands and tell me why are they a wasteland. Africa is not destitute.

Clean your damned homeland up because if you don't trust me I will clean it up for you and it won't be pretty from my venting. ***LIVE FOR LIFE AND NOT DEATH.***

The whole lot of you have no shame and pride in yourselves. You came out of the Garden of Eden and God has been shielding you and none of you are listening to him, look at the lot of you now.

Look at the Genocide in Sudan, Rwanda, Ethiopia, South Africa, everywhere in Africa *and I am to be proud of the Mother Land. Give me something to be proud of. Let me hold my head up, let my children hold their head up, let your children and future generations hold their head up and be proud to know that Great People, Great Kings, Medicine, Knowledge, God himself resided in Africa, Nubia, the Motherland. Take a good look at all the African Nations and tell me what is there to be proud of today. Your own history you cannot tell of. You are making people that are not Africans tell you lies and spreading lies about God.*

Come on now stop letting your people hold their head down in shame. More importantly stop letting God hold his head down in shame and disgrace.

Tell me something when did God become death - Doctor Death?

Come on now who the fuck are they to tell me about Africa when they don't know Africa or how Africa came about.

Tell me Africa when did God give you religion of men to follow?

When did God die?

Tell me how the hell can God die and all of humanity still lives- death and evil still lives?

How the hell can any African nation take up the bible, the quran, torah and say yes this is the truth about African civilizations?

It's time now to cut the bullshit out and stop adopting shit that other people cast at you and say it is food.

It is not of God.

No other nation should tell any African about them because they don't know nor do they know the truth so why are you doing it?

Why are you letting people that are not of African descent teaching you about your history based on their lies?

Respect God come on now. God truly loves you and every African Nation has spat in God's face.

We sell each other out to the highest bidder and now we have nothing. We can't even hold our heads high and proud and say we are blessed and highly favored. Not one of us can and any one that does I can point to the disarray of every African nation upon the land including Jamaica. Stop letting people cast you dry bones and telling you it's good food. Come on now. Like I've said you can hate me but God is there ready and willing to bless you. Come on now God is waiting to bless you please turn from your dirty ways and go back to the Garden of God and accept him. Please we

need God right now and we have to go to him in truth and live in truth. Let God bless Africa and bring all African nations back to his fold.

No one should come in and tell you about Africa. No one do you hear me. No one should come and tell you how to live because you've been around from the beginning of time. You are in time and was created in time. Know this.

Forget it white people when you say I am racist. Your ass is not excluded out of this because your ass was in the Garden too. You were and still is apart of Africa. North and South America broke off due to violent earthquakes. It separated and shifted the land. Yes this was due to the sins we committed on the face of the land. So kiss my ass when you say I am being racist.

Yes you Jamaicans, the lot of you ain't no damned better either because God took you out of Africa and brought you into the true Garden of Eden, Paradise, and look at you now, like drangcrow harvesting and feasting on the dead. Look at the name of your island you dumb fucks. See what God has done for you.

Yes I am pissed so gang up now and hate me.

Fuck the lot of you and fuck all the races on the face of this planet because none are better than the other. We all fight against each other for what? What someone else have. Then we turn hypocrites and say I am going to church to praise God.

What the fuck has any of you done for God?

What?

Tell me what have you done for God and don't you dare say you pray because you are not praying to God you are praying to death.

You ask God for help and he has helped you and what's the first thing you do, you go into your filthy and dirty churches and give Satan thanks. You'll spit in God's face then trample him down and you wonder why your life can't be better.

If God has blessed you lift your hand and say God thank you – I truly thank you. Do it right there and then. Make God happy but don't spit in his face because he is helping you. Don't even say thank you Jesus because like I said Jesus is a story. Just read the story of Hercules and Zeus.

Don't give away your blessings to the devil come on now.

Some of you if you do do you want something in return. Yes you George's right hand man you only want the OIL in South Sudan and by the grace of God I hope he (God) evicts your ass out of Sudan and show the world your true agenda

Africa does not need the bullshit that you are spreading they need true help. People that are truthful and honest to them and yes I am questioning your integrity and motives. Both races have raped the land and it is time for the bullshit and pitting to stop. We are human beings and we don't need any more people to come in and rape us of whatever little dignity we have left. You cannot continue to rape the land and then turn around and rape the people all over again. It is not right nor is it fair because I am infinitely sure none of you would allow anyone to do this to your homeland as well as ancestral land – European land.

So fuck you George because you are just a puppet on a string for the goon that sits beside you. Yes your intentions maybe pure but know what the fuck you are doing because I don't buy it. Know who you are representing – shacking up with.

If you care so much about Sudan and what is happening over there let the world see it and don't let these people use you. Your heart seem to be in the right place from what I can see but the motives of the people, that man beside you stinks to the core and God himself see's this. This man doesn't care about the Sudanese people and to be honest I don't think you do either so prove me wrong and let me eat the pains of my words by apologizing to you.

They are black and he could care less. All he see's is ***OIL. Listen to him talk why are you not talking about the OIL in the South of Sudan why does he have to mention it all the time.***

What the fuck do you think? This is a black country so take your fucking hypocrisy and bullshit handout someplace else. We're not dogs begging you for a bone. You went into Sudan not Sudan come to you and you the people of South and North Sudan should be ashamed of yourselves as well as hold your heads down in disgrace because if either side continue to let blood spill on the land because of evil – the devil I give you my

word and go on record as staying this that I hope God make the land of Sudan so desolate that not even drangcrow want the land.

Grow the hell up and help each other. You're not children. You cannot let evil stand between both lands. What the hell sense does it make. Killing each other for what a place in hell? Well let me tell you something with all the fighting you are doing amongst each other you're all hell bound because God does not fight. Good cannot fight with evil. There is something called clean prayer and asking God for protection of your land. If everyone prayed clean and ask God in truth for this, no evil formed against you shall or will conquer you know that.

As for you Dr York, Mr. Mahdi if you think I cannot do this think again so duly warn your people of the nonsense they are carrying on with because you claim to be so you should know me, who I am and what I am capable of.

George separate yourself from this man because God is waiting for his ass.

Do the lot of you think this is Iraq?

There is no fucking FOOD FOR OIL BULLSHIT HERE.

Who the fuck do you and this goon think you are fooling? Black people are gullible but we are not all stupid. God shows us what the lot of you are doing and we the children of God see it.

103

You can't fool God so George be careful of whom you lay with because they are the ones to bring your ass as well as your family's ass shame and disgrace.

If you want to help Sudan help but know how you help. Let this help truly be about the people of Sudan and not their OIL.

Know this it is only a matter of time before war breaks out and you will hear the motto FOOD FOR OIL BEING ECHOED AGAIN. IT WAS DONE IN IRAQ AND OTHER PARTS AND IT WILL BE DONE AGAIN IN SUDAN. SO TELL ME HOW COULD ANYTHING THAT YOU DO BE ABOUT THE PEOPLE AND NOT THE OIL.

KNOW FOR A FACT IF AND WHEN WAR BREAKS OUT ANY USE OF FOOD FOR OIL, ANY USE OF WE WILL HELP YOU IF YOU GIVE US YOUR OIL, ANY USE OF THE TERM OIL IN ANYWAY WHEN IT COMES TO HELPING THESE PEOPLE THE WORLD WILL HAVE A RIGHT TO QUESTION YOUR INTEGRITY BECAUSE NOW THEY WILL KNOW THAT YOU ARE NOT GENUINE.

We know it is all about the oil but what you and the world do not realize is that GOD gave those people the oil - Black Gold. God gave those people the land and you nor anyone has the right to take it from them.

None of you have the right to use North and South Sudan and pit them against each other like that. It is not fair nor is it right. You should be bringing both

BLIND OBSESSION REBUTTAL THE TRUTH IS NOW OR NEVER

sides together and let them iron out their differences peacefully. If you have good and clean intentions God will open positive doors for you. God will not refuse you because your intentions are pure good and clean. The oil belongs to them and God will not under any circumstance take it from them and give it to you. According to the bible God made this promise to Abraham when he blessed Ishmael with twelve (12) princes so why do you Mr. Clooney and your Goon want to take these people's birthright from them. Why are you pitting South against North. If you want to talk, talk but bring North and South at the table to talk peacefully. Damn I wish I could sit down and talk to both sides but I am not politically inclined. This resolution I leave in God's true and capable hands to work everything out correctly in peace and not through war.

Do you not have anything important to do with your time and effort?

Didn't your ancestors rape us enough?

Didn't they rape us of our pride and dignity enough?

What do you want to do seal the casket now? Well fuck off and royally kiss my mother fucking ass because I won't let you. Blacks need to start solving their own fucking problems for themselves. We are human beings like I've said not dogs and none of you can fuck us anymore because we have a right a GOD GIVEN RIGHT to live on this earth in peace. No one have or has the right to take this away from us or anyone for that matter.

I'm going to be racist here people but where the fuck did God say his abode was for whites only?

Where is it written?

Come on where and don't you dare bring me books of men either.

Show me where, anywhere in earth, on earth, in heaven and in God's abode where it is written that God belong to whites and whites alone and only whites can get into his abode. Show me and I will show you that you are a damned liar. Anyone that say God's abode is for their race only I can tell them they are a fucking liar because God the true and living God does not discriminate based on colour of skin or anything for that matter. If God did this then none of us would be living today. Take a good look at nature and all that God has given good and evil to maintain and sustain their lives. Yes I am harsh and ignorant in my writings but that is how my spirit is when writing at times.

George, look before you jump and if you want a cause take a look at New Orleans, take a look at the ghettos of New York, California. Blacks, Whites, Latino's are suffering there why not help them if you want a cause?

Clean the shit out of your damned backyard first before you try to clean the shit out of others. Please. I love you, infinitely truly love you but stop letting these people ride on your coat tail you are too damned good for that. You are not their puppet.

People you can slam me all you want and curse me but I don't care. I see the goodness in this man and when I hear him talk when that Goon is around I get embarrassed because George seems like he does not know what he's talking about.

People maybe I am reading too much into George's body language and thinking how misguided he is but look. Looking at the 2011 tapes how many times did his Goon mention Oil in the South of Sudan and that really unnerved me because I know if war breaks out the food for oil bullshit will surface and this is why America will not send troops in Sudan now. If war breaks out OIL will become a factor and play out in their dirty little game and trust me God see's this.

As for you Dr. York back to you, Al Sayyid Imaam Issa Al Haadi Al Mahdi. You say you are of Sudanese decent, the descendant of Al Mahdi, one of the Twenty and Four Elders incarnated but yet you are allowing bullshit like this to happen in Sudan. This is your homeland bitch clean it up. Clean up your fucking homeland. How the fuck can you say you are cleaning up America, the people of the west and bullshit like rape, genocide and murder is happening in your country? Don't even say it because I can say fuck you and kiss my ass because I tried praying to God for my people and vomited big time because their sins have reached too high.

If you were apart of the Mahdi family as you claim the bullshit between North and South Sudan would not be happening.

If you were apart of the Twenty and Four Elders you would be talking directly to God and petitioning God for the people of Sudan not to let the land be divided based on RELIGION OR ANYTHING FOR THAT MATTER.

If you were one of the twenty and four elders all of Sudan would have known this because God would have revealed this to them and they would have been living for God and not MAN.

If you were one of the twenty and four elders you would not come to man – humanity – the West with any form of religion because God the True and Living God never ever infinitely never ever gave any of his messengers – prophets as you call them religion to kill and misguide man – humanity. This I infinitely know and can attest to.

If you were all that you claimed to be you would ask God to truly save your people and not let evil befall them nor divide them.

If you were all that you claim you would have known that God would listen to you because you have direct contact with him and he would not let anything happen to your people because you were sent by him

As you teach and going from your words. God or Allah as you say would have opened their Barathay Gland for them to see and know the true truth

But because I know differently and that you can't do fuck all and you are just a fucking waste of time, a fucking waste chute that is just waiting for the opportune time to unleash more terror on the United States and bring more shame and disgrace to your land, your people another African Kingdom. You work for Satan because you speak Arabic a Babylonian tongue. You say you are black what the fuck makes you black? You tell people you come to clean up the cesspool of the West why the fuck don't you clean up the cesspool in Sudan bitch. Are they not your people. Bitch you are not my people. You don't belong in the black genealogical pool because you are one of Satan's minions hence you speak his language and practice his religion so take yourself out. No you are out so that's okay because I know you have a place in Hell just waiting for you. Yes death is smiling bitch and saying come on I'm waiting this is your spot Michelle and I reserved it especially for you. Sudan will divide because death walks upon the land and trust me death is waiting for you.

Yes your land like many lands across the globe have accepted spiritual death in the form of Christianity and Islam and because they have closed their minds to the truth war and genocide will forever plague the land.

If you were from God your first and foremost agenda would be saving your people and teaching them, the Sudanese people the truth. They are your people as you claim. You claim to be Sudanese but yet with all the money you have earned in the West, off the backs of black brothers and sisters you cannot help your own people. You cannot bring the truth to them.

You say you have the truth but you are so far from the truth because you spread hate and lies.

You say you are but are not because as one of the twenty and four elders you should have known that there is no religion in paradise and God would never give you religion to give to man and humanity.

You should have known that Christianity and Islam is death, death in the spiritual and physical. Once you accept it and die being a Muslim or Christian, whatever form of religion you take you cannot enter into the kingdom of God you can only enter the Kingdom of Hell – Satan's land and not the abode of God. This is part and parcel justification of the truth when Jesus said in my father's house there are many mansions and if it was not so he would not say so.

Tell them the truth the true truth of you. Stop telling people they have to change their name to Mohammed this is sinful and wrong because God's last name is not Mohammed. Satan's last name is not Mohammed either and if you were of God you would know the true and real last name of Satan and his people.

God gave us all a name and it is sinful and yes an abomination of sin for anyone to change their last name to something else.

The only time you can change your last name meaning add your name to someone else is through marriage.

No forget that because in retrospect those that have changed their names are married to sin so forget that. They have no part and parcel with God anymore because they were converted and they legally changed their last name to reflect the devil's own – well one of his own. Sorry black people "NO GIVESY BACKSEY". No for real. We do not look into things before we forge along and this is our downfall.

Tell them if they continue to walk this way what will happen to them. I've told you above about the grave tell your people the truth and not hide it from them. Tell them the many mansions that Jesus talked about are the mansions in hell because where God resides there are no mansions, houses because no man or woman whether spiritual or dead can tell you what the inside of God's abode look like. God have to give you permission to do so and no one that is living on the face of this planet or in the grave is clean enough to do so. You should have known this so why not teach and preach the truth. That's if the truth is within you to teach.

According to the bible Jesus is known as the first begotten of the dead. This Revelations revealed unto us but then you should have known this if you were one of the four and twenty elders. You should have known what Jesus was all about and what he did and more importantly you would have known the truth about the existence of Jesus.

Tell the people the truth that Jesus was not a Jew.

Tell them he was Muslim.

Tell them that Jesus was added to the bible because Revelations is just a rip off of Daniel and Isaiah just solidified and justified the lie.

Tell them the full truth if you can but then you can't because you have not the truth hence you teach lies and claim to be when we the Children of God know you are nothing but a FRAUD.

You are a fake. Remember Back to Eden where you got your pack of lies. Anyone that read your shit or any of your shit under the name of Dr. York can find some of your wording word for word in the book Back to Eden. Hey you could be the author of that book who knows but in a nut shell you used that book. Hey you are good but guess what you are not good enough and soon people will find you out because all black people have to do is go to any black bookstore and read some of the black books they have on the shelf.

Books like:

Back to Eden
The five books of Moses
The Macabes Bible
The Egyptian Book of the Dead

Let me educate you on the Angels of God. They are not Muslim nor are they Christian. They are not affiliated with religion and could never be because religion is a lie.

The greatest no ONE OF THE GREATEST LIE that was told to control and dominate man – humanity.

Religion came from the devil meaning wicked and evil people had to devise religion to keep humanity fighting and killing so that Satan – Death could stick around. The more we kill and hate the longer death lives and the more he strives.

Religion is death hence we kill for it – we kill for religion of men.

We have to buy death but no one can buy Life because life is free. And the way we buy death is through our offerings – alms – tides.

No religion on the face of this planet can save anyone because with life – good life and living a good life you cannot die nor do you need saving because you are living by life – the truth of God.

No one can buy life like I've said but we sure as hell can buy death.

When you are associated with religion you have to kill – bring a sacrifice to the alter and this is a must hence "THE WAGES OF SIN IS DEATH" you have to die. Your spirit and soul must die because we accepted death and gave our body and spirit over to death – Satan – Evil.

This is your blood sacrifice because we are told by the heads of these churches to drink blood and wash in blood. This is nastiness and like I've told you God infinitely does not deal in nasty he deals in cleanliness.

The next way we give evil his pay or sacrifice is by bringing other people into the church or your church. Those people that you bring in are your sacrifice – your pay onto evil which is their souls and this cannot be disputed nor can the blood sacrifice be disputed because both are infinitely true.

God's people don't bow down to the floor because the ground is where we put all manner of filth in like I've told you.

If you were an angel of God you would be wearing the colors of God's angels.

More importantly you would have the hair and you don't have it. You can't rock the hair because it is an abomination unto you. You can't wear it because you are not Ja-Mai-Can meaning you were not made by God nor are you of God.

You pay homage to the dead, bow down to the dead, sacrifice unto the dead and more importantly you speak the language of the dead. You have your father's tongue because Arabic comes from Urdu and Urdu is a Babylonian tongue and all facet of Arabic came from this language.

If you were of God you should have known all these things and more.

If you were of God you should have known that the devil hath not 666 years to pollute but 24000 years to pollute and corrupt.

If you were of God you should have known that 666 represent the 3 daughters of the devil in the spiritual world.

If you were of God you should have known that in the spiritual world evil is female and that when an evil person dies in the physical it is a woman in the spiritual realm that receives their soul. Evil have to tell her they love her.

If you were of God you should have known that the square represents the devil and the square is not the perfect containment unit.

If you were of God you would know the seal of Satan because it is not 666 like that there is a line above and below the 666.

If you were of God you would know the truth the full truth of the Star of David and not tell people lies that it is a seal. It is not a seal because God hath no seal that is known to man except one.

If you were a child of God you would have known that the Mogen David – the star of David represents Male and Female.

You would also know that when the Mogen David – the star of David when interlocked represents the union of good and evil through marriage, therefore this star must never infinitely never ever be interlocked because God's children cannot be interlocked and they can no longer marry evil nor can they continue to marry wicked and deceitful people – people that are not for God or in the fold of God.

If you were a child of God you would know that the devil himself sits at the head of all churches including your temples, mosques, synagogues.

These places are the devils domain – control over humanity. The way they control is by telling lies upon the True and Living God by making you believe in things that are unclean and unholy – things that defile the True and Living God.

If you were a child of God you would know that God ordains no one to speak for him because he God can speak for himself.

If you were a child of God you would know that none of God's messengers can interfere with in the life of the living.

If you were a child of God you would infinitely know that no messenger of God, not one can say they come to one specific race of people because God's people are of varying race and colour.

If you were a child of God you would know that God does not discriminate against anyone because if he did like I said we would all be dead and he God would die as well because he practiced sin – hate.

If you were of God you would know that God's messengers cannot interfere with Evil's children – race because God did not send us or anyone to interfere with the devil's own. What is for the devil must stay for the devil and what is for God the True and Living God must stay for him.

When God send his messengers they have to go and speak to his people – his children and it does not matter what part of the globe they are in they have to do the work of God truthfully and honestly and they cannot use books written by men to deliver the message. Yes the bible is an exception this is why it is known as the book of sin because Egypt was invaded and the Babylonians had to gain access to the books in order to change them by including them(the Babylonians) in these books and once they did that the books that were written became contaminated – condemned because they were no longer truthful, they contained sins – lies. And if you were true you would know this as well as know why Moses was sent into Egypt. You would know the significance of Moses and the Mountain.

If you were a child of God you would have known that . You would also know true time

You would also know the true time of God

You would also know about time in time and the different times

You would also know the existence of life before time and in time

If you were a child of God and a messenger of God you would be able to go into Hell and take people out – meaning those that are on the border line – the ones that did not know the full truth of Life and Death

If you were a child of God and a messenger of God you would know that even though we die without knowing the truth the Children of God can save the not too far gone in the grave and no I am not contracting myself because God does not deal in the dead meaning God cannot save the wicked – Satan's people because Satan does not want to be saved.

Hell is hell but in the Grave – the ones that truly did not know the truth can be saved. This stage is different from hell. I know I've just confused you but you will see what I mean further on because I did not mean to throw any of you for a loop. And no this is not a contradiction because sometimes my explanation is shabby hence certain things I would love to explain face to face where you can question me and yes you can bring all your books to rebuke me.

Forget they YEAH THINK and smile.

So Dr. York or whomever you are does this say much for you and your lies?

Your people need your help but yet you can't help them. You go around raping other people's children of their souls with your lies. You rape them of their dignity and self respect then turn around and call yourself a child of God.

There are many mansions in HELL hence in my father's house there are many mansions bitch so step off my God's coattail and go ride on yours – the devil's coattail. Bitch Satan knows you hence you get the people of the West to change their last names to one of the devil's own. So go fuck yourself and suck seed because you have to kiss Satan's ass to survive in his world.

> *Jesus couldn't take our souls and will never take our souls. Nor will he petition God for anyone because Jesus does not exist. He does not exist in the spiritual world but then you are of God and you are one of the twenty and four elders so you should know this. You should have known that the story of Jesus is just a story and nothing else. A story that was fabricated to fool the true Jews. It worked though but the story did not fool all of us did it because we kept the truth and know the truth and because of this truth we must rise and retake the kingdom of the living which is the kingdom of the true and living God. Yes I know one went around professing to be Jesus but tell me in all his professing is the world saved? In all that you Al Madhi, Dr. York, in all that you have done have you cleaned up the filth of the West? What can you do to clean up the West?*

Tell me something Mr. one of the twenty and four elders why did you come to earth?

In all the books you have written and the millions you have made why have you not done something for your people?

You've been on earth for decades but yet the war and strive brews more and more?
The killing of innocent lives escalate more and more?

In all that you have done and the time spent on earth what have you done to help God's people including my homeland?

How many millions have you donated to any of God's land on the behalf of God?

My country my place of birth need help what have you done for them in the name of God – the True and Living God but then again we don't need your help because you are a FRAUD – a motherfucking fake that is riding on the coattail of the True and Living God. Word of warning stay the FUCK OUT OF MY LAND – GOD'S LAND and yes I know what destruction is in stored for them. Keep your pity and dry bread we don't need it because I've petitioned God on their behalf but their sins have gone too far so now they have to pay with their lives - death.

You are one of God's angels what are you doing on earth?

Did you come to earth to screw us over like Satan with your pack of lies or did you come to earth to finish what Satan could not finish?

God's angels cannot come into a dirty land you know this. No I should not say that because that is false. No it's true because it is the death angels that come. Just to clarify this for others that do not know.

Tell them the truth of you because God's angels cannot reincarnate or incarnate into anyone we are too filthy meaning we are not clean.

As for me and those that bought into your deception and have petitioned God sincerely to forgive us and help us to walk in his footsteps.

Those of us that try I know there is a home in God's abode waiting for us.

Look at you, does this say anything for your character. You are Sudanese help your damned people and show them the true way of life, God's way of life and light. Tell me what's so important about America that every nation – every Islamic nation want to wipe them off the face of the planet?

What threat does America pose to you?

No for real.

What is so significant about America that they are on your hit list for war – your bullshit – so called Holy Jihad.

America does not speak your Babylonian tongue

America does not kiss the ass of Satan.

Let me ask you something is it the fact that they have the ALL SEEING TRIANGLE – ALL SEEING EYE ON THEIR DOLLAR BILL AND YOU CANNOT COMPREHEND THE SCOPE AND BEAUTY OF THIS ANCIENT MARK?

It it the fact that no one can.

Are you Jealous?

Jealous of the fact that you cannot have what they have which is the truth. The truth of God because in God the True and Living God we trust.

Is it the fact that American was once a part of Africa – the land of the Ameers who were black?

Look around the Triangle was given to God's people. It is a seal that is embedded in them because the Triangle is the beginning of Life and life goes up not down hence God's people must house this mark whether it be embedded in their flag of the country that they live in or embedded in their skin and no it is not a tattoo.

America and Americans do not know the importance of the Triangle nor the eye within the triangle because if they did they would never associate with evil or evil secret societies.

God's people know the significance of the Triangle because we know about life and how life came into being. When you have the triangle you are all knowing as well as see all. This is your gift because you have the gift of truth – Life. This knowledge no book can teach us because it is engrained in our DNA and as a messenger and child of God you should have known all of this.

If you are one of the four and twenty elders God will not refuse you but help you. God will show you what to do so that the people will truly listen to you.

Look now the FOOD FOR OIL bullshit will now be on the land of Sudan and if it does get there I will hold you personally responsible because you say you are a man of God, Allah, one of the four and twenty elders and you are allowing this to happen to your people. The people you claim to love and come from.

You boast of the fact that you are of Mahdi but yet doing nothing in the name of Al Mahdi to help your people.

You are doing nothing in the name of Al Mahdi to bring peace to a beautiful region and more importantly you are doing nothing in the name of All, Allelujah, Allah as you say to bring peace to your people.

Go figure.

Yes you can slam me all you want but guess what God see's what you are doing and like I've said woe be unto you when God is through with you for the lies and deception that you have spread.

Woe be unto you for killing the souls of the West with your Islamic bullshit. Remember David killed Uriah and he could not build God's temple because blood was on his hands.

How much blood is on yours?

Tell me how the hell do you think you can bring the Crystal City back to earth?

How the hell can you build God's temple of praise if you are raping the people of their souls, souls that rightfully belongs to God.
Clean your damned country up. You should be ashamed and disgusted in yourself to see what is

happening in your land and say you are of God and ignoring your own homeland.

I would love to tell you to kiss my ass but it is too good for you to kiss. Help your damned people because I am sick of hearing about what is happening in that country.

Fucking sick of hearing how we are killing each other and for the life of all the mother fucking African nations none of you all are taking heed.

Killing your fucking selves for what?

Hating your fucking selves for what?

Africa is the mother, the center of the earth you dumb fucks, respect your damned selves and heritage.

Look at all of you, wallowing like pigs in a fucking pig pen and listening to others tell you about yourselves and heritage.

I am so sick of the lot of you, beautiful set of people living like the pigs and Jesus told your asses when the Samarian whatever culture she was. She came to him and ask him for bread and he told her 'WHY SHOULD HE TAKE THE MEAT OFF THE TABLE OF THE CHILDREN OF ISRAEL AND CAST IT UNTO DOGS." Read it for yourselves it's in the bible and yes Dr. York you know exactly where that quote is in the bible because I read your books; followed you but God showed me you. The liar and deceiver you are. You're a viper of the leper race hence you are a condemnation of sin and a condemnation unto the spirit of man – humanity because you are sending innocent souls to hell to be imprisoned and killed by death.

Who the fuck are you to do this?

Who are you to spread lies and tell lies. You're raping people of their wealth and souls you dumb fuck.

How dare you use God as a bargaining chip to seal the faith fo God's children in hell?

You're a fucking demon and a condemnation as I've said and woe – truly woe be unto you you conniving piece of crap.

Look at Africa and the people right now and tell me if the world isn't saying the same thing. Telling you "why should they take the food off their tables and cast it unto dogs?" We have become dogs to the world and none of you, not one African nation can say otherwise. Not even Jamaica can say otherwise because we have become dogs accepting any bullshit that is thrown our way. Ask us about Africa and our heritage and none can tell you but ask them about Pagan and Paganism and they jump up and tell you proudly. Ask them about the true and living God and none can tell you. All they can do is quote from the book of the damned meaning the book of the dead - sin.

Tell me where is the book of Life?

Where is it?

Where is the book of Life?

If you have balls tell me because you surely don't know or know of it.

When are we going to step up and truly love ourselves?

Help your damned people asshole. I don't care whether you are White or Black or Chinese. When people talk about African they only see Black People and for the Arabs they are Asian, Saudi Arabia is not apart of Africa it is apart of Asia, predominantly, just look at the map of the world and you will see so technically they can't call themselves African's because they are not and never will be. God separated the lot of them from Africa.

So Mr. Mahdi what are you going to do? Are you going to continue to let people deface the African nation by saying "they don't take the meat off their tables and cast it unto dogs" because we are like dogs unto them. We are looking for a handout when we of ourselves can help ourselves if we would just stop the fighting and killing of each other.

Come on Mr. Mahdi how much more Sudanese need to be displaced and killed before your people and the rest of the African nations stop the nonsense they are doing and help?

How much more of your people, women and children must they rape and rob before you do something? The wicked, evil and wicked men reside in your land, how much more should your people; African nations go through because of evil and wicked men – people like you?

How much mother fucking more?

Shit, take a look at your people, look at them and tell me you truly love them. Look at them mother fucker look. They are your people and you have done nothing in the name of God to help them. You have not called on the name of God nor have you talked sincerely to God to help them.

All you do is rape and rob the blacks in the west for your personal gain.

Who the fuck are you to do this?

You are sending them to hell bitch.

And we the blacks of the West are fucking worthless because if were solid in God meaning if we were the true roots of God condemnation of sin like this one would not fool and deceive with lies – sin. We would be free because we would never accept Death and Hell. We would never accept physical and Spiritual death because we would know the truth and live by the truth daily.

Look at God and tell God you truly love him

Look bitch, look, look at Sudan, your people and tell me you truly love them. Help them asshole because they need your help. Fuck Jihad, you heard me FUCK JIHAD these are your people not the devil's clan. They are not of the devil's race well some of you are. Most of you are God's children that he protected. They are not the children of the outside Garden you know this so why are you representing the children and people of Nod. Why take up where Jesus no this man left off by bringing in the shit of the Amorites - Bohemians and feeding it to your people, my people, more importantly God's people.

Fuck I am sick of the shit that is happening in the world. Sick of it in Africa and around the globe and yes sick of the shit that is in my life because I make mistakes and still making the same mistakes.

How much more of your people should this man kill before all of AFRICA wake up and go back to God?

How much more innocent lives should be lost before all of Africa, Libya, Egypt, Ethiopia, Kenya, Rwanda, Ivory Cost say no more. This shit has to stop and we are going to stop the shit in Sudan. Why the fuck are they turning a blind eye to this? This is an African nation. Work together to help each other.

No more man, not one drop more, no more God no more, not one more drop of blood should be shed in AFRICA-NUBIA. The Land of the New Beings as you so called them.

Come on Dr, York I dare you to make a positive difference. Don't just claim to be, BE. If you truly love GOD-ALLAH as you say live for him and do right by him. Show God that you truly care. *Petition him because you have full connection to him. You claim to be one of the four and twenty elders, petition God and ask him to open the eyes of your people and let them see the real truth and turn back from their evil ways. You are of God a direct connection to God he will not refuse you, you know this. God does not refuse his people because all that they do they do for God. Remember all that God created was good so why are you doing bad? God's people cannot be bad meaning wine and dine with evil. They cannot sit with them nor make shrines and temples unto God because God does not require shrines and temple. God does not require worship all he requires is Praise meaning you are to thank him for what he is doing for you as well as what he has done for you. That's all he requires and we can't do that properly. Stop deceiving people because I know and God know that you are not one of the four and twenty elders because there is none. I know this and you know this. You know nothing of the spiritual world. You know nothing of hell. You know nothing of the mark of the beast and what it represents but now you know. No one that is of God can use religion you know this because God is not a religion he is real. God cannot die nor does he want anyone to die. Eve accepted death and she died. We as humans have accepted death and this is why we die. We gave death the power and if you were a child of God you would have known this. Moses and Noah did not take religion to the people so why are you doing it? And for me to say Noah I am misleading people - humans because we are living in the time of Noah. We are the people outside the Ark of God and do not know it because the True and Living God is the Ark as well as the Mountain. The door of the Ark is almost closed and none of us know it. People this is Noah's time because soon we will be banging down the door of God to get in and can't. We need to straighten up and live right or we will hear "TOO LATE, TOO LATE". Trust me every human being on the face of this planet will hear the death angels sing and sing clearly so that you can fully hear 'TOO LATE" and when you hear this know for a surety that it is too late. Right now we are giving everything to evil and refusing God. Don't expect God to save you when you hear your song because God did try and like our forefathers we cast Life aside for Sin. So because of this God must leave you to sin. He cannot interfere with Sin because you choose sin and sins offerings. Yes water is for now but true death is fire and this is what will devour man if we do not change and clean up ourselves. Like I said you are not one of the four and twenty elders and you should know but bitch you know fuck all. Go back to the beginning when I broke down the mark of the beast. Now you can kiss my ass with your four and twenty elders because 24 represents the time line of evil – the square and because I know you are a fraud and can never be a part of God's kingdom but the devils fuck you. With you telling me and the world you are an incarnate of the four and twenty elders now the world know that you are a part of Satan and his kingdom – his domain because you are a part of his religion hence you bring Islam to people to destroy and kill them. Oh but then again since you are one of the four and twenty elders you are one of the 24 hours of sin. You are one of Satan's henchman – murderer, yes hit man – assassins.*

You are not for God and will never be for God. You cannot represent God you can only represent the devil and his domain. Let me break it down a little bit further for you and get ahead of myself. Go to revelations and read it when it said "WOE BE UNTO THE JEWS THAT CALL THEMSELVES JEWS BECAUSE THEY ARE OF THE SYNAGOGUE OF STATAN". Simply put you could never, infinitely never be a Jew. You don't even know the meaning of the word Jew. You can never represent the God's people so when you tell us you are Islamic Hebrew, You are Ansaars, and whatever name you use we do not listen to you because we know the truth that you are of the synagogue of Satan. Every last one of you including the Blacks that you have converted and indoctrinated in your pack of Babylonian lies are a part of the synagogue of Satan. You represent Satan and have to represent Satan because you are infinitely apart of his seed. You of yourself said it because you are of the four and twenty elders – the 24 henchman not horseman. Oh trust me the square as well as 24 mean a hell of a lot more. There is significantly more to the four and twenty elders, yes the 24 thousand years of Satanic rule so step off and help your people.

You claim to be do better ***because like I said if you let the OIL FOR FOOD bullshit hit Sudan I will hold you personally responsible because you claimed to be one of the four and twenty elders and you could have done something about this and didn't.***

Remember you said the four and twenty elders is of God so where the fuck are they?

What the fuck do they do?

Oh yeah I forgot they are in hell waiting for you.

I am solely going to blame you because you let the bullshit in your country happen as well as escalate and gotten this far. Way out of hand.

You are to blame for all the mess in your homeland because you said you are from God and God gave you a task to do and I infinitely know the first order of business was to set your homeland right. You were to clean up the mess in your land and more forward in a positive way to clean up the other lands of God.

Come on and do something right – positive for God. As you petition for the East I will petition for the West as well or you can petition for the North West and I will petition for the South East. You take two and I will take two and hope my Peeps and True Loved Ones and Your Peeps and True Loved Ones join us both so that it is not just the two of us petitioning God for the people of earth but everyone petitioning and showing God that they care and they are sorry.

PLEASE DO NOT USE CHRISTIANITY AND ISLAM TO DO IT. DO IT OUT OF THE TRUE LOVE OF GOD BECAUSE GOD IS NOT A RELIGION AND HE DOES LOVE AND CARE ABOUT US ALL.

Come on Al Saayid you claim to be one of God's chosen step up or shut the fuck up. How dare you

use God as your scapegoat and bargaining chip for your hidden agenda?

How dare you use the Blacks of the West in your deceitful and corrupt plans?

Who the hell are you to do this?

You blatantly lie to blacks and none can see your hidden agenda.

Why the hell should they fight for you or bloody their hands for you and a race of people that refuse to help themselves?

You don't like them nor do you care about them because if you did you wouldn't be killing them. So for now Dr. York or whatever name you use know that God is watching you and he did pour his cup out on you so what are you going to do? Are you going to change your dirty ways and come back to God or are you going to continue to whore and spread lies?

The hand of God is stretching out to your court what are you going to do?

Yes Africa you are justified to hate me now and I have given you reasons as well as given the rest of the world reasons to hate me because I let my anger get in the way but you know what let it be and *please do not lash out at Jamaicans because my views certainly and most definitely do not represent them.*

This is my ranting because I am so tired of it all. The oil bullshit; the killing; raping, genocide, displacement of people for what Satan and his people? Tell me is it all necessary? Tell me what makes the North superior to the South and the South superior to the North? (For those of a higher knowledge I know the significance of North and South and it has nothing to do with man per say). Yes the poles people – Polaris.

Tell me something are you not one people?

Are you not of the same bloodline?

Are you not God's people? So what the hell are you fighting about?

Is Islam any better that Christianity?

Is Christianity any better than Islam?

Are they not the same religion?

Both compliment each other?

Both are accomplishing the same goal, which is to bring as many people to hell as it possibly can?

What are both sides in a race to outdo each other?

Has the competition gotten so intense – serious – fierce that you have to go against each other and play dirty politics for sin?

Tell me if there is one God why are you fighting?

If there is one paradise why are you fighting?

If there is one way to get to paradise why are you fighting?

Is God partial?

Is Allah partial?

God gives the wicked and the just air to breathe and he is not partial, why are you?

What sense does either side make?

As it is right now none of you are going to paradise or heaven whichever you call it.

None, absolutely none because blood is on all your hands.

No it's not you say.

It infinitely is because one kills and the other drink blood.

How can a man, a country say they are of God when they wage war amongst each other and against each other?

Where the hell did God say he was about war?
Is God Hades?

Is God Satan?

When Cain killed his brother what happened to him?

Did he not have to leave his mother's abode so tell me Sudan and the world if this was done why the hell do any of us think that we are going to get to paradise?

This goes for me too. I have sinned big time but all I can do is pray and petition God to let me in. Let my good deeds outweigh my bad. I am not righteous people. God is righteous, perfect and just.

Yes I may vent but that is me but this Lion – Lyon (s) has a roar meaning I have to roar okay. Put it together and no I INFINITELY DO NOT CLAIM TO BE I AM JUST MICHELLE and we will keep it so.

Africa I truly love you dearly but I had to do this for you to wake up and respect who you are. Like I said you are an ancient civilization and you should never let anyone take your birthright from you. Nor should you let someone come in and give you watered down crap and tell you it is your history. No one can tell you about you but you yourself. God gave you a beautiful land – a piece of him so stop casting God aside and respect you. Respect God because when it is all said and done you are causing Satan and his people to look down on you and yes you are causing them to look down on God. They are laughing at God because Evil's intention is to bring God shame and disgrace. His ultimate agenda is to destroy you God's people and destroy God in the process.

Evil must destroy LIFE because evil knows it has no part and parcel with life. Evil hates – no loathes God that much so the more lies he feeds you the more God moves away from you and the more his people and all the goodness that he has given us dies.

We are to have pride and ambition as well as truly, infinitely truly love the land God has given us because it is well given.

No I've never been to Africa but respect your heritage because your heritage is a part of God – the True and Living God.

You can hate me for my words but I tell it like I feel it and yes I am harsh but forgive me. I am just angry at the bullshit that is happening and you as a people need it to stop. You have to stop this. You cannot put band aid on the situation over there because it does not help. As a people and as individuals you have to want and need change for yourself. You have to respect yourself and respect your country as well as your heritage. We can't say great civilizations came from Africa but yet the west depicts Africans as barbarians. Shit they tell us we come from monkeys and we buy into this bullshit. They give us dirty and filthy religions to worship and pray in and we buy into it. We kill for it. When God gives you the right food to liberate you, you tell God no thanks and keep wallowing in our filth. Then when it gets unbearable we cry to him and say God help us.

Why the fuck should God continue to bail our asses out of our messes when we keep going back into them? Eventually God is going to stop listening to us and walk away and this is what he has done. He stepped aside and left the devil – evil – sin – death to have his way with us because this is what we are telling God we want

We don't listen. We would rather the Pagan way of doing things. Now they tell you one man is going to save you and you listen. Wake up and see what the devil is doing to you.

You have to save yourself. Each and every one of you have to start truly loving yourself. Truly love yourselves because you are a family. Look at how many countries you have. Forget about North and South America because we know these lands broke off from you.

We were separated. You know better so do better. You cannot let people that do not have the best interest of the African Nation as a whole tell you how to live. You are from the beginning of time so why are you not representing time in time. God have not forgotten about you. You are the ones to forget about God and give up on him. You are the ones to take up all forms of ritualistic crap and bring it to God and for this God has walked away from you because you have polluted the land. Greatness came out of Africa so why are you letting people tell you otherwise. Why are you letting people class you as monkeys and apes? We are spiritual beings that can tell time, have true time but because we have adopted nastiness from other nations we have lost our sight. We can no longer tell time – spiritual time. We know the dead. We know what the dead can do. We know how to defeat evil and deliver our people from the dead because we can talk to the dead face to face. We know how to do this but we have lost this gift. Every element of sin and death we kept at bay and have lost it and now we wonder and live in sin. We wonder why our countries can't be better. We wonder how our lives are filled with so much sorrow and can't be better.

The two truest Psalms are Psalms 23 and Psalms 1 but because of sin Psalms 23 is no longer effective to keep sin at bay. Sin knows the rope. Psalms 23 cannot aid us in keeping sin away anymore. It is not effective and time and time again God has shown me this but I could not comprehend until now. ***Psalms 1 is the only Psalms that can help us. I repeat Psalms 1 is the only Psalms that can help us because when we live by this Psalms the devil cannot hurt us nor can he get in.***

Yes my Peeps and True Loved Ones I am not going to take it further but I am going to get back on board because I fell so far off track and I truly wish someone could cut up the pieces of the map and join them together. Yes without the oceans, seas but just keep the four rivers of Genesis.

So George Clooney and the man beside you tell me this is truly about the people of Sudan and not the oil. Take the satellite down do not use it because if you do you will be held accountable. ***You and your family will die, his family will die. I am begging you for the true love of your family and all Americans let this be about truly helping the people of Sudan.*** White people will die and they will have no one to blame but you and this man. Innocent people will lose their lives and this is wrong. Please I am begging you to let this your mission be about truly helping the people of Sudan and not about the oil. People will further hate

Americans. I am not threatening you but telling you like it is. You bring back satellite images and say this is what is happening in the South, America and the international world will send troops into Sudan. More innocent Sudanese people in the North and South will die and people will see you as the cause of this and you cannot blame them. People especially Black people will not look at other nations they will look at America because we were taught to hate Babylon and Black people see America as the new Babylonian empire. ***Jamaican's have been saying this, preaching this, singing this for centuries. You the American's want to become the new seat of Babylon and with all that you are doing none of you can see that you are not. The true Babylonians are playing your asses like a fiddle. They are taking the dark light off them and putting it on you and when they are ready, trust me it will be too late for the lot of you because hell would have done it's job and made American and all the land its domain and there will be nothing none of you can do about it. The hadan will be called for war and Jihad will be full blown and trust me they will more than bruise your heel as stated in Revelations. Your woes and pleas will not be heard because each and everyone of you did not listen to God. Each and every one of you spat in his face and walked away. You all killed him and no God isn't Jesus.***

Join the pieces of the map together and see that America was once apart of Africa and the land separated because of violent earthquakes that we call the great flood. Whether you want to believe this or not it is up to you but it was. So know this.

George by sending images to the ICC to say yes this is what`s happening like I've said the global nations will send troops in and America will be the first one. When you do this my peeps take out economics out of the picture because the world will be at war and you America will feel the brunt of it. *I am going to stop here but before I go I am pleading to every American that has joined the Islamic bandwagon to truly walk away because these wars do not concern us - you. We cannot take up another man's fight and say it is ours it is wrong. Not one of us can lay claim to Africa in that way because not one of us know what African land we were taken from.*

Listen despite how our forefathers ended up in America though what we read in history you cannot commit treason by standing against your homeland. It is not fair and despite our struggles America is your home. God saw it befitting to secure you and you have no right to let someone come in and cause you to cause your country shame and disgrace.

You say you are loyal and you love your home then truly love your home because you stand under the banner of the UNITED STATES OF AMERICA meaning you are all united in your cause. Look at your motto it says "the land of the free and the home of the brave" so live free and know the land that which you were born in.

Listen every country have their issues and problems but you cannot let people that do not have your best interest at heart mislead you or cause you to go against your country. When you

<u>do this you are committing treason of the highest order. If a man don't like you then they should stay the fuck out of your country plain and straight.</u>

<u>Fuck these assholes. Do not go against your country for bullshit wars – wars staged by the Babylonians. It is not fair to you nor is it fair to God. It is infinitely not fair to your country.</u>

BEFORE I GO ON MY PEEPS KEEP ON READING. I WILL CATCH UP WITH YOU BELOW.

Americans and the globe forget the hatred for a minute. Truly forget the hatred of me for what I have said above.

No

Damn people wasn't the hatred of Blind Obsession enough for me. Man this hate, come on because all I want is for each land to look at themselves and see what is happening. We cannot continue this way. God is calling out to all of you and he is showing you what he needs each and everyone of you to do but none of you are listening. Hey I am not the anti-christ well many of you are saying that I am and I can't change you, never can and never will. Anyway Revelations speak of war but what type of war.

Right now America is not learning and not seeing. Western Nations are not listening and taking heed to what is to come and must come.

I don't like politics and this is a sticky situation because to me politics is like religion. They go hand in hand in that they are both lies. They are like make up and it is when politicians tell the people the truth then we can move forward.

Government can only do so much and to promise this and that is a lie. If you cannot do it do not tell the people you can. And we as a people need to know that there is so much a government can do. Governments are like businesses and they can go bankrupt as well. So people do not put so much pressure on your governments because there is so much they can do. As citizens we need to start thinking and doing. We say we love our country but what are we doing for our country. We need to start holding the politicians accountable. We are trusting them to run the country properly and not spend our hard earned tax dollars unwisely. Come on now. We all have a future so why should our government squander it – rape us of it. When we retire we should get our pension. Governments need to secure this. We can't be electing officials that keep on sinking the country what about your future, your children's future. Who will secure theirs – their future? ***And no people do not go out there and cause a riot.*** We can talk civilized to these politicians. They need your votes and don't go on their promises because promises mean nothing to them when they get in office. Let them tell you what they are doing now to secure your future, your children's future. We need honest politicians not ones that tell lies. There is nothing wrong if a politician say he cannot do this. We know there are limitations as to what he or she can or cannot do. No more promises just the truth that's all you need.

I hate to bring this in this book but if I have to I have to and can't run from it. Lord knows that I don't want to but it must be.

The West have to stop fighting the East because the West cannot win and will never win.

Please do not gasp people. We are fighting a losing battle. The people that we are fighting have been fighting from the beginning of time and none has won. Yes David and his army but was David in the West. Think. Many are saying the Arc angel fought with the devil and won but I say unto to you this is infinitely false. It is a lie. The devil can never ever infinitely never ever enter the domain of God because the devil is a murder, a liar and a deceiver. He stinks and God infinitely do not like stink he cannot take the smell. Know that Satan as you call him was never in heaven with God and could never be because God does not deal with filth nor does he deal in dirt. God is clean and even though I write these books I too have to be changed in the spiritual realm in order for me to go to God. Every good person has to.

The Western Hemisphere cannot win on their terms. We can and will never win the devil in his domain. We have to outsmart and outwit the devil. These people were bred to fight. They were the ones outside the Garden of Eden. They took us out by coming into our land. Watch 10000BC this movie is accurate as accurate as you are going to get to the truth. And I will show you further below. These people are the people of darkness, they know the land better than you and me because they are physical beings hence the bible refers to them as

MAN. They will keep you fighting by blooding your hands and no matter what you do you will never get into God's abode. They were never spiritual but were always physical. Just remember the God of War.

Take a look at Revelations and see.

We are fighting for OIL for which the Western Hemisphere has become dependent on. There are other factors but the key factor is oil.

Right now the East have the West by the balls especially America.

Please people stay with me and if I am incorrect please forgive me because I know nothing of politics and don't want to either. And America and all the governments of the world do not kill me nor crucify me over this. This is just my theory and going off what I read in the bible and what I see.

Americans look at the debt you have accumulated. You are the only nation on the face of the planet that has a debt in the trillions. Take Italy and Russia out of this because the Vatican can pay off Italy's debt in one go and still have money left over to do its work. I could be wrong because I do not have statistics or financial reports but in hindsight I am not wrong because every Roman Catholic Church must report to the Vatican and besides they don't pay tax so they are ripping off Caesar. So yes they can pay off Italy's debt. I am so not an economist nor do I hold certificates, MBA or whatever in this field so I am so opening up myself for economists and the likes to crucify me.

Now with all this debt accumulated lets say if China, Japan, European nations say you know what I want my money and I want it now. I don't care if it starts a war I want my money now. How would you America pay back the loan? Please just say okay. Look into it and don't say it won't happen because Revelations spoke about this but it called it Armageddon, WW3. I am not going to elaborate; I am just getting you the people of the West to think.

Hell no I am not getting into your politics nor do I want to.

Revelations:
Eagle .   America
Dragon   China
Bear   Russia
Loin   Ethiopia (but this is false Ethiopia is
                   not the lion because it is not Judah
Snake   Man but this man and snake represent a country but which country I have yet to figure it out. Meaning it has not been revealed to me yet but I have an idea but cannot say because I do not want to be wrong.

See where I am going with this. Now read Revelations and get full comprehension. *The war as it stands will be played out on the economic forefront not on the battlefield and China is ahead of the developed world when it comes to economic stability and money.*

Hey I could be wrong but Revelations said so. The Dragon which is China have to come to the aid of the Eagle which is America. Don't quote me because I do not have the bible in front of me.

Correct me if I am wrong. (Just a note China is not the true Dragon but Japan and this could be disputed.)

Now look people America uses 23 billions barrels of oil to keep the country running. No other country uses this much oil. Not even China who has more people.

Now if the East say to hell with you. For the hell of it I am only going to give you 3 billion barrels of oil and see what you are going to do. How will America survive? I know you have reserves but forget about the reserves and see where I am going.

No I am not doing this to start WW3 so get the hell out of here with that intention and this is where F You comes into play. Just think, this is what if?

Yes they are Arab and Muslim states so as it is the East have the West by the balls and none of us know it.

They will defend the oil – see where I am going people. Now the bombings are just an excuse in my views – economics is the key right now and this is my view (s). We of the West have nothing to stand on because slowly the East is creeping up economically and taking over.

Exclude China for a minute. Who is the West dependant on for oil Black Gold Crude Oil? We need this oil to survive. Heat our homes run our cars whatever.
Stay with me here and just see with me. Am I making any sense?

No

Okay

What I am saying is the time we spend, the money we spend on warfare could be spent to lower the deficit of the country, pay back some of the loans we owe. I am not saying not to protect your country you have to do it but *look at your economy because it is a key factor in the war that is to come.*

What we of the West need to do and this was shown to me is to invest in **Renewable Energy**. I don't know much about energy. All that was shown to me is Renewable Energy so whatever renewable energy is we need to look into it because it will be the saving grace of the West. With the temperature of the earth's core rising and with the glacier's receding we need to find alternative method's of survival. I could say the oil fields of the East are going to dry up the end of 2012 but I would be lying because I do not know. Meaning I do not know when it is going to dry up.

All I know is renewable energy is what we of the West should look into. I don't know how expensive this is, and like I said I know nothing about renewable energy but this was what was shown to me in a dream and in another book I told Jamaicans to start looking into it because hey I wanted them to be first to develop a viable, clean, cost effective method of renewable energy. (My Peeps now you can call me biased and want to take your book and hit me.)

So my Peeps we have to really take a look at our economy and make it work for us. Make it work for the West. We cannot afford to let anyone hold us by the balls or hold us hostage for their product - produce. Hey this is just me and my opinion and no one have to listen or should have to listen to me on that.

Now I am caught up. George and your right hand man think. Like I've said if you care about the Sudanese people let it be about them because once the ICC gets wind of whatever picture you are going to show them and the world to say yes this is what the North is doing to the South and once troops go into Sudan. These pictures will give developed nations ammunition and it will cause North and South Sudan to go to war. You know it will only be a matter of time before sanctions are placed on the people of Sudan. You need to think because this will signal the start of the war. *__World War 3 will begin and you and your friend will be the cause of it and America nor it's allies will win this war.__*

__Do not take my word for it read Revelations because your eyes are now open. Yes I said I will stand by my statement that Revelations have to do with the economics of the world but rest assured these people will turn it around because they are good at it. If they took Adam and Eve out of Paradise, turned every child of God against God what wouldn't they do to you. This plain is the devils plain and no one can win him in his domain because we opened the door to him. We gave evil an all access pass to do to us what he wants to do. This is his, it's his birthright because he knows__ *heaven is not his home, will never be. We gave the devil an all access pass and he's using it because he knows his time is limited.*

So you, your friend, the ICC think before you act. Do not think that Black people will not stand up and fight we will especially Jamaicans because Africa is our motherland and we love Africa more than any other Caribbean Island. We will blindly stand against you for the people of Africa. We will not use religion because as it is Blacks see America as Babylon. We were taught this and we will see this act as an act of war this time around. We will rise up and defend Africa at all cost. That land is our birthright, it is yours as well but we cherish and hold the land true American's does not because all they see is colour. They don't see Africa as their homeland. Apart of Africa and originally it was. America was once apart of Africa but you forgot, do not care about it but we do.

So once again think about what you are doing. Once this start the only thing I can tell white people is do not travel into any black lands especially Jamaica because your blood will run like river as the bible states. They will be killed; interracial couples will now be divided because blacks will be pitted against whites. Marriages will not withstand this great divide so know and for all you couples that are interracially bound do not let this be the cause of your divide. Truly love and be truthful to each other. Help but help Africa and America honestly not deceitfully.

America I am not getting into your politics or your government and refuse to but think. Truly think because Muslims will not sit on the sidelines and watch this time around. They will not fight their own. You may think they are but whether Sunni, Shiite, and Ansaar whatever sect they have they cannot fight amongst each other. This is their code of honour and it cannot be broken. This is their fate. They are bound by it and cannot break from it. To break from this code is an act of treason, meaning it is going against the faith; their God.

You cannot win against them because they are cunning. They were born this way. Bred this way. They are the dark forces, the ones to take us out of Eden. God's land. Egypt was a prime example, they enslaved the people, cause us to worship idols, devised religion to mimic every facet of our lives and we followed and we are still doing it today. They burned our books and stripped us of our dignity and self respect. They taught us to sing songs unto their God. They taught us that their God will come from the skies to save us when they know this is false – a lie - wrong. Bob Marley told us the truth when he said "no great god is going to come from the sky".

We made burnt offerings unto their gods

We performed animal and human sacrifices unto their gods

We committed abominable acts of sin before our God . We defied and defiled our God and got cast out of his kingdom because of them

We accepted them and now we are without a home God's home

People you can call me crazy and say whatever but TIME WILL TELL. Pull it up on your computer and listen to the song. The song is by Bob Marley. I will not be the only one you've called crazy, many have come and gone and years later you have to prove us right. God's children can no longer kill themselves for Satan's children. It is wrong because Satan does not respect anyone including his own. Satan's children are cold – cold blooded murderers hence they are depicted in history as the snake. The snake people that hisses and crawl on their belly. And yes this why Genesis depicted them in this way because there is no true love in their hearts nor can they comprehend true love – truth, the true nature of peace and the true beauty of peace – the true peace and harmony that surrounds God and his people – children.

Remember Noah how he told the people the flood was coming and the people laughed. Remember God told him to go into the ark and take his family. Lock the doors and God sealed it. The flood came and all perished except Noah and his family and a few animals. So truly think because Noah's time is now.

You all know that the Babylonians had to invade Egypt and distort the truth to include them. They polluted the truth and changed the dates to reflect the past knowing full well when they did this humanity would be confused – think all came to pass when things did not come to pass as yet. Listen, there are no revolving doors, evil had to do this to keep us sinning as well as keep us ignorant. I told you so rise and live up not just for God but truly for yourselves because shortly you will have to – you will need to.

I refuse to scare anyone. If you want to screw around with your life then so be it, it is your choice. Know the truth now and not wait until you are in the grave because for many it will be truly too late.

Each individual on the face of this planet have a right to live and it is unfair for others to take it for their own personal and evil gain because life does not stop in the physical it moves on – rises to the highest heights of God. This height is where we need to strive to be. When death dies life lives because LIFE INFINITELY CANNOT DIE so I do not know why we believe that someone have to die for us.

God makes no one sacrifice their lives for no one because God know and knows the beauty and sacredness of Life. Life is what he gave to us not death.

And yes this is why I say stop letting people feed you lies to take your soul with them to hell.

Think, truly think because death is not pretty. Woooo Nelly trust me death is not pretty. Woe have mercy God because humanity truly do not know. Wooooo, there is no smile in death trust me. Death makes no jokes hence he's serious when he's taking you.

People don't let me get started with death because I know death and no I am not the death angel. Nor am I doctor death.

Trust me when you start walking right with God the right and proper way in truth he will start showing you things so that you know and yes so that you will never stumble or fall. Yes you will cuss too maybe not in the way I cuss. No you won't get up and cuss like that. Your cussing is in defense of God. Hey maybe you won't but this is my way yes ever since I was a little yiddy biddy.

Remember Sodom and Gomorrah how many people survived?.

REMEMBER GOD ALWAYS SEND US SOMEONE TO WARN US BEFORE DESTRUCTION COMES. THINK AND MAKE THE RIGHT DECISION BECAUSE DESTRUCTION IS COMING. YOU CAN BE LIKE THE CHILDREN OF OLD (ISREAL AND JUDAH) OR BE LIKE THE PEOPLE OF NINEVEH AND REPENT AND LIVE CLEAN.

George and your Goon the same Dr. York has been in your country for over twenty years recruiting Blacks and the likes for his Islamic jihad - agenda. He has the money and the resources. We have been brainwashed and this is why I am petitioning him to do something but not use religion or Islam. I am crying for peace because what he is doing is wrong.

Dr. York, Al Mahdi I am asking you to squash this because whether you like it or not you cannot blame America or any country on the face of this planet for the mess that is happening in your homeland. I blame you because you claimed to be and have not truthfully gone before God and Man and ask God to squash the nonsense in your home land.

You cannot rise up Blacks of the West to fight your battles. This mess have been brewing for centuries because every black nation on the face of this planet have and has taken up other peoples garbage and culture and say it is ours when we fully know that it is not ours.

We cannot blame the next man for wrong when we of ourselves are doing wrong. No come on now. You are doing wrong.

You are teaching blacks falsely and by you telling us to hate other races you are wrong because God never told any of us to do this because skin colour means nothing as you move forward in the spiritual world and you should know this.

You claim to know but claiming to know means nothing when you are doing wrong and instigating war so squash this.

If you truly knew the truth then none of this would be happening. You would be moving towards making this earth – world a better place for everyone because God's people – children are not blacks alone.

You chose Islam. You chose the dirty land over the good land – God's land so do not bring God's people in your Islamic and religious bullshit. Like I said fuck Islam because it's not God's own.

Fuck all facets of religion because none is God's own.

I will reiterate it and stress it. God – Life do not and infinitely does not deal in Death. God is clean he is not dirty so take your filth to your own homeland. Go back to your original land with this shit because your original land is the land of Nod. The land in which evil was born and raised. The land of vipers and murderers – yes the land of the snakes.

Once again I am asking you to squash this because Islam do not and infinitely does not belong to God's children because it has become polluted and associated with war – hate – violence. It is no longer peaceful but hateful – warful.

America, George this man will rise his people up against you because trust me you will invade North Sudan and this will be enough reason for his people who are many, they are not just in America, they are in Canada, they are across the globe, this will give them a reason to gather and fight. Every Islamic nation will come to battle because you have just given them justification to and JIHAD WILL BE ECHOED in the most violent of ways. Know this and listen keenly because if you let this be about the oil know that you will die and your family will die. I am not threatening you but telling you what will happen because like I've said this man is Muslim and Sudanese and he has been recruiting blacks for decades like I've said earlier. So think and do not let whatever you are doing be about the oil because Revelations said the last will become the first. That which you think won't come together will and they will destroy. So I am pleading with you George and your Goon to truly make this be about truly helping the people of Sudan.

Truly know what you are doing because God is warning you. God will not help you if your intentions are false – deceiving – wrong. God can only save you if your intentions are good – clean – true. So please do good therefore making your efforts clean - good.

No one is keeping an eye on the last because we have forgotten about the last but the last was always there. It never died and Revelations told you this.

Yes the warning signs were there but we were ignorant to it meaning our eyes was closed to it because we got a little taste of the truth without knowing that ¼ truth of a story does not make it truthful it just makes it false.

First off he gave us religion and no child of God can come to you with religion because God hath no religion

Life is not a religion and every human being on the face of the planet know this.

No one on the face of the planet can tell you or me the religion of Life.

Evil deals in religion because it is religion that captures our soul and spirit and hand it over to death and trust me death gladly takes it because his life continues meaning Death still have and has a job.

Don't ever think you cannot give death his pink slip because you can and the way to do this is to choose life and live clean, good and truthful.

Black people listen to me now many innocent lives will be lost. This man is Sudanese and he has brainwashed us, my people because he gave us a little bit of truth but not the full truth. Just as they did to Eve in the Garden they are doing it today.

They told Eve that she would not die but become as Gods. Remember her eyes were not open to evil and she sinned. She died right away spiritually and eventually died physically. All Eve knew was the spiritual and not the physical, she could see and talk to God and after they were cast out could they see God? Not even God could see them because they sinned. They were not perfect anymore. This is why God said "Adam where forth art thou." And Adam said "Here I am." Read the rest in Genesis.

Just like Eve died you too will die because everyone forget to tell the truth that Christianity is physical death – it is automatic and Islam is spiritual death but with Islam you have to go through spiritual slavery first and trust me it is deadly hence you die after your allotted time in hell.

You can say I am lying but pick up a bible and read ¼ of the truth.

Let me tell you something Satan – evil is like the perfect pimp no not pimp. How do I explain it. You know when you want someone – meaning you want to lay with someone or get something out of someone you tell the sweetest lines to peak the person's interest and get them going knowing full well you just want to get what you want out of them. Well Satan and his people are the masters at this – deception. Trust me infinitely they know how to play on your emotions and this is what they do. When you've gotten what you want and wanted you dump the person because you have satisfied your needs. This is Satan. He got what he wanted out of Eve and in the end left her holding the bag to die and she did die. She lost it all because of him. This is what this man is. He's a master deceiver and a master planner because when it is all said and done you the blacks of America and across the globe will be the ones holding the bag because you will lose it all.

He would have led you to the slaughter house and trust me the pain you and your children will feel is nothing compared to the hell and anguish – pain that you are going to feel in hell.

You can walk away now because you have the chance to.

Yes Eve made a choice. She accepted him and hopefully I will get to Adam because he was added into the picture and hopefully I will get to him later in another book.

Dr. York, Al Saayid Imam Isa Al Haadi Al Mahdi I am truly crying for peace. Please do not let more innocent people die at the hand of the devil. You can do something about this. These are your people please truly talk to the leaders of both sides and squash this madness. How more of our people must die because of the devil?

How much more should the black race suffer because of the devil?

I am tired man come on now. I am tired. I can't shed anymore tears.

You want to wake up our people the black race then tell them the truth man. Please I am pleading with you don't kill us anymore.

God is life and we must live for life and not death. You cannot give us vinegar to drink and say it is wine it is wrong. Please do the right thing and help your people.

The black race cannot fight for the devil anymore because you know and I know as well as God knows that the devil has turned things around on us to take all eyes off them .

The devil and his race make us look like the evil ones.

He devised Jesus and say he is a black man like the angels and you know that he did this for one reason and that is to turn every nation against the black race.

When the full truth comes out he will say you see it's a black man that caused this, the black man that has been lying to you all along.

For the true love of God stop. We don't need you feeding us bullshit anymore. Tell me something, what have we done to you and the Sudanese people to warrant such hatred?

What have we done to you and the Sudanese people for you to want to kill us?

I am speaking to you the true children of God. If America and other nations want to take up the plight of the Sudanese people as well as other Babylonian nations and become the new seat of Babylon leave. Get out before it is too late. Do not look back – leave because EVILS' FIGHT IS NOT GOD'S FIGHT.
Evil will say we are the evil ones, the devils, the cursed ones. You know he is going to do this.

You know God has nothing to do with religion.

If he did then tell me WHAT RELIGION IS GOD because you claim to be from God.

If the True and Living God dealt in death would you be alive today? Come on man do good and not evil. Do good and live.

You know you cannot fight the devil in his domain and win because he knows everything about it and God infinitely do not deal in war, he is peaceful and shuns all facet of evil.

We are not physical beings but spiritual beings. These people know this so stop look and listen because God's people to not fight. They do not hurt people and wherever there is dirt and filth they separate themselves from it. God's people are passive people that do not like to see injustice. We are friendly people, easy going that troubles no one so fucking leave us the hell alone. Keep your filth and bullshit and go further corrupt and condemn your own land and people with your condemnation because you are and your kind meaning Satan's minions are more than a condemnation of sin. You're all the living DEAD that breathe, sleep, eat and drink filth - Islam because death is your mother and sin is your father. We're not your fucking lambs going to the slaughter house anymore. We will wake up and rise in God's goodness and truth and trust me evil and condemned people like you will never use us again nor will you ride on our coattails because we will all know the full truth and truth of you and the devil's race.

Enough is enough now man. You need to stop this madness.

Why are we the black race giving evil dominion over us?

Why the fuck are we the black race fighting for the devil when his race loathe the very ground we walk on?

Why are we killing ourselves to fit into the devil's domain?

They hate us so why are we killing ourselves for them?

Why are we killing each other and ourselves to be in his wretched domain?

You know that evil cares about no one but evil. You know when all is said and done and if evil wins whites and blacks will be enslaved yet again.

This time around slavery will be more brutal and deadlier in the physical. We need not have to worry about spiritual hell because there will be no escaping this judgment.

Every which way you look at it we will die and you know this.

Truly tell me why are you condemning your own people and my people to die. Forget the money and the benefits the devil offers you and truly tell me why are you condemning and killing your people and my people?

Why are you signing them over to the devil – evil?

Why are you aiding the devil in killing us?

Every race under the face of the sun hates us and instead of letting us hold our heads up high in pride you're further giving evil ammunition to crucify and kill us.

Do you hate us that much that you would side with the devil to kill your own? Remember you did say you were one of us and you did give reference to the hair. So if you are one of us why are you giving us religion – and sealing our spirit in hell to burn?

Why tell us to change our name – first and last name to accept the devil's own. We know why this is done because with everyone using the same first and last name you cannot tell each other apart because I or anyone can say Mohammed so and so did this and thousands will stand up and say I am Mohammed so and so and I have no access to your land. How can you blame me when I am here? Can I be in two places at once? Yes it goes deeper than this but like I know and many others know, evil has his own agenda and that is to dominate and control and if you refuse to be dominated and controlled you must be destroyed – eliminated by any means necessary because you are deemed as a threat to evil's political, economic and hidden agenda.

But it's funny the one thing that evil and his people fail to tell you as individuals is that Life is the spirit within you. It is energy – that spark because like I said and will forever tell you the flesh is the prison – the physical prison for the spirit – the energy inside of you and it is it that feels pain – emotions. Spiritual prison like I've said is deadlier and more dreadful than physical prison – pain. The pain you feel inside and out is your spirits way of saying taste a bit now because it gets worse in hell – the spiritual realm. So take heed and truly know what you are doing.

Dr. York, look at all the black lands of Africa and see the dreadful condition they are living in. You have the money because you caused us to work as slaves for you. The poor blacks of America and Canada as well as across the globe built you, some even signed over their worldly possessions to you. You used them and when you are done with them all you are going to do is say father – Satan I did this for you where is my reward? I did as you asked me to and I delivered on my promise where is the kingdom you promised me? And like a fool he will point to a beautiful mansion – a house in the sky and when you get closer and go inside you will smile because the floor is outlined with gold – yellow gold and you will beam with joy and say thank you I am in heaven and when you take a stock all that gold was fools gold because death will tap you on the shoulders and say – remember me. Remember all you did for me in the name of Satan well here is your true reward and you will scream like a bitch as you are being tossed in the pit of fire – spiritual fire because the fire man talks about is not like the fire we know, it is a special fire that is infinitely hotter than the sun hence it's hue – colour does not look like the hue – fire of the sun.

You made God's people stand in the cold and heat and work for you and in the end you betrayed them by converting them and giving them over to the devil.

Stop telling people to burn incense because no one can burn out evil with incense. Evil burns fire – use fire in the spiritual world and that is why some people see evil as a ball of fire which just simply means they are in hell.

True evil must use fire, it is a must hence you and some church use fire, and simply put you are paying homage to hell the God of fire.

For those who do not know fire is the first stage of true evil. Some say smokeless fire but you cannot have smokeless fire – fire must accompany the smoke meaning you see smoke first then fire. I hope I have explained this properly.

Tell me something Dr. York how much more blood how much more human sacrifices of my people your people should the devil have?

You know that the devil is a liar. Not even his own people he will care about in the end because with the devil it is DEATH FOR DEATH and you know this. The devil hath not life meaning he cannot live for life he can only live for death because he is death. This is why it is said the devil cannot blow breath meaning give life.

Tell me something Yannan when the devil's people the people of Nod conquer us yet again how are you and your people going to eat food? How are they going to pay their bills? Where are they going to find jobs? Which doctor will they find to look after them? Which hospital are they going to go to?

Remember Genesis told you the devil has his own race of people but you should know this. Genesis said God put enmity between the devil's seed and his seed but you know that's a lie an infinite lie being told on the True and Living God. God never ever infinitely never ever put enmity which is strife hate between his seed and the devil's seed. Hatred was already there and it is still there until this day. The devil's race hates us and will forever hate us and instead of separating from them we live amongst them, marry them and commit their sins with them. You should know this because you are one of the four and twenty elders. Evil is the one to bring hatred into the picture. Evil is the one to put enmity between his seed and God's seed.

If God had truly put enmity between his seed and evil's seed why is evil still living today?

Why is evil still breathing God's air and more importantly why is evil still eating the fruits and goodness of God?

No come on now. If you teach a child sinful ways will he or she not grow up in sin and do things that are sinful?

If ou teach a child to hate will he or she not grow up to hate?

If you raise a child in sin will he or she not grow up to live in sin – do all that is sinful?

So how can anyone say that they are of God when they do all in the name of sin – evil – the devil.

Tell the truth because all that we do we do not give thanks unto the True and Living God we give thanks unto sin – death.

If I was to teach hate I would not be true and more importantly I would not be true to the God of Truth.

I will be harsh and I will swear and yes I will tell you when I am being racist but infinitely do not judge me if you do not know me.

Every child of God know and knows that God infinitely do not deal with the devil and his people. God cannot interfere with the devil's own. God can only deal with his own. God's own is God's own and no matter he left apart of him on earth he did not do it because he loves evil he did it for his people. Yes to prolong their lives and keep them safe but no matter how God tries to show and teach his people the truth they refuse him. We keep doing things that is not pleasing in the sight of God and when we crash and burn we cry and say why me God why me?

It's time for us to grow up or shut up. If you cannot be faithful to God then continue to serve the devil because no one can pay back the devil. Absolutely no one can pay back or pay off our debt on the devil's terms.

Evil play for keeps and there are no refunds or returns when it comes to sin and evil – death.

Do not get me wrong GOD INFINITELY DOES NOT SHUT ANYONE OFF OR OUT OF HIS ABODE. We are the ones to shut ourselves out of his because of the filth and nastiness we indulge in. If evil's children want to abdicate the throne of death they can do so but they have to live clean. They have to repent and give up their evil ways meaning if they worship idols, man, woman, animals they have to relinquish this practice infinitely. They must not teach their children these ways. They have to infinitely relinquish blood and animal sacrifices as well as human sacrifices because God infinitely do not practice these things because they are nasty and unclean, they are death.

If you say this is wrong then look back at ancient civilizations that condoned these rituals and tell me where they are now – today?

No child of God can give false and dirty religions and say it is clean.

No religion on the face of this planet is clean because each one of them profess they know God, profess they are of God, profess their books are divinely inspired but yet teach hate, intolerance, greed and sin.

These practices are not of God because no human being, no religion can tell you fully about the truth of God if they are not clean and truthful. None.

Every child of God must strive for absolute truth which is perfection. And yes this is attainable even in this state – the physical state. Let's put it this way if you cannot live truthful, yes peaceful in the living – the physical state you cannot live truthful – peaceful in the spiritual state.

I WILL REPEAT "THE LIFE YOU LIVE IN THE PHYSICAL DETERMINES WHERE YOU GO IN THE SPIRITUAL".

George innocent people will die. Look at the internet if they have not taken their page off. Read his books and what he claimed to be. He told us they are Ansaars, then that was changed to Islamic Hebrews and now I do not know what they are going by.

He said he's of Mahdi of the great fighter that can trace his bloodline back to the prophet Mohammed. Do not quote me on the Mohammed part but I think this was what he said in one of his books.

But as black people, white people, and I am excluding the mongoloid nation (Chinese) and if you read further you will know why. We do not dig deep into things. We just get a little piece and think this is the truth when it isn't. Brainwashing is easy because it is ¼ of the truth and not the full truth.

Do not bring me into this because I have told God if he ever make me deceive you the people he will not like it. Trust me he won't. I am telling you right now I told God if ever I find out that my words are false and not true he had better shut me the hell out of his paradise before I die because I will be kicking his door down and question his integrity in front of his face. Like I said I have come thus far to find out I was deceiving. Hell to the fucking no. I don't care how mighty God is he will not like me because I will be worse than Madea. No I will not use guns and ammunition my mouth and writing will be my guns and ammunition and trust me God will not like me. He will stand afar off from me so he had better not use me in any way to spread hate, or deceive. Too much shit happening in this world and in my life for me to deceive people. Hell no. My life is not straight and I am trying to make it straight, he should be helping me and you and not pitting.

People of the West think. THE DEVIL CAN BE SHUT DOWN BELOW WILL TELL YOU HOW BUT YOU KNOW WHAT I AM GOING TO TELL YOU HERE. PRAYER, PRAYER, AND MORE PRAYER AND A CLEAN LIFE. WE NEED TO START LIVING A CLEAN LIFE AND PSALMS 1 TELLS US HOW TO LIVE. NEVER STOP PRAYING. NO IT IS NOT EFEECTIVE IN A DIRTY STATE BUT ONCE YOU BECOME CLEAN IT IS INFINITELY EFFECTIVE. CLEAN UP YOURSELF AS PSALMS 1 TELL YOU TO AND SEPARATE FROM EVIL. NOT DIVIDE BECAUSE DIVISION IS A LIE.

GOVERNMENTS YOU DON'T HAVE TO DO THIS BECAUSE YOUR AGENDA IS DIFFERENT. MY PEEPS LISTEN TO ME HERE. RIGHT NOW BECAUSE YOU WILL KNOW THAT I TOGGLE FROM TOP TO BOTTOM AND FROM BOTTOM TO TOP. PRAY FOR ME. NOT ME. PRAY AND ASK GOD TO SHUT DOWN PHYSICAL AND

SPIRITUAL EVIL. PRAY AND ASK GOD TO SHUT THESE PEOPLE DOWN. DO NOT PRAY IN THE NAME OF JESUS BECAUSE JESUS WAS ONE OF THEM AND WHEN YOU GET BELOW YOU WILL SEE. YES JESUS NEVER EXISTED BUT YOU STILL BELIEVE IN HIM AND THAT IS WHY I USE HIS NAME. EVERY CHANCE YOU GET PRAY THAT GOD PROTECTS YOUR LAND, YOUR FAMILY, YOU AND NEVER LET EVIL COME INTO YOUR LAND. PURGE IT OF ALL EVIL GREAT AND SMALL IN BOTH THE PHYSICAL AND SPIRITUAL. WHERE YOU CANNOT SEE EVIL, WHERE EVER IT EXIST ASK GOD TO CLEAN IT PERMANENTLY.

DO NOT DO THIS IN THE NAME OF JESUS LIKE I'VE SAID OR IN THE NAME OF ANY PROPHETS (PROFITS) OR MAN BUT IN THE NAME OF GOD.

IN THE NAME OF GOD THE TRUE AND LIVING GOD I BOUND THE DEVIL AND ITS AGENTS TO THE PITS OF HELL NEVER TO ESCAPE AND HURT US AGAIN. NEVER TO CAUSE US ANY MORE PAIN.

In the name of God the True and Living God I bound spiritual wickedness to go back to where they came from.

In the name of God the True and Living God I infinitely bound spiritual wickedness to the confines of hell so that they never hurt anyone again.

In the name of God the True and Living God I infinitely bound evil's children to the realm hell so they can never infinitely never ever deceive or walk amongst humanity again.

In the name of God the True and Living God I bound all that is evil, all of evil's empire to crash and burn and go directly to hell which is their true home so that they can never ever infinitely never ever pollute humanity or rob God's true people – children of their souls, spirit and prosperity anymore.

People remember the oil belongs to them and they will not give it up. Economically they have us with the oil and we have become dogs to them buying their bone to survive. Think of your future because any how we let them conquer us economically we will be like the people of Egypt and 10000BC. The slavery that you saw in the movie, the slavery that happened in Egypt will happen again and this time around it will be worse because according to your bible God told Abraham "the iniquity of the Amorites is not yet done." Each and every nation will become slaves. Yes you too white people you will become their slaves and you will have to accept the mark of the beast. This time it will not be money this time it will be your condemnation and your ticket to hell and you cannot refuse the mark. You will have to accept it and bow down to their Gods. So take your pick. People make your choice. Yes some of you already made it – accept the mark of evil by desecrating your bodies with henna, body art, tattoo's, body piercing and the likes but this is your choice. No one can condemn you for it. You made the decision and it is a decision you have to live with for the rest of your life. Yes until you die a miserable death.

All I can do is pray sincerely and truthfully and I am telling all of you to pray sincerely that evil does not overtake your land and home. Once you have done this pray out of the true love of God, step aside. Yes it is a song by Mrs. Tamela Mann. Step aside, like the elder white lady told me let God do his work. Once you pray sincerely and clean step aside and let God do his work. Do this I am not telling you anything wrong. Go to God, and not Jesus or man but God. Infinitely trust God. Like I said I am learning and I do get mad at him (God) not because I hate him but because I truly love him and I've made him my friend – my all. Trust me God is my true friend.

So George and the world think before you act because War is not pretty. Do not fight for their oil and look into renewable energy because none of us know if God is not going to dry up the oil sands meaning take away apart of him from them. God is fed up hence I am writing this book for God's people.

We cannot say we love God then turn around and hurt him. No come on now. Love hurts but true love cannot hurt nor can it deceive. If I say I truly love you and I'm hurting you, it meant I did not truly love you, I only love you hence I hurt you. There are no lies in true love because I am giving you the truth and the truth cannot hurt the good but it sure as hell can hurt the bad. And when I say this I mean because evil cannot accept the truth – they refuse the truth they can only accept lies and when you come to them with the truth they say you're a liar and a deceiver. Once they say this they will go out of their way to destroy and kill you because they cannot accept the truth. The truth is a lie to them hence evil kills – destroys.

Yes this is also why God does not send his people – messengers unto the wicked – evil because we know and he God knows that evil will never accept truth they must reject it at all times and they (evil) do reject it – the truth. I hope I've explained this correctly for you to see.

Come 2013 you have 19 years to get on the ark of God and if you don't then this is your problem because no great God is going to save you.

Like I've said we are all accountable for our own sins.

I am not accountable for you sins you are accountable for yours but this changes drastically when it comes to God, the True and Living God. The lives that he has entrusted you with and I will repeat, THE LIVES THAT HE HAS ENTRUSTED YOU WITH you are accountable for them. Their sins become your sins and you as a messenger of God have to give account for their sins. Meaning you must teach honestly and clean. You must teach truth truthfully. If the person that God has entrusted you with does not adhere to the messages that was given to all by God then you are not held accountable for that person. That person is held accountable for his or her sins.

If God has not entrusted you with Life – the lives he has given you then you are not accountable for the next man's sins.

If you say you are the keeper of Souls meaning the souls in your congregation or church belongs to God whether it be the God of Life or the God of Death you are solely responsible for those people and it is your responsibility to teach them according to life or death. If you do not then you are held guilty of sin. And yes those people can charge you for sin because you did not truly take care of them.

And no people you can't just stand up and say well God told you to take care of me so take care of me.

Which God told you this? This will be my first question because I know God does not say Michelle, Joe, Frank take care of Lucy, Jane, Patricia for me. God does not do that. God entrust the lives of his people in your hands and every messenger of God knows how he does this. We cannot fool you and yes people you will know God's messengers from the fake ones that are robbing you of your hard earned money and souls.

Listen, God is telling you that RENEWABLE ENERGY is the way to go. Invest in renewable energy. Maybe this is what God is trying to tell you that he is going to dry up the oil and for us to start using renewable energy. People do not say it will take hundred's of years because none of us know God nor do we know what he has in stored for these people. Look at it. How many years did it take for Noah to build the Ark and how long did it take for the water to come when Noah closed the door?

Hey call me crazy and shrug me off like a damned fool. Call me psycho, shithead, whatever you want to. Kill me, abuse me, spit on me, set me up, do all that you can in the name of man but guess what GOD CAN NEVER BE WRONG. HE HAS SHOWN YOU TIME AND TIME AGAIN AND NONE WOULD LISTEN. THIS IS WHY I KEEP TELLING YOU ABOUT THE TIME OF NOAH. NONE LISTENED. THEY CALLED NOAH A FOOL. TOLD HIM RAIN WAS NOT GOING TO COME. THEY DID ALL MANNER OF EVIL AGAINST NOAH, BUT HE KEPT DOING WHAT GOD TOLD HIM TO DO AND HE WAS SAVED. BUT THE PEOPLE WEREN'T SO like I said you can do unto me like Noah and turn from God but when war comes, starvation comes, oooh nelly let's not forget the fire, yes fire because you read Noah had water but we will have fire trust me infinitely on this. When the fire comes, the lack of rain and dwindling water supply comes and the angels of God lifts the hand of God from man what are you going to do?

When God's protection is gone from the world just like in the time of Noah what are you going to do?

When God's protection is gone are you going to call to God and say father I am so sorry, forgive me I did not know. Do you know what God is going to do? He will not hear any of you because you told him I was whacked, you did not listen, you continued to do your own thing.

You showed him you did not care.

Trust me many will be singing too late.

I will be singing too late.

The angels and yes God will be singing too late. Oh yes Allelujah too late. Too late will be your cry and right there and then you are going to say if only I had listened. And no matter what you say too late will still be singing because it is truly too late for you.

Trust me I have told God to follow his heart and not let us use him anymore because time and time again we have shown him we don't care. We say we are with him but we are not. We are against him. I told him walk away. He's not a damned big head bud for mankind, humankind anymore because we refuse to listen to him. We don't care about him. From the beginning until now we have failed him. I asked him if he's a sucker for punishment. Told him he does not love himself because if he did he wouldn't be eating the scraping off the table that we are throwing to him.

Look at it we are giving him scraping because the majority of us will go on doing what we are doing and not listen. We need to listen. DO NOT LISTEN TO ME PEOPLE LISTEN TO GOD. HE IS CALLING YOU SO RETURN TO HIM AND LET HIM GUIDE AND PROTECT YOU FROM THESE PEOPLE.

TRULY LOVE YOURSELF and for those that are sympathetic to the cause, they weren't sympathetic to the Egyptians because they made the Egyptians worship them, build shrines unto them but God's children outsmarted them. God took the most important thing out of Egypt and that was Life. God took life out of Egypt and to this day they are still looking for it.

How many people died?

How much more of you will die?

In every aspect of life God has tried to save you. How much more saving can God do? When is enough with you? We tell lies on God and say the world is coming to an end just look at the war and all that is happening. We say God is doing this.

Stop lying on God. God did not deplete the ozone man did.

God did not cause the fluxuation in the weather man did.
God did not create herbicides and pesticides man did.

God did not make viruses and bombs to kill each other man did

God did not make bombs, guns and weapons of mass destruction man did.

God did not create diseases man did

God did not create hate and strife man did with the aid of evil

God did not deplete the resources of the earth man did

So tell me why are we continuing with the lies.

We are killing ourselves and the ultimate death is yet to come unless we change it. We cannot change the past but we can change the future you all know this. If God wanted humanity to die would he be trying to save you?

He gave you Renewable Energy capitalize on it.

Look back at Noah and learn. The people did not listen to God and they died according to your book of lies because Noah's time is now and man's ultimate destruction – death will come at the hands of fire – heat if we do not change the course that we are on.

Eve did not listen to God and she died. She accepted the offerings of sin and where is she today? Is she not dead never to come back to life again?

We do not have a very good track record when it comes to God do we? We need to start listening to God. We have to save ourselves because in the end none of us can hold God accountable for our deaths because he did give you the answer to saving the future as well as saving yourself.

Stop listening to people that tell you there are many false profits (prophets).

We know they are false profits (prophets)but yet we believe and I repeat we believe in God.

Trust me infinitely on this God will never ever infinitely never ever send anyone that is dirty to save you.

God is clean why would he send a dirty person to preach and teach to you. Come on now are you telling God and me that God is dirty.

Are you telling God and me that he's unclean – unholy?

Are you telling God and me that he's the devil – the evil one? Come on now.

In order to be clean you have to repent of your sins and live clean in order for God to use you.

You have to have true love the true love of God.

Trust me you will be tested and tried from your conception meaning birth until the day you find God. You will never be accepted by humanity because humanity wants God to be who he cannot be.

If you don't see this see below and put the 3xy together and use the races then if that is all you know.

Now back on track because I have taken you all way into left field that the majority of you are now lost. Let's hope not. Come back on board with me now. We were talking about hate and I was talking to Dr. York.

Solomon was pure did not mix; this is according to the bible some of you are saying. Some are saying he was black and comely because this is what you read in the bible and many blacks use this as a bargaining chip. Especially you black Muslims because many of you were taught this.

Read it again

Now let me tell you the full truth it was a woman who wrote the Song of Solomon she was black like the tents of Kedar and the other women around her were fair skinned. So for you blacks that harp on this stop misleading the people. Besides the Songs of Solomon had nothing to do with Solomon persay. It's poetry of love true love written by a woman to Solomon. She was telling him how much she loved him, truly loved him. But Solomon did not truly love her because if he did he would have seen her beauty and clung to her. Instead of returning true love to her he followed after women that God told him not to follow after and he lost his crown. "A bundle of Myrrh was he to her". Man how beautiful. I wish I could write poems of true love in this way. The Song of Solomon wow, I could just read it over and over again because you feel the love she's talking about. She truly loved this guy.

Men in those days Myrrh was precious. Damn Solomon had someone that truly loved him and he let her go much like a lot of you men of today. Some of you have good women that will do anything for you and instead of treating her good, protecting her, and making her feel comfortable and truly loved, some of you beat her and run after women that you are not suppose to run after. Women you are included in this. Who cares if he or she is chunky, don't look like the top models of society or fall under society's category of beauty. Do me a favour take the make up off some of these models and see their true beauty, imperfections are many. I bet a lot of you would be surprised. Beauty has nothing to do with flesh but true love. Solomon knew this you know this. You Dr. York should know this so why mislead?

THE TRUTH EDUCATES YOU and YOU Dr. York are well educated. Well educated in the art of Sin and Evil. You have not one ounce of goodness in you because if you did you would not kill. When I say kill I mean give people the books of poison and damnation to read. When you do this you are killing them physically and spiritually and this is why I say you kill. If you are of the truth you cannot be rocked by my words because all that I have written in this book you would substantiate and say she is correct but I know otherwise. You will fume but guess what I don't care if you fume because I know you know me and have seen me in the physical and spiritual. You cannot deny me sorry you can deny me but you cannot deny the words in this book because they are not my words alone but God's words – meaning I am doing what God requires of me because he asked me to.

YOU ARE OF GOD, AN ELDER INCARNATED SO GIVE THE PEOPLE SOLID FAITH, THE RIGHT FOOD TO EAT. TAKE THE FRIGING DIRTY SHEET OFF YOUR BED LIKE I AM

DOING OFF MINE AND EDUCATE THE PEOPLE TRUTHFULLY. IT'S NOT ABOUT THE MONEY IT'S ABOUT THE TRUE LOVE OF GOD AND KEEPING GOD'S CHILDREN IN HIS FOLD WITHOUT MISLEADING THEM OR LETTING THEM GO ASTRAY AGAIN. TRUE LOVE CANNOT CONDEMN BUT THEN AGAIN YOU KNOW NOT OF TRUE LOVE BECAUSE YOU EDUCATE IN LIES.

STOP POLLUTING THE PEOPLE BY GIVING THEM THE RELIGION OF HELL TO DESTROY THEM. YOU ARE IMPRISONING THEIR SOULS AND SOLIDIFYING THEIR FATE IN HELL. YOU ARE GIVING YOUR PEOPLE OVER TO EVIL TO DIE YET AGAIN. TELL ME SOMETHING WE KNOW ISLAM IS A SPIRITUAL PRISON SO TELL ME WHO IS GOING TO GO INTO HELL OR THIS PRISON AND SAVE YOUR PEOPLE? TELL ME WHO IS GOING TO SAVE THEM BECAUSE YOU CAN'T DO IT. YOU WON'T BE ABLE TO DO IT BECAUSE YOU OF YOURSELF WILL BE WITH THEM IN PRISON SO WHO IS GOING TO SAVE YOU? I SURE AS HELL WON'T SAVE YOU. AND TRUST ME I KNOW ALL ABOUT HELL AND HOW TO GO TO HELL TO TAKE GOD'S PEOPLE OUT.

PEOPLE DO NOT TAKE MY WORD FOR IT. ASK GOD.

GO AHEAD AND ASK GOD TO SHOW YOU THE TRUTH.

GOD IS WHOM YOU HAVE AND GOD IS THE ONLY ONE THAT WILL SAVE YOU SO ASK HIM TO SHOW YOU THE TRUTH IN HEAVEN AS WELL AS ON EARTH.

CONDEMN ME ALL YOU WANT. LASH OUT AT ME ALL YOU WANT BUT DO ME A FAVOUR ASK GOD. TRULY ASK GOD FOR THE TRUTH AND LET HIM REVEAL IT TO YOU WITHOUT PARABLES. REVEAL THE TRUTH TO YOU CLEARLY AND SET YOU FREE. SET YOUR SOUL FREE.

MALACHI ZODOK, YANNAN, YES YOU DR. YORK. YOU SAY YOU ARE OF GOD AND TEACHING RIGHT KNOWLEDGE BUT YET CANNOT TELL THESE PEOPLE THAT THE LANGUAGE WE ALL SPEAK IS NOT GOD'S LANGUAGE. YOU CANNOT TELL THEM IT IS ONLY A SELECTED FEW THAT HAVE SEEN THE LANGUAGE OF GOD AND CAN WRITE THE LANGUAGE. ONCE YOU ARE OF GOD AND TRUTHFUL TO HIM HE WILL SEAL YOU WITH THIS LANGUAGE AS WELL AS PROTECT YOU, FEED AND CLOTHE YOU BUT WE HAVE TO CHANGE OUR FILTHY WAYS.

YOU CANNOT TELL THE PEOPLE ABOUT THE BRIDES OF HEAVEN AND WHAT IT MEANS TO BE LOVED TRULY LOVED BY GOD UNLESS YOU ARE CLEAN. UNLESS YOU REPENT AND BE REDEEMED BY GOD.

DO YOUR DAMNED JOB. IF NOT GET THE FUCK OUT. STEP ASIDE AND LET THE ONE

THAT TRULY LOVES GOD DO THE WORK OF THE SUSTAINER BECAUSE YOU ARE NOT.

TELL THE PEOPLE THE TRUTH ABOUT TRUE LOVE AND HOW BEAUTIFUL IT IS. TELL THEM ABOUT HOW BEAUTIFUL AND WONDERFUL THE CRYSTAL CITY IS. TELL WOMEN ONLY ONE MAN SHOULD ENTER THEIR VAGINA BECAUSE IT IS THE OPENING FOR LIFE - BIRTH. THIS IS WHERE WE RECEIVE LIFE AND GOD DOES NOT LIKE IT WHEN MORE THAN ONE MAN ENTERS HER. YES GOD HAS GIVEN PROVISION FOR THIS MEANING THERE IS A PROVISION FOR DIVORCE.

Stop raping us of our dignity but telling men to have more than one wife because God does not like it. It is confusion and an abomination unto him and if we continue to live in this way none of us will see Paradise.

TELL THE MEN TO ONLY SLEEP WITH ONE WOMAN BECAUSE THEY ARE THE GIVER OF LIFE. TELL YOUNG GIRLS AND EDUCATE THEM ON THE BLESSINGS OF KEEPING THEIR VIRGINITY UNTIL THEIR WEDDING DAY.

TELL AND TEACH WOMEN AND MEN ABOUT KEEPING THE VAGINA AND PENIS CLEAN AT ALL TIMES BECAUSE GOD DOES NOT LIKE ORDOUR. HE CAN'T STAND IT AND HE WILL MAKE YOU SMELL YOURSELF IF YOU STINK BELOW.

STOP SPREADING HATE ABOUT HOW GOD FAVOURS THE BLACK RACE OVER THE WHITE RACE BECAUSE THIS IS A DAMNED LIE. I WAS SHOWN THE PAST AND I SAW BLACKS AND WHITES LIVING AS ONE IN PEACE, IN THE ENCLOSED GARDEN AND IT WAS THE CHILDREN OUTSIDE THE GARDEN, THE CHILDREN OF A LESSER LIGHT, DARKER SKINNED THAT WAS OUTSIDE THE GARDEN. THEY WERE THE ONES TO ENTICED US NOT THE OTHER WAY AROUND AND YOU KNOW WHO THESE PEOPLE ARE. (The Babylonians – meaning the children of Babel hence they babel – lie).

I DON'T HAVETO SAY ANYMORE BECAUSE THE TRUTH IS THERE AND YOU KNOW IT. SO STOP BECAUSE IT IS NOT FAIR TO GOD AND IT IS NOT FAIR TO HUMANS ON A WHOLE.

PARADISE WAS NOT MEANT FOR ONE RACE SO STOP. I AM ASKING YOU AND PLEADING WITH YOU WITH THE LOVE THE TRUE LOVE OF GOD TO STOP MISLEADING AND SPREADING HATE. IT IS A SIN AND YOU KNOW IT.

THERE IS NO GUILTY BLUE EYED.

*BLUE, **DARK BLUE** NOT LIGHT BLUE IS A POWERFUL COLOUR THAT DRAWS AND INTERCHANGE IN THE SPIRITUAL REALM. MEANING EVIL CHANGE FROM BLUE TO BLACK AND FROM BLACK TO BLUE BECAUSE THEY ARE NEGATIVE COLOURS,*

MEANING EVIL WEARS DARK BLUE AND BLACK CLOTHING AND CAN INTERCHANGE OR CHANGE THEM AND IT IS ONLY BY CALLING THE NAME OF GOD CAN THE AGENTS OF EVIL WHO IS WEARING THIS COLOUR (DARK BLUE) FLEE. THIS HAS TO DO WITH THE SPIRITUAL REALM. THESE PEOPLE WHO WEAR BLUE AND BLACK ARE THE SPIRITUAL WICKED. TELL YOUR PEOPLE THE TRUTH AND STOP SPREADING HATE LIKE I HAVE SAID. IT IS NOT NEEDED BECAUSE GOD WILL LET YOU GO DOWN WITH THEM IF YOU CONTINUE TO DECEIVE. TELL THE PEOPLE THAT WHITE IN THE SPIRITUAL REALM IS DEATH. MEANING WHEN YOU DIE IN THE SPIRITUAL YOU ARE CLOTHED IN FULL WHITE TRUE EVIL. (This stage is tricky because if you truly do not know about the spiritual realm you will be deceived because good meaning your good family members can wear full white to visit you and when you see this they are telling you that they are dead meaning not of the physical realm – the living. I hope I did not confuse you here but it I have let me know in a good way).

WHEN PURE EVIL DIES (this is the evil you have given yourself over to because I did not clarify this earlier.) WHEN IT DIES LIKE I'VE STATED EARLIER EVIL DIES CLOTHED IN WHITE AND AS A WHITE PERSON AND THIS IS WHY EVIL POSE UP A WHITE GOD. TO BE CLOTHED IN WHITE AS A WHITE PERSON IS EVIL IN ITS PUREST OF FORMS.

SO WHEN A PERSON POSES UP A WHITE GOD THEY ARE POSING UP TRUE DEATH – THEIR GOD. AND YES PEOPLE TO BE FAIR AND CORRECT THE TRUE MOTHER OF DEATH IS A BLACK WOMAN. YES THE YING AND THE YANG IN ONE CONTEXT.

The black represent the mother of death in the physical and the white represent the father of death in the spiritual. Yes physical and spiritual death but the Ying and Yang go a lot deeper. Hence it is imperative to know – truly know about both worlds because both worlds go hand in hand.

TELL THEM THE TRUTH IF YOU ARE A BLACK DEVIL OR DEMON MEANING YOU PRACTICE AND LIVE A WICKED LIFE IN THE PHYSICAL YOUR SPIRIT OR SOUL DIE AS A WHITE PERSON IN THE SPIRITUAL REALM AND THIS IS WHY THE ANGELS OF GOD DO NOT WEAR FULL WHITE. ANOTHER COLOUR MUST BE ASSOCIATED WITH WHITE. IT DOES NOT MATTER IF YOU ARE WHITE, PURPLE, PINK, GREEN AS LONG AS YOU ARE EVIL AND LIVE FOR EVIL WHEN YOU DIE IN THE SPIRITUAL REALM YOU DIE IN WHITE AND AS A WHITE PERSON.

Tell your people that blue is not just worn by the spiritual wicked but it is used to teach you; show you. Evil goes from black to blue to white. So the colours of evil are black, dark blue and white. Just as the angels wear the colours of God, evil wear the colours of their God who is Sin. (This is not the best explanation but it is the best way I can explain it).

ONCE YOU CALL ON THE NAME OF GOD EVIL CAN NEVER AND WILL NEVER CONQUER YOU SO TEACH RIGHT BECAUSE EVIL HAVE TO FLEE.

Teach your people the importance of colours. If you are of God why are you doing wrong, educating wrong, claiming to be when you are not. ***You are just a mere man that has read a lot of books that have misguided you.***

If you are of God why are you not representing God?

If you are of God why are you not wearing the colors of God?

If you are of God why are you claiming to be an incarnate of one of the twenty four elders?

If you are of God you cannot claim to be something or another person because God does not incarnate and neither does sin.

Neither God nor Satan can incarnate or reincarnate so stop spreading lies on Satan and God.

Come on now even I have to draw the line and stop you. Satan does not incarnate, reincarnate and possess like that even I know this. I will not let you lie on Satan because it is wrong. As vile and evil as he is you cannot tell a lie on him it is simply wrong.

If you are of God then you would know, infinitely know that good and evil are born. They must be born and they cannot possess anyone or anything just like that. Evil can never, infinitely never posses you without you giving your soul and spirit over to evil. You have to give evil permission and yes people this is where debt and generational curses and sins come in.

Right is right and wrong is wrong and you have to draw the line on lies and I am doing so. You can hate me but I don't care. I live for God and not man. I live for God and not evil and truth is truth it cannot lie nor can it deceive and I will repeat this until I can't repeat it anymore. You have to live life and you also have to live for you. We cannot live for God alone we have to live for ourselves. Meaning we have to live in truth and for truth.

If we live in lies we cannot be truthful. No one can and this is why the quest must be for the truth. We need to put down lies and start accepting the truth. This is the only way we will be able to fully live. Once we have the truth and live in it we cannot grow old because the truth cannot wither nor can it age.

If you were of God you would know this. You would also know that no angel of God can incarnate, possess or be reincarnated in man. Angels are pure and void of sin. They are free of sin and were never created in sin. God never made them in sin. Man – humanity is a sin meaning we are sinful.

We accepted blood. We baptize in blood and drink blood. We eat the flesh of the dead meaning we are cannibals and no one can say otherwise because this is what we do at communion time. We wash ourselves in filth – blood.

Angels are pure energy they don't just come up to you and say I am going to take over your body. This is not the movies. You have your spirit and they cannot possess it.

What do they do just discard your spirit and start talking for you?

What about your spirit?

What about your sins?

I guess they just say I will take your sins over just go on into heaven until I come back and take you into God's abode.

Get real Dr. York this is not fiction but reality.

Come on now. If you were an incarnate of the four and twenty elders you would know this. You would also know that angels rarely speak. They only speak when it is necessary and if you speak to them and this goes for God too.

Tell me something if you are of God why aren't you the first in this day and time to stop Satan and man from destroying this planet and God?

Why aren't you the first to commission God and tell God enough is enough and the war and hatred on the face of the planet should stop?

Why aren't you telling God to contain the Moon? You know the significance of the moon and how it affects time and life but not just life and time in the physical but life and time in the spiritual.

Why aren't you telling God to stop this age old fighting with spirit and man?

If you were of God why has the fighting of the past the fighting long before good sinned with evil stopped? Why does it still continue?

If you were of God why is the fighting of the past relevant to the fighting of the future, the now and tomorrow generation?

Before you came to earth why did you not shut down spiritual fight of man?

On earth why have you not totally shut down all physical and spiritual devils –evil? Yes wicked and sinful people. Why have you not done this and do not tell me about a holy Jihad or war because I infinitely know that God would never ever infinitely never ever use wars of men to get his point across because God is infinitely peaceful. He embodies himself in peace and tranquility and this is why his people seek peace and tranquility and yes some find it. God's people have no desire to be in this sinful world with wicked and greedy people. They shun all facets of evil so don't come with religion to me because religion creates war and strife and like I've said over and over again God is not a religion – he is clean, he cannot be dirty because if he was he would be sinful like us.

Why don't you educate humanity on the significance of the moon in relation to war and how war is formed?

Tell them how war comes to the planet earth

Tell them. Tell your people and humanity about true life and how humans came into being. Meaning how they were created because Adam and Eve were never and was never the first creation when it comes to life – human life.

Before you came to earth you would have told God you will only come to earth to stop evil and all that evil is doing. Meaning stop the violence, the war, the hatred and lies and reclaim the earth and the goodness of earth for him God as well for his true people but yet you did not do this. You can infinitely never do this because you are a warlord – Aries. You are a scavenger looking for dead bodies to prey on and yes you found some but woe be unto them. Woe be unto them. Woe be unto them because your condemnation has become their condemnation and trust me they will pay and pay dearly if they do not repent and change their dirty ways.

You would have told God you want to shut down all evil on the moon and make the moon pure and void of all spiritual sin – war – wickedness.

God would have given you the power to do so.

God would not refuse you. God would have been so happy and pleased with you because you would have been the first to do what the others before you could not do.

If you are of God tell me what does God look like?

What does the inside of the Crystal City look like?

What did the inside of the Garden of Eden look like?

What does hell look like?

Who were the men outside the garden?

What race were they but then you would know because I told you from I mentioned 10 000 BC.

You would also know this beforehand because you are of the four and twenty elders.

If you are of God show me what the language of God look like? And don't bring Arabic to me because I know Arabic is another form of Urdu. It is the mother tongue of Abraham or better put Abram.

Stop telling people Black is not a colour because it is a colour. You cannot accept this nor can the people of this world accept it because you know from you accept this colour which is Black you accept God and you will have to accept his truth.

People will use colors to represent people but it has to do with energy. For those who know heaven and hell. My Peeps know the colours of heaven and hell.

For better clarification when I say God is black I am referring to colour of skin now.

You need to know the significance of colors and how it is used in the spiritual realm. Colors is not important here in the physical but it is more than important in the spiritual realm and it is important for you to know this. I don't care if you think I am crazy or I am a demon know the truth. Know the knowledge of God because like I said belief cannot and infinitely will never ever get you into God's abode. Don't wait until you are dead to find out the truth because you will be singing the blues when you sing TOO LATE.

KNOW THIS *EVIL CANNOT LIE TO YOU IN THE SPIRITUAL REALM BECAUSE THERE ARE NO LIES IN THE SPIRITUAL REALM. KNOW IT BECAUSE THIS IS THE INFINITE TRUTH.* EVIL CANNOT LIE IN THE SPIRITUAL BUT EVIL INFINITELY LIE TO YOU IN THE PHYSICAL. TELL EVIL TO TAKE HIS LIES TO THE SPIRITUAL HE CANNOT BECAUSE HE IS CAGED LIKE A WILD ANIMAL. HE HAS NO ACCESS TO HEAVEN BUT HE DOES HAVE ACCESS TO HELL AND EARTH. Evil in the spiritual realm teaches you about itself. Evil cannot teach you about Good nor can it teach you about God, it can only teach you about itself. They tell you what they know. God how do I put it for humanity to comprehend and know? People this is hard to explain in writing because I do not have the right words to explain it to you correctly.

Good whether white pink black purple once you die meaning when you die in the physical and you move on to the spiritual realm you are changed and the colour of skin you are changed to is black and this is why we see the angels, the brides of heaven and the children of God as black. It does not mean that when a message is being relayed to you that you cannot see a person in their original state you can. I hope I have explained it right so not to confuse you.

White is not indicative of heaven and the angels of heaven because when I saw the devil, the **_man_** with 666 he had a man clothed in full white beside him and yes I did see the devil as a white man. When I saw evil die I saw evil as white. So everyone that is evil dies as white a white person and they are clothed in full white. *This is how I saw it in the spiritual realm and this is how I am relaying it to you.* This cannot be disputed. If you dispute this refer to the Ying and the Yang. It does not matter if you are white, black pink or purple this is how you are going to die in the spiritual world.

In one of my vision the one in white was trying to get people to come into his fold and he did not go into the churches he was on the streets doing so; had pamphlets, paper in hand. So *white alone could never be representative of heaven and does not represent heaven, this is why God's angels do not wear white alone.* When you die in the spiritual world the colour you die in is white. Meaning the clothes you will be buried in is full white. The skin colour you take on is white meaning you die as a white person in the spiritual realm. Evil whether Black White Chinese Pink Purple you name it you die as a white person just to repeat myself. So white cannot signify purity when it signifies death.

So Dr. York the same thing you did to the young blacks in America and Canada is the same thing this man was doing. There is no difference in the two because you are the agent of the devil – sin and evil.

My Peeps and True Loved Ones this has to do with Will/Sin and I will explain in clarity at a latter date. Please do not be discouraged nor cry. ***Remember God has a way or working things out perfectly for you. If I have confused you I am sorry but this is the best way I know how to explain it. When we meet face to face hopefully I can clarify any misunderstanding and please do not throw pie in my face. (Smile)***

Always remember the people you hate God will make you become their footstool, give you over to them.

AS FOR YOU DR. YORK I WILL TELL YOU AGAIN THAT THE TRUE LOVE OF GOD EDUCATES AND CAN NEVER LIE AND YOU NEED TO TEACH THIS BECAUSE PEOPLE NEED TO KNOW THIS. ONCE YOU HAVE THE TRUE LOVE OF GOD YOU ARE PROTECTED. YOU KNOW THE TRUTH AND NOTHING CAN TAKE THIS FROM YOU. YOU SHOULD KNOW THIS AS WELL AS KNOW THAT YOU CAN'T GET THIS KNOWLEDGE FROM ANY BOOKS SO WHY MISLEAD AND MISINTERPRET.

IF YOU ARE OF GOD YOU SHOULD KNOW THAT THE SEPTRE WAS PASSED ON.

IF YOU ARE OF GOD YOU SHOULD KNOW THAT GOD TRULY LOVES EVERYONE AND NOT FAVOUR ANOTHER RACE OVER THE OTHER BUT WHEN YOU GO AGAINST GOD, SPREAD LIES ABOUT GOD, DO THINGS TO DISHONOUR AND DISPLEASE GOD IT'S ANOTHER STORY. YOU WILL NO LONGER BE CALLED A CHILD OF GOD.

WE PICK UP THINGS THAT IS NOT OURS AND INTERN DISPLEASE GOD.

WHY DO YOU THINK WE CAN'T FIND OUR WAY UNTIL THIS DAY?

WE REFUSE TO LISTEN SO GOD HAS GIVEN US OVER TO THE FALSE GODS WE WORSHIP AND BELIEVE IN AND THIS IS WHY EARTH AND THE HEAVENS IS IN SO MUCH CHAOS.

WHY DO WE ALL OF A SUDDEN HATE EACH OTHER?

PIT OURSELVES AGAINST EACH OTHER

FIGHT AGAINST EACH OTHER AND TELL EACH OTHER ONE RACE IS SUPERIOR OVER THE NEXT?

YOU CLAIM TO KNOW SO DO A HELL OF A LOT BETTER BECAUSE WHEN GOD LOVES YOU HE WILL NEVER GIVE YOU OVER TO THE ENEMIES. YOU KNOW THIS. YOU HAVE

TO GO AGAINST GOD AND DO THINGS THAT ARE NOT OF GOD FOR HIM TO GIVE YOU OVER TO THE ENEMY.

So, Dr. York, Al Saayid Imam Isa Al Haadi Al Mahdi, I am asking you to stop. You can stop this madness. Black people especially you the American Blacks I am asking you to truly look into what this man is doing. You are not Sudanese but Americans and you cannot turn against your home for this man.

You cannot fight this war for him because you are not of Sudanese decent. This is Sudan's fight and not yours. This man said he is of God and one of the four and twenty elders and if he was there would not be a great divide in his land. Muslims and Christians would not be fighting because they all worship the same Pagan yes Babylonian God. They do not speak the language of God so why are you defending them. If he truly loved his people none of this would be happening to his people because he would have went directly meaning face to face with God and tell God to squash the conflict and show the people of Sudan the truth through him. God would not say no. God would have opened up the right and truthful way for him to do so and the people would have listened because the truth reside in every human being on the face of this planet. It does not matter who you are the truth is within you because the truth is life and life is God.

You are Americans and you have to respect America. It is your home. You have an obligation to your homeland and you cannot let someone come in and destroy it. Do not disrespect the home that God has given you and do not bring slavery into this because we of ourselves sold our own people into slavery. We are still doing it today and this is what this man is doing to you.

He is selling us. He's selling you into slavery and it must stop.

We sold ourselves out in the past. We sold our own people and we too are to blame. This battle that this man is preparing for you to fight is not right.

It is not your fight. This is the devil's war, his war ad if anyone of you go against America your homeland you will be committing TREASON against your own and home and more importantly you would be committing treason against God. Despite how crappy the laws are you are free in some ways. No land is perfect. Every nation has their conflict but you are free in freedom of speech. This is your right and let no one take this from you because with evil you have no rights. You are shut up, imprisoned and sometimes killed. What this man and all religion is doing is taking away your rights and we see this each and every day in Islam and Christianity with them you have no rights because they use fear as well as use God as their weapon – bargaining chip and this is infinitely wrong. Any avenue that takes away your fundamental and God given rights is not of God but of Satan – Evil. God gave you Life as well as rights to make your own decisions when it comes to good and evil so why give up your rights to man – men that cannot save you – truly help you. Come on now this is your soul, your spirit it belongs to you because you need it. Listen, God infinitely never ever told anyone to choose him. He is giving you all the goodness of Life why throw it away for death. You need to know the difference between life and death. No one should push you to choose death and no one should push you to choose Life. You have the pros and cons, you know the difference between the two, the decision is up to you and you alone.

If God said Eric choose Life God would be wrong – infinitely wrong because God would be taking away your right to choose

If Death –Evil said Martha choose Death, Death would be wrong – infinitely wrong because Death would be taking away your right to choose

If I said Glen choose Death – Evil I would be infinitely wrong because I would be taking away your right to choose

If I said Arlene choose Life I would be infinitely wrong because I would be taking away your right to choose

Innocent people will lose their lives Malachi Zoodok, Yannan, Dr. York, and so forth.

Innocent blacks and whites will die and you will be the ones to blame.

Black people and White people you cannot take up Sudan's fight when you know it is wrong. God never gave you religion of men to condemn him.

202

God never gave you religions of men to preach to people. God never infinitely never gave you religion of men to kill and hate anyone.

One of Moses law specifically said thou shalt not kill so why are you preparing to kill. Why are you listening to a man that tells you to hate – kill?

America is your country and no one should come in and tell you to go against it.

No one should tell you to fight for another man's land. America is your land. As pompous and rude as they are – you all are you cannot go against your home. It is infinitely wrong and God will not stand for it nor does he stand for it because despite what we were taught we too did wrong. We sold God out because we were the ones to let evil in and because of this evil has and have polluted the entire globe with its hatred and lies.

We also sold our people into slavery and no one can dispute this. We did wrong unto ourselves and have done nothing to correct our wrongs. Instead of correcting ourselves we let people prey on our weaknesses by lying to us about Life – God.
Let me ask you this can a ditty man teach you how to be clean?

Can evil teach you how to be clean?

If you answered no to all of these questions then the question I ask you now is why are we following after unclean and dirty people?

Why are we letting them teach us how to be dirty?

Why do we continue to let them make us dirty?

We were taught to take up the ways of the Babylonians. They are the pagans that we have been telling you about for centuries and you are still not listening. Instead of walking away from them we continue to honor them and give them our riches – blessings.

We were taught to dress like them

Whore like them

Worship like them

Sing like them

Sin like them

Die like them

We do everything like them and it must stop. If we do not stop it we will never be better. Leave the Babylonians alone. Let them keep their damned pagan and voodoo worship.
Don't have them teach you about God because they know nothing of God. They cannot represent God nor will they represent God. They can only represent their God who is death. Yes their white Jesus.

Why soil yourself, your hands for him.

Remember I tell you this the day you shed blood you will never infinitely never ever enter God's kingdom because you know shedding of blood is wrong. It is an infinite sin. You all know this. You will never see the True and Living God whom I call God but rest assured you will infinitely see Satan – Death.

There is no remittance of sin in shedding blood. It is an infinite sin and trust me I give you my word of everlasting truth that he will never inherit any part of the kingdom of God.

He will never infinitely never ever see God's abode.

His children, your children, no bloodline of his or yours will see or inherit the kingdom of God or live in God's abode if you shed blood because he forgot to tell you about DEBT. The debt that is handed down from generation to generation and yes we it generational curse sins that have been passed on from generation to generation.

Trust me because of the lies and hate Islam and all religion spread I assure you and give you my word whatever it takes to shut down evil in the physical and spiritual realm I will do. I will not have these people disgrace God anymore. I refuse to and I refuse to let them continue to put my race to shame and disgrace because of their lies because God's children and not Blacks alone they are Whites and Chinese as well. This is how I saw the mountain and this is how I am relating it back to you. Three races alone were on that mountain all others were excluded not because of race but because of the lies they spread and believe in. God infinitely does not block anyone from entering his abode we are the ones to block ourselves from it with our beliefs – lies. If you say God do I will refer you to nature and the book of Daniel because Daniel dealt with nature as well but man do not know this. If God blocked anyone from his abode evil's children would have no food to eat or water to drink, they would infinitely be cut off from the goodness of God.

No Babylonian or Pagan will inherit and see the kingdom of God if I can help it if they continue with their lies. Trust me they would have to truly repent and live for God meaning they have to live clean and truthful.

I've had enough of their lies and bullshit.

They represent the dead – Satan and not the True and Living God

I've told you Islam is a spiritual prison.

You should not be going against your country for him or anyone. America is your birthright. Your home and you cannot go against it because a <u>MAN</u> told you to do so.
Tell me something when did God tell you to go against your home? Come on tell me. Yes I am yelling. When did God tell you to go against your home?

Did God tell you to do it? God didn't so why are you going against God because <u>of a mere man.</u>

Let me tell you something knowing what I know now do you think anyone can tell me to go against my sweet and gorgeous Jamaica?

Do you think anyone can tell me to go against Canada?

Do you think anyone can tell me to go against the lands that God's people reside in?

Trust me infinitely the foul language that would come out of my mouth as well as the gestures would not be becoming of a lady and trust me kiss my ass won't do because it would be chicken feed – wine to the other words I'd be telling you. Yes my mouth gets worse. Mek mi put it a likkle vulga fi yu. Di bingo bag would come down. Now ask a Jamaican tegareg what happens when di bingo bag cum dung. Better yet ask any true Jamaica whether white or black. Hey Sean Paul don't be shy if they ask you tell it to dem.

Like I said I refuse to let anyone take God from me again and I refuse to go against God for anyone. Fuck them and their bullshit because Mr. Pagan doesn't live here anymore. He was infinitely evicted never to return.

I will defend God until my last breath and trust me I will not use weapons of mass destruction to do so. I will use my words and arrogance because I am arrogant meaning I am a fighter but with words not my fists or with weapons.

Go against my homeland for who?

Nigga please your fight is not my fight. Fight your own damn battles just don't take your shit into my homeland because that's a different story.

Remember the saying where no bones are provided no dogs are invited and since I did not invite you into any of God's homelands fuck off and stay the fuck out. You and your kind are not welcomed nor are they wanted and you are infinitely not needed because no bones are provided for Satan's dogs.

Keep your shit to yourself because what don't concern me I leave it the hell alone and Satan don't concern me hence I leave his ass alone but when you come into God's land with your bullshit then it concerns me because I am of God and not of the Devil so therefore I must defend God and get the Jinns and Janns out as you call them.

I infinitely respect God and despite my wrongs he's the one to correct me and show me the errors of my ways.

I am not perfect people I do make mistakes but the beauty of making mistakes is knowing that God truly forgives me because he's allowed me to learn from them so that I can teach others not to make them (the same mistakes).
Like you I need to be solid in God. My past is not clean it is filthy but I refuse to let my past hinder me from doing what God has asked me to do. I have to do it honestly despite my flaws – sins of the past and present.

Trust me it is not easy on God when it comes to me and if you read my other books you will see and know why. So when people dreg up my past to destroy me look to God and say God they're fools because she done told us she sinned and her past was sinful and not clean.

Look to God and say thank you God, truly thank you because she was truly honest with us. She did not fake anything or lie to us. I refuse to lie to you despite my sins because we all sin. I would truly love to be perfect and one day I will but in the mean time the Michelle now will have to do. I'm just like you, no different. Like you I stress and have problems but I have infinitely learnt to leave my troubles with God meaning I talk to God about them and he does answer me whether it be in a song or someone calling me he infinitely answer me. Yes I quarrel with him and tell him he needs to talk to me so I can hear him but guess what God rarely speaks. His language is different from mine and yes it does take time sometimes for him to answer because of the distance in time between him and man. Know this.

As for going against my land, the land that God gave me fuck you Al Saayid and that is mild to the language I wanted to use. You can kiss my ass when it comes to fighting for you. Bitch my life is precious because God gave it to me so fuck off with your war and your Islamic bullshit. I am not dead because I was not born under the banner of death I was born under the banner of Ja. I was given life but you were given death. You were born under the banner of death hence you spread hate and lies. You cause nations to die. Like I said you are doctor death because you came to us with death and hoping all of God's children would accept death but I walked away. I infinitely refuse you and in the name of God his children will see and know the truth and refuse you also.

You can't tell me to destroy my land to suit you.

You are telling me to go against my people for you.

Tell me something the freedom I have in my homeland can I have it in yours?

Can I tell your government to kiss my ass if I want to?

What about my freedom of speech?

What if I want to denounce the profits (prophets) especially Mohammed if I feel he is incorrect? All these things and more can I do?

Can I call your elected official a buffoon if I wanted to?

I bet not so why would I give up my own – my freedom for you?

Why the fuck would I give up God for you? Your shit stink like anyone else. What makes you so important? So what if you are from Africa. Have you forgotten that a lot of lands broke free from Africa long ago.

Why don't you tell the people the truth as to why lands were separated from Africa and please start with slavery and tell us bullshit about the

Europeans invaded the land so I can blast you and school you in our true history.

Keep your fucking dead god. Mine the True and Living God that I cry out to by saying Allelujah suits me just fine.

Jah short for Allelujah suits me just fine. He's the one that has seen me through many storms so fuck the lot of you because I am not giving him up for no man or spirit. I call on God and when he touches me the right way I say Allelujah praise your wonderful name thy will is done.

Me Michelle give up God for the lot of you come on now. I am gullible but I ain't no fool. I know God and I have him. Me give up God for a Babylonian or a Pagan. Bitch step off and move out of my way because the God I look up to and truly love is no Babylonian or Pagan. Keep your Pagan way of doing things just stay the fuck out of the lands that God has and have given me.

No matter how crappy some of our laws are I am free. Listen people especially my black people whether we like it or not God took us out of Africa.

Some came out the harsh way and some the not so harsh way. We were disobedient to God. We did not listen and we cannot blame anyone but self.

Whether you like it or not it is the truth. Learn, truly learn from your past and stop letting people turn you against your home because in the end you are the ones to go to jail and be held for treason and he would be in his homeland free.

<u>I am asking you my people walk away. Do not go against your own because this man said so because he is wrong.</u> Please step aside because it is not right for anyone to tell you to go against the home God has given you. It is not right for someone to tell you to go against the laws of God.

God has given you something and it is well given. If you do not take care of it would it not wither – rust – decay? Truly think because when it comes to being indebted to evil you cannot repay evil. You infinitely cannot repay evil. Death's pay is death there is no ands ifs or buts about this.

I do not care what evil offers you, you cannot repay evil.

I know they said Jesus will save you but can a dead man save you that is in the living?

I know about death people and that the good that has moved on can save you but those spirits are not dead. I am talking about the dead dead – death.

No for real can death save you in the grave?
Not convinced. Look at a dead body. No don't go to the morgue but at times you see dead bodies on television or in the movies. Can those dead move and don't come with your zombie bullshit or vampire bullshit. Just had to sneak that in there for those who are going to try.

Those dead bodies cannot more right?

The body hath not life right?

If you have answered yes and no to the two questions above now tell me why would you want to die?

Why do you want to live to die?

Why do you let people convince you to die?

There is no happiness in death. Take a good look at some of the faces on the dead and truly tell me if this is what you want to become? Lifeless and stiff – void of truth – Life.

You cannot let the Babylonians win because if they do your homeland will be in economic turmoil. Your children will suffer and you will be enslaved again. TRUST ME THE BABYLONIANS WILL ENSLAVE YOU AND THIS TIME AROUND IT WILL NOT BE PRETTY. No one should tell you to dishonor your land for theirs, it is not right. It is unjustified because God did take us out of their lies. What are you telling God you want back into their lies and hatred – slavery? Come on now. We love the beating that much that we would deceive ourselves for it. Please I know the cruelty of whipping a person – beating them to the point where they curse God for creating monsters like them. We faced it and some of us are facing it today. God took us out. Yes we faced pain but who is to blame for the pain that we faced? Our ancestors faced. Truly look back in history so no one can feed me bullshit. We all have to take the beam out of our eyes before we can take it out of the next man. I'm no different and this is why I refuse to hate any race because it is not warranted. Every race is guilty of something and that something is sin – hate. Like I said my hate is too good for evil. Evil has a job to do and he's doing it. Life has a job to do and life is doing it despite the nature of man – humanity.

If you are against what I say take up the bible and read it then. We are the ones to leave God and each time God rescues us we go right back into our mess but not this time around because the Babylonians are playing for keeps. You will die and this man knows this.

Sudan is his homeland he should be talking with God about saving it and not pitting you against the home you were born in.

I don't care how long he's been in America what he is doing is wrong and from he said he was an incarnate of the four and twenty elders this should have sent up alarm bells but we including me did not know.

Do not go against God for him. God is your right and no one has a right to take God from you not even me.

He has us changing our names to suit him and his religion but did God tell you to change your name and accept a Babylonian name. All of you have a birth name and many of you have dishonored it by changing your names. Your name sets you apart from them. The name you were born with whether you know it or not is your birth and death certificate and you cannot change it. If you change it then you would have sinned. You've become a liar in the eyes and sight of God and you will die – you will die with death. The name your mother and father gave you is your true name and this lesson I learned from my eldest son. Your true name is vital and to change it means you do not respect your family nor do you respect God. It does not matter if we change our name latter on, you were recorded at birth with your original name. Meaning if your name is John Alexander and you change it to Joe Chretien you will stay John Alexander in God's record books. Meaning your birth and death certificate will remain John Alexander. But because you changed your name and say your name is now Joe Chretien and have everyone believing you are Joe Chretien you will not see God because you lied. You're deceiving and lying to people. You are giving them false or wrong information.

Now for those that say and said but the bible said God changed Abrams name to Abraham this is an infinite lie.

Why would God change Abrams name and not change Moses, Daniel, even my name and yes yours? God cannot change your name and will infinitely never ever change a person's name to please him or anyone. If God did this then God would have broken his own law. He God would be a liar and a deceiver. Yes he God would have committed sin and because he committed sin no one should listen to him God because he's a liar and deceiver like Satan. He's no different from sin if he changed your name. So know infinitely know that God did not change Abrams name to Abraham.

The country that you reside in sets you apart from them.

The name of your land and the name you were born under is infinitely significant. You cannot accept the name of Babylonians and think you are going to be right with God because you are not. You will go down in hell with the devils people and you need to know this.

Do not think that I don't feel it for you because I do feel it for you. Please just ask God for yourself and free yourself from this man.

If this man was of God and of the four and twenty elders would Sudan be facing turmoil?

The genocide and conflict that is happening in this country he would have fixed it long ago because he has direct contact with God.

Sudan wouldn't be depending on anyone.
The country would be prosperous and pure, economically stable and void of sin.

All that he asked for from God, God would have granted it to him. He could fix the problems of the world because he knows God personally and he is of God and an angel incarnated.

Look into things and don't bring Moses or Noah or the messengers of old into this because none of them were a direct descendant of God meaning none of them were angels incarnated like this man.

Listen my homeland has its problems and trust me I've asked God to spear them and trust me he has. God stayed Jamaica's destruction twice and they don't know it. Trust me this destruction that is heading their way will destroy them if not wipe them off the face of the planet if they don't change their ways. I've prayed for them (the people of Jamaica) and have vomited big time. Their sins are too far gone so I have to step aside and let destruction come because I cannot cry and vomit for them anymore. The lawlessness and sins on the island have reached too high so what they sow is now what they will reap. Meaning they sowed the seeds of sin so sin will now destroy them. Yes I know I am repeating myself. Dem naa listen because ole people no lie when dem sey fiya daa muss muss tail and dem tink a cool breeze. Truss mi when fiya hit dem rass soon dem ha go halla an ball because they refused to listen.

God gave them everything including the music and they had musical messengers then and now and they still refuse to listen.

Listen to time will tell by Bob Marley. <u>He told you GOD WOULD NEVER SEND A BALL HEAD TO HIS PEOPLE TO TEACH THEM OR EDUCATE THEM.</u>

HE TOLD US NO GREAT GOD IS GOING TO COME FROM THE SKY TO SAVE US AND HE IS INFINITELY CORRECT. AND I WILL TELL YOU WHY BELOW. SO KEEP READING ON.

None of us can say we truly love God and is doing for God when the world is in such disarray. Come on people it's time we stop following men and start following God. Come on now. When will you stop follow people that are leading you astray and telling you nonsense about God?

Do not wait until you are in the grave to find out the truth. When you find out in the grave you cannot and will be sorry because you will cry and trust me there will be no turning back for any of you. You are going to wish you listened and then you will remember the song, TOO LATE, TOO LATE, TOO LATE. ALLELUJAH. YES LORD, ALLELUJAH TOO LATE.

Wasn't the Garden of Eden enough?

Trust God and he will show you the past. He will take you back; show you things that no books, pastors or imams can teach you. God will teach you so that you will have greater faith, right knowledge. Stop being stiff necked and stubborn. Prayer ***alone*** cannot and will never save you. You have to live according to God. You have to respect God and what he is teaching you. You have to live a clean life. ***GOD IS RIGHT PEOPLE; GOD HAS RIGHT KNOWLEDGE, RIGHT EVERYTHING.***

For all you haters out there here we go:

Egyptians stop the bullshit and stop your hate. Yes I am on your cases now.

Stop the damn lies because some of you have black in your GENES, you have black in you. Stop saying that black people were only slaves. Some of you go as far as saying there were no black people in Egypt you were all white or pale skinned and yes Hindu.

We know who you are. The ones that are saying there were no blacks in Egypt we know you are from Hindu descent. You spoke the original language Sandscript. You educated the people on worshipping idols and other gods. Enslaved our people, we know you used the back door to get into Egypt. Remember Egypt is apart of Africa and not Asia. I know why Ethiopia was conquered as well as why Egypt was conquered. You can't fool God's people anymore. No matter how you enslave and kill us we will find the truth because the truth is in us. It does not matter if it takes thousands and thousands of years the full truth will come out.

Stop people and learn, stop going off, this is why when Moses came to free the people, his people, he went up to the Mount to get the teaching of God which was written, it was never spoken, ***but written***. None of you know the significance of the mountain because we all think the mountain was a physical mountain. Look within and know the truth. Know the mountain and that's all I am going to say.

Read your bible.

He came back and saw what?

Saw that the people made a ***golden calf.***

Think people.

So yes Egyptians say there were no blacks because I know it was your race that was outside the Garden of Eden, residing in the land of Nod and now in Egypt, Persia which is now Iran. You are also Phoenicians because this was what God taught and showed me.

Egypt was not the first place you conquered and polluted. Ethiopia was. You intermarried with the blacks of Ethiopia. You caused them to disgrace and pollute the land by trampling on God. Ethiopia was one of the mecca – hub for civilization because they knew about time meaning the elements of nature and time. Man the beauty of this land and you brought shame and disgrace to it. We polluted this land because of you. It was no longer pure and this is one of the reasons why you include Ethiopia in your book of lies. Every country you go into you seek to control dominate and destroy. You hate the black race so much that you and your race will do anything to eradicate us off the face of the planet. You want this planet to yourselves. Your race want to be supreme. Your race want to control everything but you forget you kill us this world will be gone. It will die and it is dying because fire is coming. The world will burn because the fire – lava is rising up from the earth's crust and humanity will die and trust me this is shortly. It is coming and if we do not change this now there will be no future in 20 years to talk about because all of humanity will die. This is no scare tactic. This is reality.

None of you know. You are his race Satan's race but Satan is not loyal to you. He's going to watch you die because it's death for death with him. Keeping hating my race the black race because when it is all said and done none of you will see God nor will you enter his abode and trust me infinitely on this I will make sure of it in the spiritual realm also.

I know there were black people in Egypt. They resided in Kemet which is Lower Egypt, the land of Nubia, Southern Egypt today. They were the wooly haired people for which some call 9th Ether.

__Take a good look at the Sphinx; take a good look at the pyramids. Better yet look at some of the artifacts that you have unearthed and tell me otherwise.__

God left the pyramids and Sphinx there for thousands of years for a purpose. He made our people build them for a purpose because he knew it would come to this. He knew over time you would come up with garbage like this.

The Sphinx are black, left there to donate and tell the world there were black people in Egypt and yes we were the ones to build the pyramids. I know why they were left there, you wanted the Ark of the Covenant but God took it out. Trust me we knew and still know how powerful the Ark was and is. We knew the healing power of the Ark. More importantly we knew what it could do and how to use it.

We build everything because your lazy asses could not. Nose too damned high in society asses that you can't take it out. Go ahead and hate me because all of you know the truth but yet want to disclaim. Now the lot of you are mixed with Black, Greek, White, you name it you are mixed. Not pure. Next you are going to tell me that Anwar Sadat was not black sorry had black in him.

It's amazing that when you ask an Egyptian if there were Black people in Egypt you all cringe as if the thought of black people burns your soul. As if it is a curse to say black. Well let it continue to burn your asses because you will never get the Ark of God. Now to justify yourselves you are going to say black is not even a colour.

Fuck the lot of you because you are all ashamed, ashamed to admit the truth. Ashamed to say yes black people were in Egypt and we have black in us.

Go ahead and tell God you are ashamed of him. Come on tell him, tell God you are ashamed of him, Go the hell ahead and tell God. Bunch of lying heathens and parasites.

Look at all of you. Disclaiming but guess what God is proclaiming. What are you all going to do now? Blow up the Sphinx and Pyramids, wipe the internet clear of the statues, and destroy all your books now, our books, books that rightfully belong to the true Pharaoh's, ***well guess what the true pharaoh is not dead, he is still alive so keep on looking to the land of the dead for him, keep on searching amongst the dead for him because you will never find him.***

It's amazing that all everyone is running from has a way of biting you all in your asses.

Napoleon's soldiers knocked the nose off because he hated Black, hated everyone because he could not and would not accept the fact that his ass was mixed too. ***Every race on the face of this planet has black in them but everyone refuse to acknowledge each other. Refuse to love each other.***

Go ahead and gasp. It's only a matter of time before two white couple's start having black babies and what are you haters going to do. Say she cheated.

I don't care you can hate all you want and gasp all you want but guess what we consume each other. We all hate based on colour, race and religion. ***Yes you Mr. Nazi guy Mr. White Supremist*** this is for you. Let me show you how God is good and show you and the rest of the haters show you too how God is good. Show us how stupid and ignorant we are.

Mr. Sewer guy sorry but I have to use you here. No disrespect because you are all doing a fantastic job but I have to come here. So please don't condemn me or hate me.

You hate Jews, Blacks everyone that is not White but yet you drink their piss and shit and yes their blood too.

Yes people GASP

Oh Lord I am more of a target now.

When you piss, and shit in the toilet where does it go?

To a sewer treatment plant for which it is filtered to get the gook out of it. Once treated it goes into the ocean and sea and from there back to you. You are drinking water that is filtered and treated from people's shit, piss and blood. And some of that shit you drink is from Jews and Blacks, the people you so hate.

Mr. Sewer and Ms. Sewer people, I know you do a good job and by no means am I saying you are doing a bad job you are doing a wonderful job. Pat yourselves on the back I am just trying to show these people how ignorant they are.

They need to think because we are all drinking recycle, piss, shit and blood.

From another angle if the first one grosses you out. The seafood we buy where do we get it from. The same place that shit, piss and blood is dumped in. ***Think and now tell me what are we hating each other for when we consume each other?***
I've told you there is no section in heaven for this race or that race, no section for this religion or that religion so stop the nonsense we are carrying on with. There is no tribalism in heaven.

People it takes seven days for nature to clean the water. Mr. Sewer guy correct me. I could be wrong. ***Yes here you can say I am a hypocrite because the undertone of my book and words spell hate.***

It sounds like I am spreading hate but by no means am I trying to. If there was another way to use this analogy I would so please forgive me. I certainly don't like hate and people do not hate these people

BLIND OBSESSION REBUTTAL THE TRUTH IS NOW OR NEVER

or protest them because it has to be so. Our waters are no longer pure, no longer safe as it is. We throw everything but the kitchen sink down our drains and toilet and these people are the ones to keep us safe. Clean up our drinking water the best way they know how to. So thank them sometimes. Make them feel appreciated.

Guys I am not spreading hate when it comes to your jobs because it takes a heart of lion to do what you do without going insane. I could never do it.

For you Blacks that hate other blacks and call us sell outs and say we must die. Fuck you because you are the ones selling out. You are not pure either. Your asses are mixed. So what if I am married to a white man or white woman. Does that make me less of a person? ***Yes you call us house Nigga's and sellouts but guess what these house Nigga's are blessed and highly favoured. It is us house nigga's that have to come back and teach your ignorant ass the truth.***

Solomon is an example you say. Go back and read the Songs of Solomon and see. He was not black skinned so you are mixed, mixed, mixed. The same thing you hate is apart of your GENES too.

Forget about the Garden of Eden because in the Garden both races resided in there. White and Black and they lived in peace. For right knowledge and comprehension you can say this analogy had to do with energy. Just as blue eyed could be used as energy in that analogy. ***God wasn't saying that people with blue eyes are evil he was telling us that we all have evil in us and that evil's energy is blue***

– dark blue. This is the correct knowledge that we all need to know. ***That person got the revelation in the form of blue eyed but it did not mean people with blue eyes are evil it meant blue which is negative energy is in all of us.*** It is in heaven, look at the sky, what do you see? Is it not blue? So when we pray and talk to God our thoughts and prayers have to pass through that negative energy or field and when God is answering us the answer have to pass back through that negative field and that is why our dreams are distorted, we cannot fully comprehend them. You literally have to figure it out to get right and exact knowledge and trust me this is hard because for some it takes years, hundreds and thousands of years before we figure it out.

All of you tell me which heaven are you all going to go to with this hate?

Tell me.

Think because as it is all of you who are condemning are condemning your own souls and walking on the way to hell. It is amazing how men use God and religion to spread hate, kill and rob.

My Peeps read revelations it tells you that man have the mark of the beast. They are the ones that want to be worshipped, they are the evil ones.

No sweetie I am not spreading hate. Revelations tell you. Hey let no one tell you that the Satan is half goat and half man that is just a fucking lie. Sorry. Baby girl let me tell you how the devil looks. He does not have pale skin like White people, nor does he have the skin of Albino's. Girl friend the man is sweeeeeeeeeeeeet. His skin is creamy, when you add the right amount of cream to coffee. Caramel but not so brown a little lighter. His body is fit and nice. I am telling you baby is hot, hot, hot. No man on the face of this planet is as good looking as him. He's that fine. Pull up Bobby Lashley on YouTube and look at his body. This man's body is infinitely finer and nicer than his. Trust me infinitely if you were to put all the world's handsomest man from the past to the present together they could not compare to Satan. He is that gorgeous and my description pales in comparison to how handsome he is.

He has the mark of the beast which is 666 in his side. This mark the naked eye can see but 666 is not all and you have to look closer in order to see the line above and below the 666. This was how I saw it and this is how I am relating it to you. Trust me baby is hot with black hair. So let no one tell you otherwise. Let no one tell you Satan is half beast and half man because he isn't. He is a man and a fine looking hottie too. If I didn't see the marks trust me I would have been gone with him. Ladies the man is fine, fine, fine. Cuteeeeeeeeeeeeeeeeeee. Any woman on the face of this planet would go with him. I don't care who you are or how religious you are you would fall for him. This is how hot he is. Trust me he's so not a one night stand. He's someone you want to keep forever and show off on your friends to stay look at the man I've got. Baby is fineeeeeeeeeeeeeeeeeeeeeee. Trust me an arm candy has nothing on Satan and I better stop because I am going to go overboard but honey is sweeeeeeeeeeeeeeeeeeeeeeeeeeeeet. Damn he's fine. Ladies ***this is one of the reasons I tell you to truly***

love because when each partner truly love each other you cannot stray and will never stray. Do not just love truly love. My Peeps and True Loved Ones if you truly love, when another man apart from your husband come to you meaning try to pick you up it becomes an abomination unto you. It makes you angry. When you truly love you can only see your wife or husband and no one else. Man your spirit will stir. So truly love so when the devil comes to you he cannot conquer you.

My Peeps and True Loved Ones I did tell you it was going to get nasty. I sound racial but trust me I am not and I am tired of defending my way of writing so if you think I am a racist so be it but like you well not like you. I just have to put the physical devils in there places that's all.

Sometimes you got to let God open your mouth for you and do the talking and trust me I did. Please do not be offended about the swearing because that's me when I am angry and passionate about God. And trust me I am very passionate about him. I will defend him at all cost with my mouth ***but I will not pick up arms against you*** because that is just wrong.

This is what God gave me. My writing and I am going to use it to teach and defend God to my last breath. Those who hate me and want to kill me are not of God. They have their own agenda and guess what God has his own agenda too and I trust God infinitely over any man and their bag of tricks and lies.

So for all that hate, know what you hate? You can hate me and refute me all you want but you will not be able to get away from the truth. ***God has a way of leaving things to make you eat the food of your own sorrows.***

Now for you White people that say you praise and worship God and that Jesus is God and Jesus is going to save you and that I am a liar.

You say you love Jesus but yet hate Black People and can't stretch your hands to the poor. Some of you don't want to live next to black people because we are the devil and cursed in your eyes.

Man do you hate blacks but yet go to church each Sunday and worship Jesus.

Put your trust in Jesus. Give him the praise.

Sister Pat I am telling you now that Jesus was and is the Son of Man. He is not God and will never be God. I am telling you yes boldly telling you that Jesus never existed in the physical realm nor can he be found in the spiritual realm. The story of Jesus is just it a story devised by the Greeks and Romans to throw the children of God off. The Roman Catholic Church devised this and this is why Satan himself sits at the head of their table and empire.

The Roman Catholic Church need to come clean and tell people the truth. It's not about the money but peoples souls. This is our life and it does not give you the right to lie and deceive nations with bullshit stories. Watered down crap taken from

Black and Hindu history. Stop deceiving the people because God does not deceive you nor does God tell lies on you.

Tell the people the truth that the story of Jesus was taken from Babylonian history. It's the story of Nimrod and Semiramus. Man this story is timeless because every culture knows about it.

Tell me something people if Jesus was God why is the world in such disarray?

Why is there this religion and that religion?

Why are we fighting to get to Heaven or Paradise? Should we not have Paradise already?

Would we not have stopped the fighting and truly love each other?

Would we not respect God and do all for God?

If Jesus is God why are we still living in sin?

Why is there so much sin in the world today?

Why are we still doing what we are doing?

Come on tell me and don't tell me any bullshit.

If Jesus was God the world would not be the way it is today so stop the shit you are all doing. Preacher, yes you deceivers stop telling people shit.

Pastor shut the fuck up because you are a conniving and deceitful demon.

If Jesus was God why couldn't he open the book?

If he was the savior for all the inhabitants of the earth why couldn't he open God's book?

To you Muslim's you are included in this if Mohammed was the seal of the prophets why could he not open the book? ***God's truthful book. Come on tell me. They are all Prophets – holy men but yet none could open the book of God.***

Sister Pat read it for yourself go on read it. Revelations 5 verses 3 and on.

What does it say?

"And ***no man***"

Stop and read again.

"And no man in heaven, or in earth, neither under the earth, was able to open the book, neither look thereon."

Read on and hear what happened to John.

He wept. Go on read it for yourself and get comprehension.

Now tell me if Jesus was God, the incarnation of God why the hell couldn't he open his own book?

He is God, he wrote it but yet he could not open it nor look upon it.

BLAST ME, GO AHEAD. ATTACK ME NOW. GO AHEAD.

You cannot dispute it and now the lot of you want to say well the book said, REVELATIONS OF ST. JOHN THE DIVINE so this is of John and not Jesus.

Go ahead and say it to justify yourself then read verse 1 and tell me if your justification is warranted. Go ahead and deny the truth now.

(

}

Finished?

No

{

}

Sister Pat I am going to come back to you.

Now to the Jews the real Juws.

Mr. Jewish man, the true Ju you cannot accept Jesus and will never accept Jesus because you know this to be a true. You know this is a story. You know that Jesus did not exist. Come on you know the significance of Latin and why it is so important to the Roman Catholic Church. Come on now and live for life instead of living for death. You know the truth but yet you accept lies, write lies and tell lies.

This is one of the reason's why Revelations 2 verse 9 said in part "and I know the blasphemy of them which say they are Jews, and are not, but are of the synagogue of Satan."

If you are a true Ju you cannot go against the laws of God.

You cannot accept false teachings and bring it in the realm of God.

You have to keep the law no matter the consequences of man

You cannot say you are God

You cannot say you are the son of God. Under no circumstances can you say you are the son of God and every one of you should know this. I don't have to spell it out nor tell you because you know. It is in you as well as in your genes.
You cannot let people think you are God

You cannot mislead and go against God

You cannot leave the teachings of God and accept other cultures, teachings

You cannot under any circumstances bring other teachings in God's fold

Being a true Ju has absolutely nothing to do with race but the true love and devotion of God himself.

You must keep the teaching of God clean and pure.

You must adhere to the laws of life – creation

You were the keepers of life so tell me what truly happened? Come on tell me. I know the truth but do you?

A true Ju will never leave the fold of God to teach others lies. He or she cannot do it. More specifically HE and if you are a true Jew you know the reason why.

Catholicism was designed to mimic you perfectly but you kept true as well as knew this faith was a lie but many of you left the fold and accepted their lies. I know why.

This is why it said "Jesus came to his own and his own refused him" because he brought false teaching, teachings of other nations into God's nation and this is why he was refused because he brought Baal and Balaam into your fold.
He brought ***Islam*** unto you

Now I ask you Mr. True Ju to decipher this dream for me.

This is my dream: dream #3

I went into a place of worship (people if I said it was a church I would be lying) I have to say it was more of a home that you worshiped in.

2 men – white men dressed in black

They were happy so they went to the front and said to this man they were ready – ready to get married.

They addressed their words to one man in particular and he stood up.

I thought this man that stood up was Catholic, because he wore a small head covering, much like the rabbi wears and yes some Catholic – Pope.

This man threw them out. Not physically but with his words these two men had to flee.

When these two men fled the children that were outside came in and they were being guided into another area. They went towards this lady and she was White but the children were black as well as mixed. His daughter was half white with beautiful black hair and the reason why I know this is because she called him dad. They were young children and beautiful. And like I said as soon as the two men fled they came inside and went towards this lady – guardian. She was the woman that looked after them. This is what I gathered from the dream.

I asked him (this man) about what he did and he said they were Muslims and not Jewish but they could sit at the back if they wanted to and he began to explain to me the difference between the two.

My Peeps and True Loved Ones I cannot remember if he said the Muslims were Bohemian's or if they the Jews were Bohemian's but I know ***Bohemian's*** is in there somewhere.

After the two men fled and yes these two men in Black were White. Yes the Jewish man was also white and had a pudgy too because I remembered touching is pudgy. Pudgy for those that do not know is a small tummy. My Peeps you know I love pudgy's and I guess that's why I touched his.

I said to him the Jewish man where I come from we have Sephardic Jews (I had read somewhere that Sean Paul was a Sephardic Jew because I did not know we had Jews in Jamaica) he was about to explain to me the difference between the Jews and the Sephardic Jews but I woke up out of my sleep.

People this man was friendly because he was explaining to me the difference between the two. He also told me that these two men could sit in the back.

End of Dream
So Mr. Jewish man the true Jews you knew Jesus was the son of man and not the son of God. He could have never been the Son of God and for us to say that Jesus is the Son of God we are blaspheming, and this is an abomination and condemnation of God. We are condemning our souls to darkness and carrying on this lie. We are fulfilling this lie.

I know some preachers will use Ezekiel and other stories of the bible to justify their claim but so be it. Like I said I am not here to rob anyone of their souls nor am I here to convert anyone.

From my dream being a true Jew has nothing to do with skin colour but keeping the word and life God has ordained upon you pure. The true Jew protects the children. You the white Jews are the protector of the Children of God so why are you not protecting them. Why are you destroying the children of God?

The children of God are not males they are females. Everyone of them were female so why is it that your Rabbi is a male? Yes I know it is not wrong for a Rabbi to be a male. He has to be but it is a female to carry life and the teachings of God.

The true Jus (Jews) do not mix religions; you protect God's language because it is pure and not defiled. This language is one of the keys to life. It is a language that is used to heal. Meaning once you have this language you can defeat evil and yes create life itself. Meaning you know how life was created and how it came to be on the face of the planet. With this language you know about time and yes you can communicate directly with God because you know the distance in time in relation to how far God is away from man. Yes with this language you can heal the sick from any parts of the globe without having to have to leave your home. People with this language have infinite knowledge and yes you know about the dead and how to communicate with the dead. Hence Egypt had to be conquered. Ethiopia had to be conquered because these two lands had this knowledge and housed this knowledge. This is why in Egypt they rape the dead until this day. They are looking for the truth – life and trust me none will possess it because if they do humanity will be more than doomed not just in the physical but in the spiritual as well.

God's language is written but never spoken. It is not mixed with Sandscript and can never be Sandscript or any of the languages upon the face of the planet. For you black Muslims that were taught that the language of God is Cuneiform toss that crap in the garbage because Cuneiform was an ancient tongue – language of the Babylonians.

There is no language upon the face of this planet that comes close to God's language.

No one in the outside world knows of it or can learn it just like that and this you hold until this day. You hold God who is the light true to this day.

You Mr. and Mrs. True Jew you hold the language true to this day. No people it is not Yiddish or Hebrew.

No language upon the face of the planet comes close or even look like it and this is what Moses got.
The bible said Moses broke the law.

Once you are given this language you cannot teach it to someone else.

It is sacred and must be kept until the day you die.

Only you can write it, you the person or persons it was given to can use it. When you have this language you can use it to cure and heal people, you have direct access to the spiritual world, yes you can see evil spirits, talk to the dead directly, this you can do no matter where you are within the world and yes I am repeating myself.

We in Jamaica call it a gift; say people that has this gift is gifted, they can see.

You will never let anyone come and defile it. Nor will you break free and let go of it or break the code to dishonour or displease God.

If Jesus was a true Jew and was true he could have never gone out there and preach. He would have never gone into the lands of the enemies of God and learn anything from them because he had the language and gift of God. He would have been sealed with the gift of God. He would have had the truth of God.

Going back to the old nursery rhyme. This was left in our anansy stories to guide us home.

"MARY HAD A LITTLE LAMB, A LITTLE LAMB, HIS FLEECE WAS WHITE AS SNOW AND EVERY WHERE THAT MARY WENT THE LAMB WAS SURE TO GO."

If you were to accept the story of Jesus as being true then you would have to accept the nursery rhyme above.

Mary had to have been the wife of Jesus. She was the one to do all the teaching but he broke free didn't he and went to study in a land that he should not have and brought their teachings back to his people. This is why he will never be accepted because he broke the code of God's honour and way of life.

People it is self explanatory because Mary was not his mother.

From this dream Islam is an abomination unto God and must never come near the children of light.

Sister Pat back to you because I am going to send you to Revelations chapter 1 verse 13.

Read it for yourself. "And in the midst of the seven candlesticks one like unto"

Unto what?

Read it again.

"Like unto the Son of Man"

Read it again.
"Like unto the son of man"

This is Jesus' revelations and not God.

So from reading this Jesus could not be the Son of God and will never be.

Cry now and get angry.

You can do all of this but you cannot change the truth and no matter how much you mask it, and hide it God will come back to it. He will give it time because the pit you dig you will fall right back into it. That is why old people always say when you are digging a pit dig two. Meaning don't just dig one for me but dig one for yourself as well because mine may catch me but rest assured yours will too.

And if the pit that you dig for me don't catch me it will catch your followers of hate, your children, your family, a family member so please don't dig one dig two.

Pastors go ahead and dispute, say it is a typo and has no meaning. Read it for yourself. The Angel that was revealing revelations to him looked like the son of man. *It did not say looked like the Son of God but the Son of Man.*

I am not finished yet people.

Now back to you white people that say you love Jesus and worship Jesus but hate black people read what colour Jesus was. Open your bibles the book you so hold in high esteem and turn to Revelations chapter 1 verse 14-15. He had hair like wool, hair as white as snow, meaning he had gray hair (we should say silver hair because there is no such thing as gray hair but silver hair) and feet like burnt brass. When you burn something is it not black.

Read it.

Now tell me how the hell can you hate Black People but yet bow down to them in praise and worship? You go so far and say Jesus is God so therefore God is black and you are bowing down and giving your worship and life to a Black God.

You even say he's going to save you from your sins.

Go figure a black man is going to save you.

The race you hate is going to save you.

How hypocritical.

Go figure you hate us so much but yet bow down to us even kiss our ass. What do you think you are doing when you go to church? You have to worship us and praise us. More importantly you have to bow down to us.

Now do you see how foolish and ignorant you are?

How the fuck can you hate the black race but yet bow down to us and worship us?

Does that make any sense?

You hate us but yet we the black race have to save your ass?
Why the fuck should we save you?

Tell me why should we save your racist ass?

(Yes people you can call me racist here).

You hate me because I am black

You hate me because my skin is black

You hate me because my hair is wooly but yet in prayer you bow down to me well not me but a black man and beg him to save you from your sins. Go figure.

Why the fuck should we save your hating and racial ass?

You hate us bitch so why should we save your ass?

Dispute the facts all you want. Go ahead and condemn me.

See how God is good. That which you hate and despise you have to bow down to.

To the Muslims you are another set of heathens.

Eat the grape of your sorrow now.

You are another set that hate Blacks, despise them, and depict Bilaal the Septre Bearer as a slave. Some of you say he is a lowly slave but yet this Black Slave did what you heathens cannot do and that is to blow the horn for the call of prayer.

The same black people that you hate you still have to pay homage to. You have to kiss it and walk around it, make pilgrimage to it when you attend Mecca. You have to honour it because it is in your five pillars of faith. ***You have to do it.***

YOU HAVE MAKE HAJJ TO WHAT?

CAN'T SAY IT.

WELL LET ME TELL YOU

A BLACK STONE.

YES A BLACK STONE.

So tell me how can you hate when you have to pay homage to it? To what "Black Stone" for which you call the Kaaba, for which many say house the remains of Adam and if you were to trace the lineage of Adam back through the genealogy of charts. And I don't even have to because some scientists and religions acknowledge that Adam and Eve had to have been Black. So guess what you are kissing the remains of a Black Man, making pilgrimage to honour a Black Man. Walking around a Black Man.

Now God's cup is emptied onto the inhabitants of earth. Now eat the grapes of your sorrows and see how ridiculous the whole lot of you are. Hating each other without knowing what you are hating.

- Hating each other because Religion told you so.

- Hating each other because Man told you to do so.

- Any which way you put it you are worshiping ***Man***

- This is why I say not one of you are worshiping God, know God. And let me tell you this, no one can worship God because God does not require worship he requires thanks.

- Now God has shown you how ridiculous the lot of you are because what you hate is what he gave you over to. What you have to bow down to.

Now that each and every one of you know

What are you going to do?

What the hell are the lot of you going to do?

Who are you all going to worship now?

Who are you going to call upon now?

What God are you going to worship?

Are you going back to worshipping idols?

Dispute all you want, hate me all you want, set me up all you want, condemn me all you want but ***the fact is the truth cannot be disputed.***

For all of you that are going to come with John, all the books of John I am ready for you because my other book is written and it will follow this.

Now tell me are you going to stop worshipping man and start giving God thanks?

Many of you won't. Many of you will continue onwards to do what you think is best instead of going to God for the answers.

Many of you will be like the people of old, especially Noah but rest assured on that fateful day none of you can use the excuse that I did not know because now you all know so there is no excuse.

I do not worship men and never will again. I will always give God the praise and honour. He deserves it. *There is no place for hatred when it comes to God and I will not spread hatred. Yes I can but I refuse to and if above seems like I am spreading hatred My Peeps and True Loved Ones forgive me. Sustainer, My Love please forgive me and I repent of my sins as I do not want to spread hatred but was just putting this man in his place. Educating the haters and your people about the truth and the light which is you. This is by no means a rejection upon you but when it comes to you and me no one crosses the line when it comes to you.*

No one classes me or judge me when I know God and what his world of true love and peace is all about. *They don't know they wanna be; trying to be but can never be.* My Peeps and True Loved Ones if God is good to you, keep giving him thanks and praise.

I will tell you again and forever tell you. *What God has given to you no one can take that away from you. You are the only one that can give it away and trust me when you give it away you will never be able to get it back because you are telling God that you don't want it.*

Going back to the Garden of Eden. God warned us and told us the people of the outside garden were deceitful and tricky and we were not to lay with them but we did not listen and it cost us our kingdom and it is still costing us today.

We the ones of the Enclosed Garden were of peace. Peaceful people that knew nothing of hate. *When*

Jesus greeted people did he not say Peace Be Unto You and we the children of God know why he said it.

So Mr. Muslim man because you say As Salam Alaykum it means nothing to me because peace is not with you.

Could never be with the lot of you because none of you whether black or pale can stand to hear the truth. That is why you kill. And this is why you tell me God kills. ***Your God is a killer, a fucking murder because he knows his time is up. His 24000 years is almost up and this is why he is trying to take all of humanity with him.***

What the fuck do you think I am?

This is why you and the whole Islamic kingdom cannot pray right. You pray the same dead prayer over and over again. Bowing down to ground and paying homage to the dead which is your god. Your God is death hence you tell us we have to die.

Your God is a rapist hence you rape us of our souls and dignity

Your God is a fraud hence he rides off the True and Living God's coat tail

Your God is ugly – uglier than sin itself hence you tell us he's a beautiful angel of God and we should want to be like him as well as look like him

Bitch shit cannot be pretty, it stinks and this is your God. Shit – the shit we pass out of our ass. I certainly don't fucking want or need him. God's people don't want or need him because death cannot compare to LIFE and my Father, My Love and Lovey is Life. He's the air I breathe and the food that I eat. He's the water that I drink. He's a part of nature and nature is within me therefore my God, the God of Truth is in me.

Your God lies and he lives within you hence you spread lies, spread hate, steal, kill, do all manner of abominable acts of sin in his name.

This is your god because you know your God is dead. Buried under the ground. Buried the same way we bury our dead therefore we dump our shit on him because he is shit. He can't give me life so fuck off and go back to Nod where you came from. Who the fuck are you to class me. Don't fuck with God's people because we know who we are do you?

My God is not dead and no matter how you mark me for death the truth is now known.

Keep praying to the ground and think God is hearing you.

When you pray you must sit upright in the form of the upright triangle.

You are not to bow down to the ground because the ground is where we spit, shit, bury our dead in. This is where your hell is. Hell is in the ground hence fire rises from the ground.

The children of God knows not to prostrate to the ground but sit around a table, on a chair, lay in bed and talk to God silently in the mind. Truthfully think of him and talk to him this is their connection to God and will always be their connection to him. The connection starts in the womb at the navel. The navel is the centre of life and the womb is the cradle of life.

In the garden there was no religion.

None of the prophets before Jesus had a religion.

Catholicism was devised to mimic the true Jewish way of praise and thanks for which you call worship.

Designed to show Catholicism as a faith of God

Designed to throw the people off in order for them to accept your new religion and your voodooistic and idolistic way of life and living.

Some accepted but those that did not you killed them but you couldn't kill all. Every religion came from Catholicism which is from you.

Jesus just perfected ISLAM that is why you call him the lamb. He's the one leading his people to the slaughter house but some knew better and this is why he was accepted by the Council of Nice.

Now today you are using ISLAM to catch more people because you know your time is almost up. You only have a short time and from we accept ISLAM, CATHOLICISM, CHRISTIANITY,

BUDDAISM WHAT EVER RELIGION upon the face of the land we will all go down in hell with you.

So fuck the lot of you because as it is none of you will enter paradise because you hate, kill and spread hate and for us me included that use to follow your doctrines written by men I ask God forgiveness and repent of my sins. I ask God to redeem my soul and cleanse me of my past sins. Forgive me for following after false hope, false doctrines and false prophets. I ask him not to just cleanse me in the physical but in the spiritual as well. I ask him to wipe my slate clean in both worlds and never let me follow after false prophets, false worship, false love and praise anymore.

Read your Bible people. When a true Rastaman greet you does he not greet you with Blessings? If he does not say Blessed, he says Guidance, True Love, touch you and go through the moves of peace and love so why the hell are we straying and listening to the dead, dead people that was not in the garden. Why are we letting the dead, dead people take our peaceful state from us and then turn it against us? They know nothing of creation and how we were created but yet we listen to them tell us we come from monkeys and that we are the descendants of slaves. We accept this bullshit but yet cannot accept the true and living God.

Shit if Jesus is the first begotten of the dead why the hell would you want to be like him?

The MF is dead. Come on now. Live man this is your life. Why follow after the dead? The dead can only lead you to the dead – death. You have a brain think and be wise.

God is giving you good food – Life so why refuse it? No for real why refuse it?

God is giving you the truth and you cannot accept it.

When God took us out of the land of Egypt what did we do?

We build a GOLDEN CALF indicative of which religion and started to worship it. Think. We take different bits and pieces of different religion and make it our own. Give up what is truly ours to follow what is not ours. These religions were not given to us. They are not pretty but like the make up that your beautiful models wear.

Now we have lost our home, kingdom, and yes God. Now we are struggling to find him and can't find him because we were told he was lost but God was never lost. How can you lose pure love? Come on now. Look within you and you will find God. Pray silently within you. Every chance you get talk to God silently and he will answer you.

Come on people stop being ignorant and letting people that do not know God teach you and tell you about God.

All you have to do is ask God yourself. God never left you he was always there.

We were the ones to leave God and no matter how hard he tries to save us we refuse his help. We tell him we do not want to be saved.

Well let me tell you something and I will repeat it until the day I die. When I see true change I will stop. FIYA DEY A MUSS MUSS TAIL UNNO TINK A COOL BREEZE.

Can a man prove God wrong?

Can God prove himself wrong?

Come on people stop doing what men and women tell you to do and do what God tells you to do because in the end God is whom that counts not man. Man cannot and will never save me or you but GOD will save us all.
By no means it mean to commit wrong all the time and expect God to bail you out, he will never do this because you know better. Once he has closed his door you will never be able to open it.

You can never open it and the people in Noah's time found out the hard way. Adam and Eve found out the hard, the children of God found out the hard way. Everyone died. They lost their soul to evil and we are doing the same thing today. We are losing ourselves to evil. The flood could have been prevented but the people of old made a choice. They chose not to listen and perished.

Eve made a choice. She chose not to listen and she perished.

The people of Sodom and Gomorrah made a choice and they chose not to listen and they perished.

Many of us today have and has made a choice and you too will die if you do not amend your dirty ways. Destruction cometh it is up to you to listen and head the word of God. You can save yourself and this planet but as individuals you have to want and need this because the future does not belong to you alone it belongs to your family meaning your kids and grand kids and so on.

Pull up these songs by Duane Stephenson on the internet and listen to the words. If you want to hear Bob Marley you know which songs are relevant but I am giving you Duane Stephenson now so listen because he says it better.
> Misty Morning
> Truth Is
> As Soon As We Rise
> Better Tomorrow

As humanity we have to start listening because it is our future. It is our life and we have to live for life not just in the physical but in the spiritual as well.

I do not want your soul. Will infinitely never ever want or need it. You need that which God has given unto you. Life is yours and you need to cherish it and truly love and live for life.

We've been taught that after we die that's it. It is not it. Life continues onwards. Truly listen to Truth is because Duane is right none of us can seek forgiveness inna dirty clothes. We need to clean ourselves up before God can forgive us.

We cannot say we are saved and sanctified if we are still dirty

We cannot say we are saved and sanctified if we are still living dirty

We cannot say we are saved and sanctified if we are praising and worshipping dirty

We all need to be clean including me. I am no exception to the rule meaning the laws of God who is Life.

We are living for death and we are going to die. Not one of us on the face of the planet is living for life because if we were we would not die.

Remember The Ark was closed and everyone perished except for Noah and his family

If you know the truth of Moses you would know that many perished in the desert and some were left to wonder not for 40 years but for more than 40 000+ years.

God has given you one more chance to clean yourself up and it is up to you to make the right choice because if you don't you will perish and you will not be able to continue on in the spiritual world. You will go directly to hell because you made the choice in the living.

No one is going to save you in the grave and no great God is going to come from the sky to save you. Trust me the man on the winged horse is real but he will not be able to save you because he did fall from grace because he was showing off. And yes for those that want to know the colour of the horse it is black. Beautiful black horse that changed into a man. It's a weird vision because I do not comprehend it so I am going to leave it alone.

Mister Muslim man I do not hate you and will never hate you because to hate you mean I would give you the victory over me and I will infinitely never give you the victory over me. My hate is too good for you. My hate is precious and cannot be wasted on people like you because in truth you are not deserving of it it's too good.

Let me tell you something, God did not bring me into this world to hate and if I do hate it's only for a time therefore my hate is not true. Trust me I truly love you because when you truly love you cannot hate and the best part of truly loving is that evil cannot comprehend it. It is our shield, our protection against people like you. Truth cannot hurt and I would never ever infinitely never ever tell anyone to hate you or your race because hate is wasted energy. Like I said don't class me. You don't know me so don't class me because I know how to walk in hell. I am the one to literally walk into hell and take God's people out if God wishes me to do so. Do not think because God is clean he cannot make his people go into your homeland – hell and take his people out. He can and I know how to so truly don't fuck with God's people. We are simple and passive people that have the sword of death and as a Muslim you should know what the sword of death is. We have it but because we are clean we do not use it. We do not dirty our hands we leave that for Death, your God. Do not take and or adapt what was rightfully given to me and my people and use it against me because I know who and what I am.

My question to you is DO YOU KNOW WHO YOU ARE?

DO YOU EVEN KNOW WHERE YOU ARE GOING BECAUSE I INFINITELY KNOW YOU KNOW WHERE YOU CAME FROM? And yes people this is a stupid question to ask but I ask it anyway.

DO YOU KNOW YOUR HISTORY OF DARKNESS AND DECEIT?

DO YOU KNOW WHERE YOU'RE FROM?

I infinitely know my truth and the truth of life.

I know how this universe came into being.

I know who God's people are

I infinitely know who you are

I infinitely know who the devil is

I infinitely know who God is

I know who God's people are and I infinitely know who the devil's people are so do not use what was rightfully given to me against me because you don't know me nor do you know my people. I am the one that can go into hell and take out God's people. I am the one that can go into hell and defeat your people as well as the devil himself so stop fucking around with my people because you are not my people nor will you ever be.

God saw it befitting to send Moses into Egypt to take his people out of your clutches and he did it successfully. Moses took **_LIFE_** out of Egypt and he did not use any books of man nor did he take any books out of Egypt. Moses took life out which is the Ying and Yang. The Ying and Yang is the very fabric of life because this is how the universe was made but you cannot have it and never will have it because you know not time and the secrets of time – the pleasures and beauty of time.

Humanity does not need your lies because you seek to control and dominate. You want dominion over the land and this is why it is said in your books of lies that God said to have dominion over the fishes of the sea and so forth. You will never have dominion over my people because God's people are not just blacks they are whites as well.

We are the Ying and the Yang. We are life because life is within us and we are in the likeness of life and that's the infinite truth.

Whether the undertone of this book stress hate it is not my intent and will never be my intent but I refuse to listen to you and your hate. You cannot tell people to hate based on colour because colour is not significant in the physical it is significant in the spiritual. The flesh dies and is eaten by worms but the spirit/souls continues on.

Our bones are our prison in the physical world. Meaning it is our spirit/souls physical prison. Our spirit tries to escape this because with this body we do not have freedom to move back and forth in the physical and spiritual freely. We do not have freedom to travel back in time and fix the problems that are still in time. We are trapped in this body until its allotted time has expired.

I know about life because God has given me life. He has given me the truth so therefore I must live clean as well as live by the truth. Evil and the evils of sin can be defeated. Satan's people can be defeated and the only way to do this is to live a clean life and by separating from evil. We must live as it is outlined in Psalms One. We cannot walk in the council of the wicked or the ungodly.

We cannot buy your food.

We cannot marry you

We cannot eat and drink from you

We cannot commune with you by going to your churches and holy places of sin

We must not bank in your institutions nor go into your institutions for medical help we must have our own that are clean and truly holy – void of sin.

I do not use religion nor will I use my words or books to spread hate, lies, and sin. I do not use my books or words to kill BECAUSE I KNOW THE BEAUTY AND SERENITY OF PEACE - LIFE.

WE WERE GOD'S CHILDREN AND STILL ARE. WE ARE THE CHILDREN OF GOD AND FOREVER WILL BE AND NO MATTER HOW YOU COME IN AND DISTORT IT. YOU WILL NEVER TAKE LIFE OUT OF GOD'S CHILDREN. AND FOR YOUR INFORMATION "ALLAH" *MEANS THE BREATH OF LIFE. You cannot and will never say Allelujah because Allelujah is what our spirit cries out to. Whether we are good or bad we cry out to life to save us and have mercy upon us.*

We have to cry out Allelujah. We have to cry out to ALL because all that is in the universe and all that is in and on the earth we came from. It is within us. All is life because all is Allelujah – All is Truth – All is the Breath of Life and life is within us all because All is God and God is within us all.
He is the heat our body needs to keep us alive, which is the sun, he is the air we breathe, oxygen, the water that flows within our bodies – blood, he is the ice we need to cool our bodies down, the food we eat to sustain the outer shell – body. *Your books can never tell me that which was left and engrained in me.*

Your books cannot tell me about where I came from nor can it tell me my heritage because God made sure he left that in me as well as in all his children. When the appointed time comes all will be revealed unto God's people and they will live in truth as well as love truly love in truth and this no one can or will take from us again.

Man will come and give me a bit to open my eyes a little and when God sees that I am committed, his children are committed he will reveal all to us. He will seal us so that you cannot touch us with your lies. He will seal us so that you cannot come near us or abide with us with your lies and deceit. And like I've said God will not use books of lies and condemnation to save us. He will do it through the truth of his own people meaning the truth he left within us – our genes. He will open my Chakra's as you call it and your seal will be broken but his seal will come together in me and all his chosen people.

I am not disrespecting you but educating you on what I know to be the absolute truth, truth without a shadow of a doubt because this is God's truth. God is the light and it is by this light and true love that the children of God must live and abide by.

As God's true chosen people we have done nothing but disrespect ourselves with you.

We have disrespected God and now is the time to reclaim God not by lies but by truth and true love.

We have accepted your religions

Accepted your idols

Accepted your way of worship

Accepted your way of worshiping man and idols

We have made burnt offerings and human sacrifices unto your gods

We have put ourselves in debt to your god without knowing that we cannot and will never be able to repay your god because we accepted death and therefore we all must die

We carry the debt we have with your god we cannot repay and never will be able to repay because he is taking us to hell with him and many of us do not know this. This was what your people failed to tell Eve. You gave her something to hold onto to but you did not tell her you were not spiritual beings but earthly beings.

Peeps My True Loved Ones and to all that is reading this do not take my word for it read it for yourself and ask God, the True and Living God to clarify it for you. Give you full truth and overstanding.

Let no one tell you you can repay this sinful death because none of us can if we could we would have done so.

There is no repaying your debt this is why Genesis said, "the day you eat of the fruit you shall surely die."

The first death was spiritual death, the second death is physical death, now there is a third death this is deadlier than the two, with this last death there is no redemption of soul, people will not get a chance to live with God because this death is the final death and it is absolute.

Now My Peeps and True Loved Ones you know the full truth so it is up to you to choose wisely. I cannot chose for you but if you truly love God and walk in his footsteps then you don't have to choose

because heaven, the plain where God resides not the heaven that I have talked about but he plain where the crystal city resides will be your home.

Yes you can solidify yourself as a child of God and say God I truly accept you and I am going to do all I can to walk in your truthful way. I am going to live my life for me which is for you because I will be walking in the truth. Not man's truth but your truth.

My Peeps and True Loved Ones read the book of Proverbs. This is Solomon's book. Read what he tells you about disobedience. He lived the life and lost it all because he listened to people tell him bullshit about their Gods. He listened to women; he did to please the flesh and did nothing to please God. He did to please women and not God. This is why his temple is not around. The children of Egypt built the pyramids and sphinx to teach you because God knew things would come to this. Hating each other based on religion and colour.

Look at the confusion of the land, each religion claiming to be the truth but none can truthfully lead you to God.

God is the one to look to and not man. When we stop hating each other and truly start helping each other watch and see if God does not turn back the hands of destruction from you.

Someone tell me why the hell do we always want better and more?
Tell me why is our God not important?

Tell me why does the God that we claim to serve and love does not matter to us?

Tell me, tell me!! (I am yelling)

Tell me why when we want something we run to him and as soon as we get it we cast him to the side. Some don't even say thanks.

We shouldn't want him.
Shut the hell up because you have given me all the right to ask this.

If you can't truly love him, care for him, praise him don't want him.

Leave God the fuck alone and continue to worship your dead prophets, idols and gods.

Don't fucking use Allah either because you know not the meaning of Allah – All.

Keep the name of your dead God and leave us the fuck alone. Go back to using Baal and Baalam, Nimrod and Satan. Use nothing of ours because we the children of God want nothing from you and your race. We want nothing of the Babylonians so fuck the hell off. We don't want your men or women because they are an abomination in the sight of God. They're fucking ugly. Yes people now you can call me racist because I am bent. Who the fuck is he – this man to class me. Mother fucker you don't know me. You don't know my history. Solomon may have wanted your whoring asses and he did whore but trust me I don't want you. Keep your fucking religions of destruction and sin and go the fuck to hell and burn.

Stay the fuck away from my God and don't use anything of ours. Find your own fucking history if you can because God is the way and the light and God is infinitely not Jesus. Keep him and all the lies he's offered in this world and go straight to hell you demon of sin. You're a fucking condemnation like religion and all the religions of men.

My Peeps and True Loved Ones forgive me but I am going off here and letting my negative side get the best of me and I will not hate you for being in a uproar nor will I condemn you for hating my ass but no one class me or tell lies on God. Not on my watch because I will defend God and if I have sound racist and be racist so be it. Like I've said I do not hate this man but don't class me without knowing who you are classing. Don't condemn me because I will make you eat your own shit of sorrow and destruction.

Your race can class us as dogs and monkeys yes even slaves but it's these dogs and monkeys yes us slaves that you have to bow down to in the physical and spiritual.

If we are slaves and monkeys and even dogs why are you using the name Allah? Why mother fucker?

Tell me come on now tell me. You class us so low then don't use Allah because it means Allah is a dog; a money and a slave which means he's black a mother fucking black man bitch and because God – Allelujah is All he created your monkey ass too.

You heard me. If you can't truly love God get the hell out of his domain.

To all of you that cannot truly love God get the fuck out of his land because you are telling him all you want him for is your needs. A frigging pair of shoes, houses, land and riches and as soon as we get it we say See Ya wouldn't wanna be ya.

Well guess what people the time is coming where all your bullshit and lies will come to an end and the lot of you including me will be sorry. Because many of you are singing Jesus is God, Jesus is going to save me, the prophets will save me. Woe be unto the lot of you because Paradise will not be your home.
That's a lie you are yelling.

Well God does not lie.

The True God does not lie but guess what Jesus is not God. Never will be and never could be because "JESUS NEVER EXISTED".

Go ahead and gasp and call me a fucking liar because some of you are. Go on pastors tell them, tell your people not to read any of my books, because I am the anti-christ. I am not of Christ but against him. Protest all you want, ***do all you have to do to me but Jesus is not God and could never be God because guess what God cannot die, nor kill himself and Jesus is dead never coming back.***

Bitch take that back or I will kill you. I'm gonna kill you. (Keep saying it). Because guess what Jesus died he is dead. He never existed and no matter how you look at it no prayer, no nothing is going to bring him back. Come on I challenge all of you to bring him back from the dead. Don't wait until the appointed time as you were taught. Right now bring him back. Each of you bring him back. None of you can because he's like those in the grave dead and none of you have yet to find his tomb. You cannot find it and will never find it. (My Peeps get mad at me because for me to challenge like this is a sin because God can show any of you what Jesus looks like in the spirit hence bringing him back. Meaning there was a man that went around professing he was Jesus long after the conception of Jesus – the story of Jesus.) So forgive me of my arrogance.

Forgive me?
Yes

Good and thank you My Father, My Love. Please forgive me also because I know you did not like what I just said.

If you are so good bring your God back, come on you bitch you are saying bring your God back. (This is what some of you are saying). Bitch come on you are so good and you think you are all that dissing on Jesus. Bitch step back because I will kill you myself. Keep yelling I hear you.

Yes I love the challenge but guess what my God cannot die and never will die and even when this planet dies God will still be alive. So nothing you do or say can kill God. Man dies and spirit dies but God cannot die. Just go outside and take a whiff of the air, better yet breathe in. Go get some grapes, an apple or mango and eat then come back and tell me that God is dead.

Now take your hand and blow into it.

- What do you feel?

- Feels good doesn't it.

- Look at the trees

- Look at the stars and moon

- Look at your veins and the blood that flows through your body

- Feel the love within your body

- Touch your wife or mate at nights

- Make love to them

- See the different races of this planet

- The animals of this planet

- Take a look at the spirit if you can see it

- This is all a part of God

- More importantly when you die, when I die, the air that we breathe is still there, cannot die and this is God and neither you nor I can kill it because we all need it.

- Man can try to pollute it to kill it but it cannot die. Humanity will die before it dies.

- Don't even go there and say that air kills you. No it does not. What we put into the air, the chemicals and shit we do kills us. If it did why the hell does hospitals give you air, oxygen to help you breathe and clean the shit out of you. So air cannot kill. We kill by adding things to it. Now you know I don't have to bring my God to life because he is there and you breathe him, eat of him, sleep in him each and every day so I don't have to prove anything to you because you prove God to yourself each and every day 24/7.

Come on people; think if God killed himself everything including the universe would die.

It would have died long ago with Jesus on the cross. I have to say cross because this is what you believe and I wouldn't be writing this book, you wouldn't even exist. None of us would exist.

Don't make excuses and say this is God; he works miracles, wonders to perform. God cannot kill, will never kill, nor will he send his messengers to the slaughter house. Nor will he tell his messengers to kill nor would he tell his messengers to hate. Yes the bible said he killed well the bible is a fucking lie. So let's scrap that. The bible was not divinely inspired. No book on the face of this planet is divinely inspired because God did not write them himself. If he did every book would have his name on it. God would be the author of them. Tell me something did God himself sit down and dictate the words that he wanted in these books to these authors or did God sent them the manuscript? Yes God will ask you to do something but how you do it is another story. You infinitely cannot use words to mislead and tell lies. You infinitely cannot use words to hate but you can sure as hell use them to defend God and the word of God. Trust me when you are walking on the path of God your spirit becomes crossed meaning evil stirs your spirit at times and this happens when you ask God to make evil be an abomination in your sight. Evil and wicked people become disgusting meaning you will find them disgusting and you will not want anything to do with them. Yes people will call you racist because of this but you cannot be racist if you are living right and according to God. Evil is a condemnation of spirit. It is also a condemnation unto to land that you reside in because evil seek to destroy in every avenue so if someone say you are racist because of this you can tell them to royally kiss your ass. ***Segregation is not a sin it is a blessing.*** Yes many of you will be in uproar and the reason many of you will be in uproar or feel this way is because of change. We all believe we can change the devil. Well know this, you cannot change the devil. You cannot change evil because no one can change DEATH not even God himself can change death. Our problem is we want to change everyone. They must change and conform to your system because to you it is the right thing to do. It is the godly thing to do. No it is not. Each individual have a choice. My choice to be good or evil is my choice not yours. You cannot tell me what to do when it comes to making choices. Not even God tells you what to do. He directs you and if you are making a mistake he will show you the mistake beforehand just like he did Eve and just like he does me. If my body smells a certain way he will let me smell me, if I am walking in the wrong direction he will let me know but the ultimate choice is up to me. It is up to me to listen and get full comprehension of what God is telling me. God cannot make choices for me and if he did he would be doing something without my permission and yes infinitely yes he would be taking away my right to choose therefore committing sin. Trust me I would love for him to tell me what to do but he cannot, he can only direct you and this is a pity. So stop trying to change people. If a person does not want to change what right is it of yours to say he is wrong? It's his decision, his life. You can show him the warning signs like I am doing to you but to say or tell you to accept God I would be wrong. I cannot take away your right. I did that In Blind Obsession and trust me I had to revise that book. I had to correct that right away because God was not pleased. He told me he did not like it and trust me I went off on him. I am hot headed and I know I put it in one of my books. See I did not comprehend what he was trying to tell me at the time but I figured it out and this is why I will tell everyone to know what God is trying to tell you. It is not easy to decipher but when you figure it out you will say oh that's what you meant.

The devil, the physical and spiritual devils know what they were doing. Some of the truth is buried in there and it must be deciphered before the end of time. It is now up to you to accept the truth.

No matter how you hide the truth God has a way of pointing his people there. True love cannot kill people. Nor does it steal. All these things men did because we cannot be satisfied; we constantly want more so we take what is not given to us. We as human kill and take what the other man has.

Come on people, why do we make God out to be a monster.

Why do we depict him as a heathen?

Why do we contradict ourselves.

Most of you trust and believe in the bible with your hearts and soul that you read no other books apart from the bible. Think and stop selling your soul for garbage.

Tell me this did not one of the commandments say "thou shall not kill" God is telling us not to kill but yet he told his prophets to kill, and steal. Take the land of other nations.

Read it for your damned selves. Read the books. God does not live by his word. He's a damned liar according to your books of lies and sin. He tells us in his commandments not to steal, and kill but yet he sends his people to war to kill and steal.

Come on people this is bullshit. How can God go against his word? Think. You are telling us to do one thing and go against it in another sense. This makes absolutely no sense. This is pure and utter confusion, pure and utter bullshit. This is not of God but whoredum and confusion. No wonder we are lost and confused in this day and time because none of us know what to believe and trust. This lie is a grave injustice unto God and none of you not one of you stopped to think and say hey something is wrong here. I didn't until recently.

None of us said wait a minute God told us not to kill but yet he is telling his prophets to kill. What are we to trust? Is this not confusion?

"The wages of sin is death", the taking of human life is a sin – death punishable by death but yet God is telling us to do it – die. Come on now. Why would God say one thing and then turn around and do the opposite – contradict himself? This does not make any sense.

We don't say hey mister preacher man or woman this book is bullshit because the wages of sin is death and killing is a sin, adultery is a sin, so why would God condone these things – tell his prophets to kill as well as have them commit adultery if it is a sin – death?

One of the laws specifically say though shalt not kill but yet he's sending his prophets on the battlefield to kill? Woe woe woe which God is this? This can't be the God of Life this must be Satan the Devil in disguise doing this because Life cannot take Life and if this was the God of Life then something is wrong. We are all doomed. So to say mister preacher man or woman that the bible is true and divinely inspired is wrong because it is telling us to commit wrongs. This book cannot be of God then because it is filled with lies upon lies. It is bullshit – false and infinitely wrong.

We don't stand up and say wait a minute God you are lying to us confusing us. You are contradicting yourself. How can you say thou shalt not kill but yet send your prophets out to kill? None of us say God you know what you are a fucking liar and I don't want anything to do with you. I don't give a fuck what you say killing is killing, murder is murder and you are a fucking murderer.

None of us say God when you tell us to do this what do we tell our children? Are we not condemning ourselves to hell as well as condemning our children?

How do we raise them in truth when we can't even trust you? You can't even be truthful to us so how can you expect us to be truthful to you?

You tell us one thing but yet you do the opposite that's not love but confusion an abomination of sin. You are not the truth but a sin. You are sinful and deceitful. You're a fucking liar and I don't want to have anything to do with you.

Tell me something if God told you to sin or commit sin would God not be sinful?

If God told you to die would God not be Death? So how can we believe the book of sin to be the book of life.

I will ask again, can death tell you about life?

KNOW THIS INFINITELY TO BE THE TRUTH. <u>GOD WILL NEVER AND WOULD NEVER INFINITELY NEVER SEND SOMEONE OUT</u>

OF HIS RACE TO EDUCATE AND TEACH HIS PEOPLE ABOUT HIM.

Never stray from this.

Infinitely know who God's people are because if you don't you will be led astray yet again and you too will become like the condemned.

REMEMBER THE SONG TIME WILL TELL BY BOB MARLEY. Never forget it because God is true time and time is important. It does tell you what is to come. It does tell you and can take you back in time. It is the key – one of the keys to life. Infinitely know this because everything is done in time. I will not elaborate on the sun and the moon here because they too are equally important but not important to time.

Now you don't have to believe but know.

Hell will be right here on earth because guess what people, the ozone is depleting, the glaciers and ice caps receding, summers and spring are becoming hotter, weather patterns have changed, more infectious diseases on the increase, hey lets not talk about pestilence, bed bugs, woe. This is Revelations. Yes Allelujah woe be unto man because the lava slowly rises. Food will be hard to find, money will not be able to buy your souls back because the gate of God will be closed so either you get on board now or all will be lost.

Don't take my word for it read your bible and holy books, your scrolls, whatever you read read it.

Don't for a minute think a meteor is not on the way because it is. Just when it will get here is another story. Scientists know this and are watching for it.

So tell me who is going to save us.

Apocalyptic and you don't believe. Good for you because knowing is the key and now you know so on the last day none of you can use the excuse I was not warned because you have just been warned.

For you that think I am telling you to stop going to church, I am not telling you to do so and if I told you to stop that would be wrong of me. I will never tell you to stop doing what you truly love to do.

What I am telling you is to know God. Know that God is real and truly thank him. Know what God need and want from you so you can serve him properly. Meaning be a good child not servant because God does not want us to serve him. He requires no servants, he requires good, truthful and honest children. Yes he needs you to be his root so that you can grow and bare good and truthful fruits – seeds.

Let all you do center around him and on him. Show him you appreciate what he is doing for you. Yes we make mistakes trust me I am still making mistakes and my faith is rocked too but I am glad I have God.

A lot of you might dispute this because I cuss but you know what I am not ***fake*** and will never claim to be. I am the one that will tell God, Baby, My

Boo, Honey Bunch, Millie Mango and Jackfruit let me and I will pick him up and put him to one side and lay it into you for him.

It's like Independence Day when Will Smith was punching the alien and telling him you don't come up in my home and start nothing I will kick your ass. (In a nut shell people I cannot quote every line). When it comes to God I am this way. I will do it on paper because I am not articulate vocally so I will use written words.

Sweeties God is mine mine mine mine mine and I truly love him dearly. Do you know what he brought me and my family out of?

Do you know how far I have come to find him to let someone take him away from me?

I refuse to let anyone come in and disrespect his kingdom and people

Hell to the fucking no.

Get the fuck out if you are going to spread hate. Take your damned lies and stay the fuck in hell. We don't want you here.

I certainly don't.

I don't need anyone controlling me. God does not control so why should I let religion and man control me? Hell no. God did not give them the authority to act on his behalf. They are not of God so why should I let them continue to spread lies on God to make their God, the devil look good. Fuck that.

Satan cannot offer me anything. Evil cannot offer me anything. All they can do is offer me stress and with God there is infinitely no stress. God does not stress out anyone. Oh baby if only you knew how beautiful life can be living stress free. Trust me many things you would not worry about. Bills become worry free because you have enough to pay your bills meaning you will now live within your means. It's a bit harder if you are a single parent but as time goes by life become a lot easier. It's even easier if you kick evil out of your home and clean it up. Infinitely trust me on that. If you know someone is evil do not harbor them in your home or you will have no peace. You will become so stressed that you will end up haggard out with lots of grey – silver hair like me. (Smile). Know who are truthfully to you and if God show you them, listen because God knows the future as well as know what he is talking about.

So yes you Dr. York I am coming back to you. Take your fucking lies and hate and eat shit. I know you accepted the septre. It was given to you but darkness surrounded it and you accepted it that is why you cannot tell the full truth you can only use it to spread hate.

I was given that same septre of power but I refused because darkness surrounded it. I do not want to spread hate nor will I spread hate. Shit I see what is happening in this world how people kill, lie, want to hurt each other and hurt each other. No this is not true love, its hate and that scepter that was given to me was not true love it was abomination, an abomination of sin; it was and is against Truth which is God. Once you accept it you turn from God and the truth and I am happy I did not accept it.

You have the Aloe and the Scepter but the scepter you have is not the true scepter. You have a rod – a staff but you could never and will never have the scepter of God. That's all you GOT a rod and nothing else. Instead of using the Aloe to heal, you use it to kill. Instead of using the rod of power to show people true love you use it to spread hate. Pity you don't know that the Aloe is nothing without Life – Water. And water is nothing without the Pineapple – the scent and aroma of God. But then how could you know this when it wasn't given unto you.

Your followers do not know. You gave them some truth but not all. Tell me who represented Islam. Jesus did. He is the Lam. ISLAM. That is why they called him the LAMB. He had to represent Islam because he accepted it. He was a Muslim. Tell your followers the full truth not just half truth if you are capable. Jesus is there Lamb the one to lead them to the slaughter house – hell.

Forget it because all that I say can be broken down further to give further and true meaning and comprehension for those who cannot accept what I say without hate. Many of you will say I hate, including you and your nation of Jinn's as you call people that are not of the Islamic faith.

Teach the children that follow you about Mary because she was the backbone to the truth and John tells you why so tell your followers if you so know the truth.

Tell them the truth about Jesus, his story mimicked John the Baptist, he didn`t bring anything new. John the Baptist spoke of repentance and word for word Jesus the son of man mimicked him and that is why they had to kill John the Baptist. He had the truth and he did not deviate from it. He did not mix the doctrine that he knew with anything else. Your so called Jesus did. He accepted and converted to Islam and you cannot prove me wrong this is why the true Jews refused him. No true Jew can or will accept Jesus because we know that Jesus did not exist. His story is a rip off of Greek Mythology.

This is why God showed me the dream with Islam wanting to marry into the fold of the Jewish way of life. Juws (Juws short for Ju – dahites but I will continue to use Jews so that I do not confuse you and Jus or Juws is hard to use.) Jews must never ever infinitely never ever marry or form any allegiance with Muslims. It's an infinite no no because the Jews are the ones that have the power to defeat evil – make them flee from the realm of God not only in the physical but also in the spiritual.

It's amazing how we let others that do not know about God brainwash us about God.

A dirty man cannot tell you about God. Come on now.

Religion is a bully. It uses Psychology, Sociology and Theology which is lies to manipulate and deceive the masses.

All facet of religion rob you of your hard earned money and dignity so tell me how is this of God?

How is fear and preying on the weaknesses of emotions of God?

Yes my words may echo hate to some in their hearts but God knows that I will never use my words to spread hate and if I did I would never truly love him. I know for a fact that God will shield all those who read my lines from hate. Make them know that I do not hate and will never spread hate. Yes I will be racist but I will tell you when I am being racist.

We teach about the oneness of God but none of us know that God can never be one. To be one means you are alone and God is never and will never be alone. My Peeps and True Loved Ones do not gasp.

THEIR GOD IS ONE. HE IS ALONE. HE CANNOT AND WILL NEVER DO ANYTHING. CAN'T DO A DAMNED THING. YOU HAVE TO KNOW THIS.

This is absolute truth. Don't cry. Pick up your Bible it is there. Genesis. We say the beginning but Genesis is in your ***GENES.*** Hence Gene sis meaning it is the genes is. It cannot change and never will change because God left it in you in your genes. So God can never be one. This is why we have the circle, triangle and square but that is a different chapter.

Now back to God. Are we agreed that God cannot be one?

No.

Do you have your Bible?

No

Sister Pat stop it, no tears I am not going to go against the Bible and what you already know I am just confirming the truth so trust me. Remember God does not lie and when he teaches you you are solid and well grounded – well taught. So go get your Bible and sit with me.

Remember I was once where you were. Now God is educating me, teaching me so let him teach you. I am not the one doing it. He is doing it meaning educating me so that I can educate you. I am but another human like you. I bleed, eat, sleep and drink in the same manner as you. Meaning I close my eyes when I sleep, put a cup and glass to my mouth to drink water and juice just like you. So we are no different in this retrospect. Now come on get your Bible. I will wait.

{

{

Have it?

Yes

Trust me?

Yes but I still don't know.

Keep trusting me and tell God to never let me fall from his grace. Do it truthfully with true love. Now smile because I do truly love you and feel you.

Yes My Peeps I can feel you. Many times I smile when I am writing because I know you are enjoying some of what I write.

Now back on board. Kevin I gave you enough time with my extra chatter. Now sit down, Pam I know you are laying on your tummy with feet up. Mother May and Mary I feel your love because I know you are hugging me. Alright Joe and Peggy I acknowledge you too.

Open your bible to Genesis. Genesis One is self explanatory for some but it goes deeper. Will elaborate later but for now I need you to go to verse 26 of Genesis 1. Sister Pat read it. It says what?

Let us

Let what?

"US"

Do what?

Make man in our image after our likeness.

It did not say I am going to make man in my likeness. ***It said let us.***

Pastor stop because it did not say God and Jesus, it did not say God and the Angels, and no it is not a typo.

Thank you Frank you reminded me of what I said earlier that the bible was written to keep us ignorant as well as enslaved.

See this is why I love My Peeps and True Loved Ones.

I am not even going to bother because I know you truly love me and not just love me. This I know. Jennifer thank you because now you know the truth and you can never be rocked. I truly love you not love you and this is what God wants you to know about him.

He needs you to know that he truly loves you. Need your truth to be solid in him so that when people like me come and say they love you and give you food to eat you tell them to KISS YOUR ASS and tell them my God the True God of Love indefinitely truly loves me.

Never leave true love and run to love do you hear me. ***God is the truth.*** I don't care if Jesus was to come now and say love. Rebuke him and say if you were of God you would tell me the truth. Tell me God truly loves me because the truth cannot and will never lie, the truth cannot hurt and will never hurt because the truth protects and my God truly protects and shields me. It's not to say that God will not lift his hand of protection from you. He will if you are doing things that are wrong. He allows you time to find your mistake. Once you find your mistake correct it. Do not continue to do wrong because when you do he lifts his what? Yes his hands of protection from you and let the devil have his way with you. My Love, My Lord, My Sustainer and True Love of my Life will never ever infinitely never ever hurt me or guide me wrong. You know this so let no one put you in debt for their god.

Let no one tell you God is One because he could never be one. ***One is death, it means you are alone and need no one.*** We can do all by ourselves. I use to believe that God was one. I bought into the misconception and deception but I know the truth. I know otherwise.

Sister Pat I am not trying to convince you I am showing you. I am letting you read for yourself. You don't have to believe me because like I've said belief is like the branches and leafs of a tree. *Knowledge is the root and true knowledge cannot kill nor can it hurt.* **It can only set you free, HEAL.**

Remember God set our ancestors in the Garden of Eden. He hid us from lies and deception but instead of keeping ourselves pure and hidden meaning instead of staying away from the children of the dark we did not listen. We saw something else that we wanted and we let that something else in because of what and we are still doing it today.

I will tell you this. I don't want anything from man. Will never want anything from man. Not even his money. All I need, I need it from God. I need his true love, need him to send me the right and perfect mate that truly love him and me and will walk in his footsteps. I don't need man's dirty money but God's true money. Honest, truthful and loving people to buy my books. People that will know the truth of true love and not use it to hate,

<u>but use the truth to truly love others, help others, turn from sin and live in love, the true love of God.</u>

I will explain the concept of marriage and divorce at a later time. Yes My Peeps in another book but in the form of a love story cause you know I write love stories. Yes I know God wants only one man to enter us but circumstances happen that it does not work out this way. By no means think that God does not forgive, he forgives, trust me infinitely on this, God forgives. Oh man does he ever forgive. People we don't know how much God forgives. Wow he is more than wonderful.

So Sister Pat God can never be One; which is alone and we know this because he gave us two eyes to see, two hands and two feet.

<u>Were I come from old people always say one hand cannot wash</u>. You need two. We know this to be true. Try washing with one hand, try walking with one foot. You cannot do it you will hop and that is not the same as walking.

Not convinced.

Can you bring forth a child without the aid of a sperm and please do not bring technology into this for all you techno geeks. Hey Charlie love your glasses no disrespect when I say geeks because honey I find geeks sexy. Just thinking of you guys yes you Charlie do something to my body. You know what I had better stop because now I am going too far and straying way way way off topic. I am going into another dimension. Sorry Father but you know how I can be.

Sister Pat please forgive me. My imagination and mind ran away with me there. Time to get serious. But you know Charlie.

No no no stop.

Charlie

No. See Charlie now the thought of you have done something to me help me to get back on track and stop making me smirk with the thoughts of you.

Come on Michelle

Forget it Charlie

Sorry people that was between Charlie and me

Now for those of higher learning:

XXX   Y   3XY

Star of David – Mogen David which represents the male equals 6

Original star which represents the females is 5
Draw it if you have to
Add them together you get 11

One plus one equals 2

Still don't get it.

Look at your six pointed star. Which is two triangles right. Yes.

Good
Count

You get 6 right?

Yes

Good.

Now take a look at the male. Spread his arms and legs apart and look at his body.

1	head
2	arms
2	legs
1	snake/penis

Everton don't jump stay with us because I know you get Genesis and what happened in the Garden of Eden. You have graduated on your own to the next level but stay with me for now. Help me to help the others so stop smiling and boasting. No you will not use this knowledge to condemn others. Stay. Sorry Peeps he's gone.

Now back on track. Add.

Do you get 6?

Yes

Excellent

So you have head, arm, arm, leg, penis/snake, leg

Or head, arm, arm, leg, leg, penis which ever way you want to put it.

Now look at the female.
Spread her apart

1 head
2 arms
2 feet

Do you get five?

Yes

What about the vagina?

It is in not out

The clitoris does not count ladies and yes you males. We know the lot of you enjoy it but it is not a factor here.

Are you with me so far?

Yes

Add 6 plus 5

Do you get 11?

Yes

Add 1 plus 1

Do you get 2?

Yes

Excellent.

Stay with me now and some of you will dispute this but it is okay.

I might lose you but I hope not.

Put the male atop the female or vise versa. Forget it for you older folks we are not children. Let me just come out with it. When you make love, have sex you become one because your penis enters the vagina which does not hang but in fact you are not one you are still two because you are still atop of her and she is still atop of you which ever method you use. This is why people say One, when you marry your mate you come together as one meaning one in love.

Confused?

Here's another angle.

Six becomes five because the penis no longer hangs it is within you. It is stiff, solid. That's why some people say you are one. When you are inside the vagina you are not hanging you are solid or stiff.

Stay on your wife for those who are on her and vise versa. Count.

2 heads
4 arms
4 legs

What do you get?

10

If you divide by 2 you will get 5 can never get six but if you add 1 plus 0 you get one and this is where the oneness of God comes in, the oneness with your mate or partner. But in reality you are two.

How?

1 giver - male
1 receiver - female

Add and you get two

Add the penis to the ten above. Even though it is inside of her you have to count it. It is not gone it is still there. So 10+1=11 and 1+1= 2.

Now we are going to get into chemistry and I am so going to lose a lot of you.

1 male
1 female

Reduce it

Take the male out

You get Fe

Which is Iron the 26th element on the periodic table of elements

You can break the numbers down differently I know.

Add 2 plus 6

Do you get 8?

Yes

Eight represents Oxygen on the periodic table of element which is O. And you need oxygen to live. Your body needs this as well as iron to live.

Yes Jeremy it is also the Octagon which has eight sides but the O also represents the circle.

Sister Pat I know I have lost you because now I am bringing Science and Chemistry and Mathematics into all of this.

Sorry My Peeps but for Sister Pat. When Adam was in the garden was he not lonely?

Yes

What did God do?

Did he not give him a help mate? A wife. A queen and that person was Eve.

Yes

So in this context God can never be one because one is lonely. Cannot live by himself. When you are one you are depressed, need someone to share your bed and be beside you at all times.

For some this is far fetched but look at it from another angle. To ease our loneliness do we not get a dog, snake, cat, and rat whatever to love and give love to. Are these pets not in our homes and bringing us joy? So think. God can never be one because one represents death, loneliness and depression.

When you die do you not die alone? I know your family is around you but it is you that is dying and not them. Your families are still alive. It is you, your body alone that goes into that casket not there's.

When we do not have our partner's around us do we not feel isolated and lonely, as if we are dying inside?

In the old folks home do these people not die quicker because loved ones are not around so what do some nursing homes do now. Some bring animals in to cheer the people up so that they are not so lonely.

Yes others can prove the theory of oneness.

But look at the male chromosome. XY

What does it represent?

X represent female
Y represents Male

So God can never be one because he is both.

Forget it men do not get your heads twisted or bloated because it is not needed here and this is just an analogy. You are not the creator – God.

You give to us the females.

We receive life from you and we bring forth life – give birth.

We are the ones to nourish and cradle in the womb. We bring forth life from the womb to live upon the land. This is true in nature and true in man - humanity.

So Sister Pat I hope I have cleared it all up for you and show you why God cannot be one.

Onwards we go, now that we know this let's break the eight down a little further. Keep dividing by two.

Now you have 4

4 is Beryllium
Hey you have to Be real now
This is where man and women came into being
Read all about the beauty of beryllium
This is where 13 comes in
Thirteen is B
Draw the number 1 then draw the number 3
Put them together do you not get B
Add 1 + 3
Do you not get 4?

Thirteen is the state of being and this is why you have 13 months exactly in a year to do all you can and that 1 day is for God.

Break it down more
Now you have 2

2 is Helium
Now you are healed read about Helium and see its uses and what it is used for.

Go further down to get your 1 for those that believe otherwise
Divide two into two
You get 1

1 is hydrogen
Yes keep on hiding Jerry because you are higher than a mother.
You are dry, in the stated of dryness
This state is deadly, very explosive
The beginning of death
Go ahead and read about it.

My Peeps read about these elements and know. Talk to scientist and chemists about these elements. They can educate you and please Mister and Miss Scientist please teach right and truthful knowledge. I know nothing of these elements but they are fascinating and I am just using them as examples so please do not crucify me or yell at me because there is a lot more to these elements. Things I cannot comprehend hence you are there. Have knowledge and full comprehension of them. So my Peeps question question question because these people are knowledgeable. Maybe one day the door will be opened to the public for us to see the uses. Hey if there is a place where we can go and be intrigued please let us know because I know of none and knowledge is the key.

Yes ministers and preachers and yes you Dr. York can condemn me but I will defend God. You all can say this is not of God you don't condone it but I am sure rub you the wrong way the language that comes out of your mouth would not be befitting of a minister.

So My Peeps and True Loved Ones now that I am finished and my conscience is clear I am happy and Sir, like I said, I do not hate you but I hate the lies and deception that you stand for and spread.

A Muslim is one of Peace living a peaceful way of Life which you call Islam.

The enclosed Garden was a peaceful land. It was a harmonious land and everyone lived in peace without hate and it is through this knowledge that God will Rise his people again and we will once again reside in Paradise which some call Heaven.

I will not look to the sky for heaven because heaven is within me. It is the light in me and that light is God.

I have to close but in so doing take up your Bible and read ***Haggai*** all of it. Yes all of it. Know that God does not smite anyone or shut up the heavens to anyone. As humans we do not know that our sins affect everything including nature itself. So when we deplete nature we are taking away its goodness. And like I've said before, if you plant bad seeds you cannot get good fruits and those bad fruits are sin. All that is happening to us is due to our sins and God cannot fix our sins because we made a choice to commit them. Like I've said God can show you the errors of your ways but it is infinitely up to you to correct or fix them – make the right decision.

Goodness is a blessing therefore we have to do good so no matter how these books are written you must know the truth the full truth of it all.

We cannot change the original books to accommodate self or any given race this is wrong. Even me telling you to read Haggai is wrong because this book also tell lies on God therefore making it wrong - sinful. Lies are in it so therefore it makes this book sinful. You do not have to read Haggai and I would never encourage anyone to do so but you need to know and see the lies – read them for yourself. Even in telling you this I do not have a good feeling about it meaning telling you to read Haggai. I originally put this part in about reading Haggai and trust me it has been haunting me but I am going to keep it in there not due to disobedience or me being a disobedient child but I am hoping the eerie feeling or weird feeling I have you will have it too and you will know what I am talking about. Your spirit may caution you not to read it and if it does listen to your spirit because now you will know how I feel and what God is trying to tell you. You cannot knowingly read books of sin. Yes I have bibles in my home but I will not get rid of it because our history is in there meaning our history has been perverted and the bible stands as our shame as to how we have lied and tell lies on God. It stands as our shame of how we have failed God over the centuries – years.

As children of God our history not history our heritage is precious and we should never leave it or dilute to please any given race or anyone.

It is wrong for a man to say the bible belongs to him and it is of God because the bible is infinitely not from God.

God does not give lies, sin does because when we do wrong we tell lies to cover up the wrongs that we have done. It does not make any sense. Tell the truth and done. Don't continue on with the sin – lies it's not worth it because in the end it is you that is going to lose your soul.

Some may say well the punishment. Take your punishment now don't run from it. Solve it here do not leave it until you are dead because hell's fire is beautiful to the eye in the physical but infinitely deadly to the soul – spirit in the spiritual.

As writers we cannot say God smite or kill people. We cannot say God punish and I've said God punishes but this is wrong the proper way to say it is God walks away from you and leave you to the choice that you have made. So if you choose sin then God will leave you to sin. He cannot interfere because you made a choice. You excluded him and he has no right to interfere with the decision you have made. Hence we have the Ying and Yang – Life and Death, Positive and Negative, Good and Evil, God and Nod.

God is with us at all times and now you infinitely know so My Peeps and True Loved Ones stay strong. I might be rough around the edges in my books but I cannot deceive and paint a sweet and rosy picture when the picture is ugly.

Come on now. God is beautiful so is his abode and trust me I don't want to go to hell that's for sure so I have to secure my Soul and you have to secure yours too.

Sometimes enlighten yourself go to YouTube and listen to these songs. Download them if you can, buy them on ITunes if you want to. My Peeps I am not endorsing the people and will never endorse any artist because like me we all have flaws. I will however endorse the song because we all need comfort, truth, healing, knowledge and true love. These songs comfort and heal. Some of these songs delivers God's message so I give them to you.

God never leaves his people hanging and no matter how we change the names of original lands we can never and will never change God which is TRUE LOVE. You cannot and will never take the truth from us because whether you know it or not God will make you leave the truth in something for us to find our way home and no stray no more.

Bob Marley
Time will Tell – listen to this song keenly when he said Jah will never give the power to a bald head. This is infinitely true. So no matter how the heathens rage and kill, steal and rape they will never infinitely never ever have God's power.

Ambush in the Night
Redemption Song
One Love
Buffalo Soldier
As a matter of fact all of his songs.

Peter Tosh
Rastafari Is
Equal Rights and Justice
I am that I am
Glass House

Encourage Yourself – **Donald Lawrence**

R. Kelly
The Storm Is Over
You Saved Me

Culture
One Stone
Holy Mount Zion
(There is Culture Club this is Boy George's group. Culture is the Jamaican Reggae Group)

Alborosie
Free Yourself

Queen Ifrica ft. Steele
New World Order

People listen to the lyrics, carefully listen, because Jamaican's have been telling you about this New World Order that is to come and if we make the Pagans – Babylonians win there will be a New World Order and all that God stands for meaning life will be doomed. White people don't even think

you are excluded because your ass will be enslaved and no matter you say you own your companies you will have to give them up because in Islam or the Pagan Way of doing things you cannot tell the head no. You have to give up everything because you are now apart of the collective and the head tells the collective what to do. You will own nothing. This is why churches – some tell you to give up your possession and you follow them like lambs going to the slaughter house and give up everything leaving you and your family penniless. This is infinitely wrong so know because the snake and his people will hold you hostage and they are not infinitely not afraid to kill – eliminate you. Queen Ifrica told you Mankind has no soul so they are acting the fool blood in the streets can fill up a bowl. No not a bowl you eat cereal out of but look at you domes your big bowls.

This will be the blood of humanity if we let the Babylonians win. You know their agenda and this is world domination and if we let them get control truly woe be unto man because we will all be doomed. Go back to 10 000BC and skip to the slavery part. This slavery will be worse and none of us can blame anyone but self. Their laws are infinitely not God's laws nor are their laws humanities laws.

If you think I am scaring you think again, just remember Egypt and the barbaric way they treated God's people.

Tell me something when they get in power and start being prime minister, presidents of your land what are you going to do? Many are running your organizations – corporations; many employ their own kind, just take a look at the global market and who is running the show. Just look at the evil's some use to get some of you out of your good jobs. Evil use evil to get what it wants – there are no level playing fields anywhere.

Tell me something when we give our rights over to evil what about our children. What about their future because they too will be indebted to evil. They will have to do what evil asks them to do and no one can complain because we were the ones to give evil the right to do so.

Do not look to the church for a saving grace because the churches are only money making organizations that make their money off you by selling God. They use God as their bargaining chip and tool and all of humanity has bought into it but woe be unto them because they will have hell to pay.

Onwards I go. You can also listen to these songs by:

Morgan Heritage
Chant we a go Chant
One Bingi
More Teachings
Africa Here We Come
Jealousy – This song I dedicate to all wicked and dreadful people especially to every Muslim and Islamic kingdom across the globe. You're all JEALOUS of God and his people. But guess what HELL a go bun unnu because it is there for the lots of you as well as there for all wicked and evil people. When I listen to this song I infinitely think

about God and what all of you have done to God because Life – God is prosperous and you're not. God created Life – this universe and it lived – everything lives and you're all envious and Jealous of God. You want to take credit for all the goodness God have done but none of you can have it because none of you can be God because you were all born from lies and deceit and you will all die in your lies and deceit just like Adam your father because Adam was not black he was a Babylonian like the lot of you hence you parade around his grave – the Kaaba in Mecca once per year in hopes to raise him from the dead but you have all forgotten death can never come to life because it is dead, it hath not life so keep parading and hoping and chant around your dead.

Jahranimo ft Jah Cure – I'm Free

Lucky Dube – The Other Side. Like he said the grass is greener on the other side until you get there and this is what evil paints. It paints a greener and better future and when you get there you live like slaves and dream of returning home. How many of us today wish to go home and can't even find taxi – fare to get there. Yes plane tickets people. The taxi fares are unreachable for some because we make it so. We don't prepare to return home nor do we think of returning home. We need to prepare ourselves because if we don't return home soon we will get caught up in this global web – mess and trust me we will be singing the blues real soon.

Like I've said God does not judge. Evil is the one to judge and charge you for guilt and sin if you have committed sin. Sin cannot, infinitely cannot get up and charge you for sin if you have done nothing wrong. Know this infinitely.

Good don't mingle with dirty and sinful people and God will never ever mingle with dirty and sinful people. Know this infinitely as well.

No one can charge you for guilt or sin if you are not living in the way of sin.

No one can charge good for sin because good does not walk in the way of sin nor do they walk in the way of wicked and sinful people.

My Peeps and True Loved Ones the truth is now or never. It is up to each and every one of you to know the truth because on that final day we can't blame anyone we can only blame self.

You cannot stand before God and say the devil made me do it because he did not make you; you made a choice to follow evil. You listened to lies and deceit of men and now they're sitting at the gates of hell laughing at each and every one of us – each and every one of you. Trust me evil's got a smile on his face because now he's not lonely anymore he has a lot of company. He has people going to hell with him. These men are the devils and they all know there is no resting place for them.

Let me ask you like I ask my people. If you grow a child to be evil will he not grow up to do evil?

If you tell a child that God kills will he not grow up to believe and say God kills?

We do evil and say they are good and when our children do them we say they are ungodly – evil. We taught them this so we are guilty of sin. We cannot blame them we have to blame ourselves because we taught them so – this.

We are the ones to let them – evil in. We go to there churches, we marry them, kill for them. We fall for their lies and deceit and spread it around.

We have to stop this. We need to make them clean their shit up and live for God. Let their churches be about God and only God and not just the money.

We cannot live our lives in a lie anymore it is not fair to you and more importantly it is not fair to God. It is not fair to your children and future generations. Why the fuck should we make them enslave us again with their lies and deceit. Come on now.

We can't keep believing and telling lies upon God by saying God kill when we know better.

Who the fuck has LIFE killed?

Death kills not life come on now. Get real because God is real, he's life and he loves his people unconditionally but his people do not love him unconditionally. They refuse to be his roots hence we accept evil and the killings of evil and this is why our homelands are in such messes – disarray.

Their god's kill rape and steal but the true and living God cannot rape and steal, he cannot die like their gods.

God will never put you in debt like their gods. Look at the Garden of Eden until now. We have been indebted to their gods until now and still have done nothing to change it. Tell me what are we doing to ourselves?

We say we care about life, love God but yet using him as a bargaining chip to do our wrongs, sell our wrongs, sell false hope, false religion and false love.

My people don't think that the devil does not have a way in.

Here me now my people, by the grace and truth of the ever living God. Know that the devil has a way in and we can shut him down permanently.

Listen to me and hear me people the devil has a way in and will always have a way in and we have to shut him down.

Your pastors and preachers will never tell you this because they do not know so by the grace of the true and living God I am telling you this.

The devil will always get in through the back door.

What did I day?

"The devil will always get in through the back door."

The back door he has a key to and he uses it when he cannot come through the front door.

Hear me people and know this.

He gets in through spiritual wickedness, the spiritual wicked, the dead that still lingers on the earth.

So in order to shut the devil down, when you are praying ask God to shut spiritual wickedness down and never let the spiritual wicked conquer.

Tell God to close every door and portal including all back doors so that evil will never come in.

Tell God to shut them permanently down. When you do this you are closing all doors and the devil has no way in. You have to close all the doors.

Don't believe me. Know.

It was revealed to me, like you I did not know and when I got the revelation I was so upset at God. I told him he did not truly love me, why was this happening to me but then he gave me the answer after I was done fuming.

The back door I saw with the window down was his way of telling me that though I lock the door in the physical, the door, the back door in the spiritual is still open and this is how evil still comes. They evil still have the keys to the back – the back door.

So we have to close the doors to spiritual wickedness as well meaning when you pray for God to conquer your enemies in the physical tell him to conquer the enemies in the spiritual as well.

Remember as it is in heaven so it is on earth.

If we do not pray for deliverance in the spiritual realm as well we will never be free, nor will we conquer the devil and shut him down. I know I told you prayer do not work meaning it is not effective anymore. I told you we have to live as in psalms one and this is infinitely correct but keep praying meaning talk to God silently. Once you clean up yourself and separate from evil you will see the beauty of God. Do not give up talking to God because we all need God just do not pray in the way of the heathens.

Know that when you are clean and you pray or talk to God truthful and clean your enemies will fall at the wayside. God will help you but you have to be true and honest – clean.

As I close well not close because I am still writing I leave Alborosie's Free Yourself with you all. Forget the picture people, the joker has no foundation here and the 8 does not mean I hate you. It represents Oxygen, an element that sustains life. The octagon.

Hear him when he said "you are the only one that can free yourself, let your spirits free to love someone else. Love yourself before someone else, free yourself."

Respect yourself and live for God. I cannot tell you I can only teach you. *God is the one that can educate you and free you but you have to accept him and let him help you.* I know the bible said many will come in the name of Jesus claiming to be, but they are misleading, are the anti-christ but I do not come to you in the name of Jesus. Will never come to you in the name of Jesus.

I can only be me and that me is Michelle, a child of God and so are you.

I will never claim to be someone else because that is wrong. I can only show you what was shown to me but in words, what I write; I will not use my words, what God has given to me to spread hate. This is your knowledge, the surface of knowledge but true love is the root of all knowledge which is God.

God is the one that can lead you to perfect truth but you have to trust him and let him lead you.

It will be hard and your world will be filled with doubt and confusion, yes at times you will want to hate but do not give into *will.*

Take a look at the Ying and Yang because this symbol is an important symbol. It is the light and dark. *Will* as we know it.

Father by your true love and grace let thy pure will, your true love and harmony be done.

Michelle

Now that all has been said you know and knowing is the key to true knowledge - life.

Turn the page

Now that you think you know I can say you truly know nothing and it is when you truly comprehend the concept of nothing and something then you can truly comprehend life, the formation and existence of life.

What but you said?

But I said what?

You still have not comprehended what I said because some of you will use what I have said to hate me, want to kill me, try to kill me, use my words to judge me, judge others, use my words against others, other nations. You will continue to spread hate, turn against the people of Nod for what. It is not about colour of skin and this is full comprehension. You cannot hate based on skin colour, eye colour or whatever colour.

Now for those of you that will burn the Indian flag, start to hate the people of India by letting hate and prejudice overshadow you tell me this.

What have the people of India done to you? Though they are Babylonians what have they done to you?

You cannot hate because hate is unwarranted. Like I said and will forever say if you do not let evil in evil can never come into your domain – land.

Therefore you cannot comprehend nor overstand the concept and root that I have been telling you.

Here now is full comprehension on the simplest scale.

Listen to Diversity by Alborosie. Forget about King Selassie because he too was man but look at his crown.

Because I give you this song does it mean you have full comprehension?

You're not even close and you're still closed minded.

Now that your eyes is open you will now know that the formation of heaven, this universe, nature, the universe is ***not based on religion nor was it formed by religion and religious beliefs.***

The formation of this universe is based on negative and positive energy.

This is what the Chinese call the Ying and Yang.

We say Negative and Positive

The laws of attraction

Light and Dark

Black and White

The principles above have nothing to do with colour of skin.

We know your complexion has to do with melanin.

Your environment, how much sun is absorbed in your body which is Vitamin D and it is the fourth element or letter on your ABC table of charts.

Get it.

No

Go back to Beryllium which is the state of being.

Where everything came in being, came to life.

Energy has nothing to do with colour of skin it has to do with negative and positive, the Ying and the Yang.

Negative and Positive, Light and Darkness so to say you hate based on skin colour is unwarranted and has no foundation to life whatsoever in the physical world.

There has to be equal balance and that balance has nothing to do with religion.

The negative and positive is what humans call ***Will*** because will is a force, energy that is the Good and Bad, Black and White, Ying and Yang.

So to base hate on colour of skin has no merit or logical foundation because each and every one of us are hating ourselves. We are hating the very fabric that makes up each and everyone of us, which is energy, the Ying and the Yang, Positive and Negative energy.

Like I've said when you comprehend the concept of nothing and something then you will comprehend life because one cannot exist without the other.

Men complicated this by bringing the colour scheme into the picture to pit one against the other.

There has to be an equal balance as I've said and as it is there isn't an equal balance in the universe right now.

Man take without replacing, we are the ones to throw the earth off balance because nature has everything to do with life, the death of life and the maintenance of life. Nature is trying to fix our mess and each and every day we give nature more mess to fix. How much can it do for us to learn that we are the ones killing ourselves? The air we breathe, water we drink, intake of food. Everything in life is important and has to be in balance.

Look at it, does nature and animals wage war, kill each other just for the sake of killing?

Look at nature, it roars and upturn life because it is trying to put the elements back in sequence but we are throwing it off. We destroy trees without planting back, we're destroying the ozone without realizing that this protects us from the sun, the heat of the sun. It keeps the glaciers intact, the ice caps intact. Everything that is in the universe is within us, each and every one of us.

This is energy, which some call the spirit and some call the soul. This is why the foundation of heaven and the universe but more importantly God has nothing to do with religion. Could never have and will never have anything to do with religion.

Religion is just a deception, designed by men of power to keep the masses in check. Keep us believing that God is a religion when we of ourselves know that God is not and could never be. Many write to deceive but it's a few that write to tell the truth and you have to know the difference between the liars and deceivers and the truthful ones. Anyone that say they come to one race or a specific race is a liar because God's children are White, Chinese and Blacks. These are the 3 races that I saw on the mountain and these are the 3 races that I am relaying to you and I will infinitely never ever change this to please and suit any given race. Like I said and will forever say God does not shut anyone out of his kingdom we are the ones to shut ourselves out of his kingdom – domain. If a Babylonian wants to get in they know they have to relinquish lies and deceit – they infinitely have to live clean.

Religion was designed to keep us ignorant because that which we hate is what God leaves us to. Hand us over to.

If this was not so why didn't God himself create religion in the beginning? When he designed the universe and was putting everything in place why didn't he say "let us make religion?"

Why didn't he say he is going to give man religion to worship him, be submissive to him, and keep us in check and in line?

You need to think.

Humanity has nothing to do with Darwin's theory of evolution because everything has life in it. ***Everything.***

The earth is life. It breathes and it too can die and we do cause it to die each and every day with our acts of sin. The abominable acts we commit in her.

She gives us life but yet we plant death in her.

She gives us hope but yet we plant shit – all manner of chemicals in her.

She maintains our life but yet each and every day we kill her by raping her of our gems, resources – her life.

She gives us clean water to drink to sustain our lives but each and every day we dump chemicals in it including our feces to kill her. We give her shit to eat and piss to drink on a daily basis and no one can dispute this because this is where we dump our waste. We expect her to clean up our messes on a daily basis. She gets no help from us now tell me if that is fair? Tell me how fair is this to her? We do not treat ourselves this way but we do it to her. We have no respect for life and the goodness of life because all that is evil we do unto good.

As humans we live to kill and destroy and when things go wrong we turn around and blame everything in the book and beyond and do not blame ourselves. We're the ones destroying this planet because our sins also affect her – this planet.

Our sins have a negative effect on earth because earth hath life just like us humans. We are made – designed like her hence she gives birth to life in every way. When you plant a seed does it not grow and if you don't take care of it does it not die? Well guess what earth is like this but when it is all said and done humanity will die first and this is because of our unfair treatment of her; the way we commit sin in her and destroy her land. Earth has the ability to regenerate itself but this can only be done when all evil have vanished away and yes this is why your bible talks about replenishing the earth.

The smallest of atoms that the microscope can see can be broken down further to the point where no microscope can see it.

Within the darkness there is light.

There has to be and must be but the darkness cannot comprehend this. This is why there is 3X to 1Y.

Every which way you look at it there will always be 3X to 1Y.

You can base this on the correlation to race if you like you will find 3 races must come together and leave 1 race.

There is 3 element of life to one element of darkness.

Sun, Moon and Stars to 1 night-darkness.

So like I said to base prejudice on colour of skin is unfounded and has no basis whatsoever because you are hating that which is inside of you.

Positive and Negative energy and this law is the foundation of humanity and all living things.

To hate based on religion is unfounded and has no merit because God is not a religion, will never be a religion and you all need to know this.

This is why I keep asking and will forever ask which heaven are you going to go to with this?

Is there is a section in heaven for Jews, Christians, Muslims, Hindu you name it is there a section for it. And this is a stupid way to put things because of what I saw, the three races on the mountain so yes there is a place in God's abode for the different races.

Do not get me wrong there is a creator. Some say there isn't everything just came into being at the fourth level which is the beryllium level but there is more. There are different stages to life that we must go through and grow.

There are different stages to life and the physical is just one stage, the learning stage.

Good and Evil must separate, but separate how?
We know for a fact that there is a heaven and hell. This is where evil is separated from good, positive is separated from negative.

If I said this is where everything is destroyed then I would be lying. If I said this is where everything comes to an end I would be lying. I have seen spiritual death yes and I do not comprehend the magnitude of it because that which we think we kill is not what dies and this has to do with evil. This I infinitely know. If you've sold your spirit unto evil that which commands you or possess your body must die also. This evil or demon must die also it cannot live – continue on.

Yes the person that dies is clothed in full white but the person you think is dead is not the person that dies. The one that dies is the one that you have given or sold your soul to in the living. Hence the soul becomes sould – sold and maybe this is why some people believe that life is recycled. We are incarnated from one being to the next meaning when you die you come back as another person. But know that death can infinitely never be recycled or reincarnated once it has died and life infinitely cannot be recycled or reincarnated because life moves forward to greater and better life.

Further this is why I tell you God's colours cannot and will never be pure white alone and you should know your colours.

Back to religion. It is not important and will never be a factor in the spiritual realm and when I say this you need to know where religion originated because it was never in the Garden of Eden. It is not in heaven and will never be.

Religion came into being outside the garden.

Religion is darkness – death – one.

Religion originated in Asia as stated in Revelations when the book said to the seven churches of Asia write this.
No it is not China but India to be exact.

Do you believe me?

Yes

Well slap yourself and call yourself stupid.

Now you see how hate spreads.

How the hell can you say that you believe this?

Now I have given all of India a reason to hate my ass and your ass too.

See how misconception is spread. Revelations said the 7 churches are in Asia, did it say where in Asia?

No it did not so how can I say it is in India, the seven churches could be in Iran, Saudi Arabia, China, Pakistan.

Know what you read and how you read. I know what I said. Sandscript is the foundation for all language and it is. Yes we know it is still used in India today, but with this knowledge can we say India is where the seven churches reside, no we cannot.

In the dream I had it was the Egyptians, Persian, and Phoenicians that led us astray.

We were not in India originally. When good married evil then our people went into the land of Nod and you can find remnants of them until this day.

We know they worshipped idols but to say India is where the seven churches are I would be lying because God never told me this and I would be spreading lies on India and that is just plain out sick. Yes they are of the land of Nod and not of God but today many people fall under the banner of Nod and not God.

Know the difference between the two meaning know the difference between the people of God and the people of Nod. Yes the people of Good and the people of Evil.

So people do not get caught up in deception because it does hurt. See how we as writers can turn you against someone, a race of people without you knowing it. Giving you bits and pieces to hook you and when you are hooked baby it is hard to let go.

What I do know is the Iranian text, Greek, English and Latin derived from Sandscript.

Idols was the first known form of worship because these people worship idols and other Gods, they were in Egypt as stated before and you know this from the golden calf as stated before. They are Persian – Iranian's, Egyptians, and Phoenicians who resided in the land of Nod. We know that Eve was the first to go against God and married a Nodite – Adam who was from the land of Nod and she had a child for him. This is the infinite truth and this is why their books say Satan was in heaven with God he was one of God's angels but Satan could never be in heaven with God because God does not, infinitely do not deal with shit – garbage. Yes they have bragging rights and can brag about this but with Eve she truly loved him because she gave up her kingdom for it and in so doing this she lost her soul – she died because she married evil – true evil.

Know too that I will go off biblical context to make a point but do not deviate from the truth because you now know infinitely that Adam was Satan and let no one tell you otherwise. If someone say, run to God and say God this person said this this and this are they correct? God can and will take you back in the past – time and show you the truth because he God is the key to time because he is time and so much more.

We also know that Abraham's father worshiped idols.

Being Jewish is not a religion. A Jew just mean foreigner in biblical context. This title was given to Abraham when he crossed over the Tigris Euphrates River into the land of Caldeas. The inhabitants of that land called him a Jew because he was a foreigner in their land. This is according to biblical text.

The worship of idols was taught by man because there were no idols in the Garden of Eden and it was outside this isle of peace that we learnt this.

Jews which are the children of God were not to mix with the children of the dark meaning children that lived in Nod because they worshipped idols and different gods but God's children did not listen. The children of God did their own thing hence they lost their crown.

When God told his messengers who to marry did he not tell them to choose from their own people – race meaning the races of God?

Did he God not warn them on the complications and troubles they would have if they choose people that were not his own?

According to your bible God told them which house to take their wives from.

Did not Abraham obey this law according to your bible?

Did God not tell Solomon the same thing and Solomon did not listen he wanted to spread his genes every where and he took women of different nations to be his wife and these women turned him from God. These women worshipped other Gods and not the True and Living God. They didn't care about the God Solomon praised hence he wrote Proverbs to tell you what he did, how he did not listen and it cost him his kingdom.

Do not take my word for it but read what Solomon wrote and get the full over standing of what he is trying to tell you. How he commissioned you to listen and do not stray from God.

Those that didn't accept these idols were persecuted, killed and or enslaved. This we know from Egypt when Pharaoh imprisoned the people and the outcome of Moses. The hardship he Moses had to teach his people the ways of God all over again.

When he went up into the mount what did he come back and see?

For the steadfast that would not break, religion was devised, and Catholicism was devised to mimic *for lack of a better word we will say Judaism*. It mimicked the Jewish way of life perfectly but some was not fooled because they knew otherwise.

When that did not work, Islam was devised to deceive and the person they used was Jesus.

He was used to draw his people into his fold but the Jews – true Jews did not accept him and this is why Revelations say *Jesus is the first begotten of the dead.*

It also said he came to his own and his own refused him.

This is why he said peace be unto you indicative of Islam.

They say peace but in there hearts there is no peace. It is filled with war and hate because they know heaven as we know it could never be there home because they are of the dark - evil.

They are negative force that pulls you in and tell young men to kill. Murder innocent life and they believe they are going to heaven, paradise but yet they do not know that the paradise they are going to is HELL.

If this was not so I would not have seen their fearless leader for whom some are going to start worshipping because now they will say he is god, the true son of god because I saw him in my dream on the third day of his death which is in the month of Ramadan, their holy month.
They will ignore the fact that I saw him in prison; he was caged behind a fence.

They will ignore the fact that he is telling them that Islam is nothing but a spiritual prison, jailhouse.

Once you are here you cannot move to the next level. You will never see God, the true and living God. This is your condemnation for life – all eternity.

If this was not so he would not have shown me him behind the fence, he would have shown me the state of his comfort, his spiritual state in a different light. He would have shown me him in paradise ***and not hell, spiritual hell.***

You cannot base God on religion because religion is a condemnation of spirit and soul. It is a spiritual jailhouse. Just as our bones imprison our spirit/soul so that it cannot move about freely in the living – walking state so does religion. It imprisons and we follow it to our prisons - the grave.

Once you chose religion in this realm you are condemning yourself in the spiritual realm and this is the truth that people need to know.

You need to know this before you can accept God who is the energy within you, the spirit within you.

This is why I ask what religion is God?

There is so many today, which religion is he?

Which religion is nature?

Look at the animals of the earth, which religion do they practice?

Some of us say we evolve from animals so if we did what religion are the animals practicing?

Which God do the animals serve?

Animals know evil, they know when evil approaches. Remember when they smell something wrong what do they do, birds take flight, some animals take cover, dogs bark and will defend the ones that they truly love.

The only animal that will never defend you is the cat.

They will let evil subdue you and kill you because cats are evil in nature, they aid evil.

So once again to say you hate based on colour and religion what is the basis of it.

Where is the foundation of it all or for it?

If you look at colour read the colour of God's angel in the bible. If John described the angel as being black how are you going to go to heaven?

Because God's angel was black and they are still black.

What are you going to tell God are you going to say God I don't want to come to heaven because you have blacks there?

Are we going to say God, I refuse to come or I am not coming into heaven because you have Jews, Homosexuals, Gentiles, Lesbians there?

As for religion are we going to say God I am a Jew and have all right to enter heaven

We kept your word and did not stray from your fold

You gave us your laws and we lived by them

You favoured us over them because they followed after abominations of sin

They worshipped idols

Bowed down to the ground to pray when they knew better because the ground is where all filth goes into, the dead goes into

And God will say the fruits I have given you comes from the earth, the ground are you saying it is defiled, filthy?

Are you going to say God I am a Muslim, the ones of peace and Paradise/Heaven belongs to us. We fought for it so it is rightfully ours. We defended you?

And the question God will ask is how did you defend me?

With blood and deception, killing is this your defense?

Is your defense judging people, saying I am going to judge the guilty blue eyed?

Who are you to judge me, tell people what I am going to do without knowing me?

Was David not a war monger?

Did he not soil his hands with blood and could he build my temple?

So how can you say you defended me when you have brought nothing but shame and disgrace to the fold that was meant for me?

You have bloodied your hands

As Christians what are you going to say?

I praised Jesus and Jesus is you and you are the petitioner of us all?

When God asks can I die, can the God that created everything die?

What will your answer be?

Jesus said in my father's house there are many mansions and if it was not so he would not say it. He said he will petition you for our sins and he is the interceder for our sins.

When God say if Jesus was me why would he have to intercede with me for your sins?

Why would he say in my father's house there are many mansions and if it was not so he would not say so?

Can I contradict myself?

Would he not have forgiven all your sins?

Would he not be the one speaking to you?

So how can Jesus be me?

Then you will be asked if a man is guilty of sin can another man petition for his soul without he himself be guilty? He knows you are guilty but yet petitioning for you?

But God you forgive sins Jesus said so?

Yes I forgive sins but you are still held accountable for them. Does not a judge hand out sentences to you when you have broken the law so why now should I overlook yours and not overlook those that are residing in hell. That would mean I love you more, favours you more than them. I would not be a just God then would I. I would be breaking my own laws that I have given to you and what kind of God would I be.

Jesus you said

But Jesus cannot speak for you, he has no authority here. I am God, the True and Living God and not he.

Did you not read Revelations when John showed you, told you that Jesus was just the son of man and I am he who that created all?

I am known as Allah to some but for those that know I am Allelujah. I am he who you cry out to when my spirit fills you, consumes you. Everything that you know and that which you do not know I am He. I am the ALL because all was created by me, designed by me, formed and conceived by me. I am in all, which is the breath of Life the spirit and soul of every living thing known to man and unknown to man so how can Jesus be me.

I am the energy, which is the life within you so how can Jesus be me. How can a man do all this?

I am the darkness and the light that consumes you so how can Jesus be me.

I am the one to give you Will to choose the latter of the two, good and evil but time and time again man has chosen the darkness without seeing the consequences – without seeing the light.

You become blinded by the darkness and as soon as something goes wrong you all come knocking at my door and as soon as I release you, you turn from me and continue to do evil, expecting me to bail you out, and expecting man to petition for your souls.

Does not evil run from the truth?

Will evil not run from the consequences of his sin?

When a man commits murder does he not run and hide like his brother Cain?

So tell me can a man run from his sins, does he not have to face them at some point in time?

Tell me if you do wrong why should I turn the other cheek when man cannot do so?

Tell me when a child is hungry do you not feed him?

When a child is wet do you not change him?

When a child does wrong do you not punish him, scold him?

So why should I not punish you when you have done wrong?

You are grace and mercy

But my grace and mercy have kept all living. I did not turn back the sun, moon and stars from you all. I did not give you and the inhabitants of the earth over to total darkness so tell me how much more graceful and merciful can I be?

None of you have abstained from the things that I have told you not to do.

I have sent messengers to warn you and tell you about false gods and worshipping idols and none of you listened. Not even Solomon whom I loved dearly. He turned from me.

You designed and made holy temples and sanctuaries unto me but yet you all have polluted it. Wore dirty shoes in my home, brought statues in my home, defiled my home with your deceitful lies, deceitful cries.

None of you have kept your bodies clean

Defiling each other by sleeping with one another when you have given yourself unto another

Not one of my laws have you kept.

Each one was broken by all of you and now I am to show grace and mercy

Have man not raped you all of your souls and now that you see the abode of heaven and hell you are petitioning me for grace and mercy after I have told you, forgiven you time and time again and you would not listen.

You are all my children but none of you listen to me and it is only when the end has come you are knocking at my door pleading for Grace and Mercy.

You are crying to me for forgiveness but still do not know that I never asked you to do anything wrong.

I never said worship or praise me but love me as you love yourself, truly love me

Love others with truth as you would truly love you

I never gave you idols to worship

I never gave you religion to worship me

None amongst the angels or the messengers can say I gave them religion

None amongst man can say I gave them religion to praise and worship me but yet you do it knowing that it is wrong

You go on deceiving yourselves with lies, instill lies in your children, instill hate and yet here you are and still you do not know

You go on blaming, hoping for a way in, a loop hole to heaven

I am not man because I know the lot of you

I know your intentions and thoughts before they surface because you are mere men

I gave you all to eat

All the herbs of the land, fruits of the land but yet you listened to man and the ones that you have listened to, do not eat the dead carcass of the land.

Know this now see your hell upon the land, in heaven

I am God and that which I give you to do, do but that which man has given to you to do, do not do because I will never lead you wrong, nor lead you astray.

Do not break the laws of man but do not bring the laws of man into my fold and deceive with it, say it is mine

Tell me something Gregg can a drowning man save you?

Can a dead man come back to life without me giving life again?

Can a man create heaven and earth, that which was, which is to be, that which his eyes cannot see?

Can a man take the spirit by his hand and pluck it out of your body?

So why live by man and not by me, my laws?

With all this said why hate based on colour, religion, nature, wars created by men?

Man has a choice and the truth does not hate. So why use this book to now hate, spread hate and become hate.

Despite all that you have learned the true light of God in you will never let you concede to hate and destruction.

Though I said I hate the lies that are spread, I've learnt to let God handle that and all those who hate.

The greatest gift anyone can have is the true and perfect love of God and once you have that no enemies formed against you in the physical and spiritual can or will harm you. They cannot conquer you because God will show you them before they and their evil manifests.

Trust God and put all your love in him and you will see the difference in your life so as I leave you yet again but I am not truly leaving because yes I am still writing meaning editing.

I leave you all with Alborosie's ***FREE YOURSELF.***

Do not just listen to the beat of the song but listen to what he is saying. Especially when he said "let nobody rape your soul."

I don't care how it hurts never hate others. I don't care who they are because when you hate you are giving the enemy or the devil as you would say victory over you. I know in my other book I said God hates Ethiopia but I asked the question "why does God hate Ethiopia" and was given the answer.

For lack of a better word we will use hate, because if God truly hated them they would not be around today. It was what they did to God, that God is displeased with them and I guess displeased is a better word and not hate. So if you get my other book I did use hate so forgive me because God is truly displeased with them but not hate them. Okay.

God does not hate anyone and will never hate anyone but he is displeased with us, and if he see's wrong he will step in and say do not go there because that person is not for you, not for me, they will take you off the path of me. He's been doing this for centuries but like I've said we are not listening. Being devoted to God does not mean giving up your life. Respect him. If you like to dance, dance, go to the movies, take that vacation, go for dinner. I am not going to acknowledge clubbing but if there is a club that is intimate where you can go for dinner and dance after, if it is clean, the music is clean, it is respectable then yes. If it is where you go to pick up people for one night stands then no. Respect God all the way. There is nothing wrong with going on a date with your special someone. ***With God no cheating is allowed***, it is so frowned upon. Eve people always remember the price she paid and we are still paying the price until this day. Now you get the gist. God wants you to have fun and not be bored because trust me God is so not boring.

God is very jealous. Trust me he is and I so love this about him. The jealousy. Because he does protect and protect well. Everything about God I love and more, yes especially the jealousy. Need I say more?

When it comes to idols, and false worship don't do it, please don't do it or you will regret it like Solomon.

Solomon showed you this. God does not like idols, nor idol worship and this is why he told his children not to go outside the garden – his safe haven. Not because of their skin colour it was

because they worshipped idols and would turn you from him and so said so done and look at us now.

We left the safe haven of God and look at the world today.

We left his protection and now we are running in every direction to get back in and can't and it is so easy.

Honesty and truth

Cleanliness in body and spirit

How do you clean the spirit?

By speaking the truth at all times that's how you clean the spirit. Water cleans the internal organs and flushes out all impurities in our blood stream and veins.

Negative cannot live in peace with Positive in the present state it is in because one will be pulling this way and the other pulling that way. God has to be in the center of it all.

My babies just listen to Free Yourself and get to know yourself, truly love yourself and be free then you will be on your way.

Infinitely remember that God is the only one that you can trust not to hurt and deceive you so let your life be for God, let God consume you, educate and teach you.

When you know God no one can deceive you or come to you with nonsense.

Learn to truly love you for who you are and if I ever said I love you know that is not so. I do not love you but truly love you because true love like I've told you over and over again does not hurt, nor does it deceives and God is that truth. He is true love and will never deceive you and each and every one of you have to know this.

So FREE YOURSELF and break the chains of slavery, physically, mentally and spiritually.

In the name of God, Allelujah Free Yourself.

Michelle

Do you have full comprehension now?

Yes

Then tell me who is God?

Man or Spirit?

Spirit

Female or Male

He is a spirit

Wrong

God is All

What?

Confused aren't you?

Yes

Scratching your head aren't you?

Yes

God is all so you still do not know God.

Okay I will let you have absolute knowledge and I will try my best to explain without going off track. If I do I can't help it.

You know that God is all both in the physical and spiritual.

Yes

Yes

Look at the Ying and the Yang symbol.

Pull it up on your computer.

(

)

Have it?

Yes

Look at it carefully.

Now you know God in the concept of man's eyes

What?

Now you know God.

No I don't because you don't make any sense, this is just a picture this cannot be God. God cannot be a picture.

True but you just saw him in the truest form according to the depiction of man. How the ancients conceived him to be.

There is no picture of God because you cannot see energy and this was the only way to depict him so now you have seen God.

No I have not and you have just confused the hell out of me now. Now I can say you are whacked and no one should read your book because you have just given me utter nonsense to know.

How?

Ying and Yang that is Chinese jargon and that has nothing to do with me.

Why?

Because China is China and they believe differently, they don't believe in God and besides above you never touched on there race. You never touched them. You touched on everyone else but the Chinese.

__Chinese don't have to believe because they KNOW GOD and it is with this knowing that I cannot touch them because they kept the faith and knowledge of God. The world sees it but don't know it. They know it and kept it.__

__Now to get fresh and feisty. Look at 10 000 BC the lady that could see was she not Mongolian or Chinese as we say?__

__And yes there were black people in China. Remember Moses and the Red Sea.__

Where the hell do you think these people went when Moses took them out of the land of Egypt? Some resided in Pakistan and some moved into China.

I will elaborate further but not now.

And why the hell do you think Black People always say they are looking to the East for a Black King. And no Black people it is not Africa.

They are looking to the East for there God and I told you the Ying and Yang is God in the form that man can depict – see him. Know this to be infinitely true. The Ying and the Yang is the creation of life. It is the very fabric of life itself as well as the creation of the universe.

The Ying and Yang represent the physical and spiritual

It represents human life

The coming together of the black and white race for some and this is in physical terms. The flesh or intermarrying of race on a physical level. If I did not explain this properly I am sorry because this is the best way I know how to.

The Ying and Yang also represents Life and death and so much more

You still don't understand or comprehend.

Okay

How do I explain it in perfect terms for you to comprehend?

I will try my best now but I will have to use this in the physical context so that you have greater over standing of the truth.

Keep in mind the Ying and the Yang okay.

The Ying and the Yang is energy pure energy.

I say Ying and Yang some say Yin Yang so oblige me in this book.

Yes Olivia I know it looks like a fish, a whale to be exact but it is the way it is. Pure and True Energy. Nothing is like it in the world know that. This is perfection and this is God in the truest form that the EYE can see.

But is this truly God?

No, but it is God in truest form that the ***EYE can see.***

I know you are confused but I am trying to explain.

When you ask God to show you him and give you his true love he will present himself in the form of a woman, man in the cloud, a perfect white door that is open. The reason why he does this is because this is the form you understand or you can comprehend. The form that your eye's and mind can comprehend. And yes this is the reason why some say that we cannot see God.

Do you have full understanding so far?

Yes

Then know that God is pure energy that you cannot see with your naked eye nor can you see him with your spiritual eye. You can feel him but to see him in his original state no one has seen him. How do I put it? It's like looking through impenetrable darkness, no that's not correct because this darkness you cannot see hence it is extremely hard to explain. It's like darkness in the darkness but within the darkness there is light. Listen it's extremely hard and hence I am confusing you.. Man cannot behold the beauty of God just like that because we are not pure nor are we in a state of purity. The naked eye cannot see him and this is why I told you an atom can be broken down further so that no microscope or the naked eye see it.

You heard of the black hole?

Yes

Can you see inside of it?

No

Well there is light inside but the naked eye cannot see it. Look at the Ying and Yang symbol within the white section, is the eyes not black and vise versa.

Yes

Now you know the concept of the black hole as well of understanding of it but not full comprehension.

Is this black hole God?

Yes because it is pure energy.

Now do you understand God?

No I am still confused. You lost me at Ying and Yang.

Okay

Look at the globe, the different races upon the face of the earth. Forget that they are Chinese, Black, White and Indian. Look at the skin tone.

Forget about the melanin factor. Forget all that I said above because that was the beginning of knowledge and I had to start at the ground floor. You are on a different plain now. You have graduated from basic knowledge or Jr. Kinder garden. Now you are in Sr. Kinder garden.

To say Ying and Yang is God is very wrong but it is the truest depiction in the eyes of man that we can comprehend.

Now you are seeing the different races. Look at the skin tone. There is only two tones is there not. Some are light and some are dark. None is purple, yellow, green, brown, red. Some are of a lighter shade and some are of a darker shade. Forget the different colour eyes we are talking about skin.

Now look at the Ying and Yang what colours do you see.

White and Black right

Yes

This is concept is God. It is also you, me, Indians, Chinese, Whites and Blacks. This Ying and Yang is what you are made up of and it is God and this is why Genesis said God said, "And low man has become one of us knowing good and evil".

Get it.

No

Everything is made up of Good and Bad which is Black and White.

Black represents the Physical – Good and Bad –death

White represents the Spiritual – Good and Bad –death

Pure over standing when you die in the physical (physical death) you die in black and when you die in the spiritual (spiritual death) you die in white. This is evil as you know it in both realms. When evil comes to earth it comes clothed in full suit of black – black clothing.

Everything that happens in the earth have to take form in the spiritual before it manifests upon the physical. (As it is in heaven so it is on earth).

Take your eyes off the different races.

Now look at the Ja mai can motto.

"Out of Many One People"

What JA meaning God is trying to tell us is that though we class each other we are all one people and he created us all meaning we are created in the same manner as the Ying and Yang – Positive and Negative energy. For those that say Blue and White you are correct because Blue and White as in the Blue and White Nile represent the Ying and Yang also.

Comprehend

Yes but

No buts now go back to the Ying and the Yang symbol. What do you see? Do you not see Positive and Negative forces acting as one, working in unison. Are they not one within the circle?

If you look at it from the highest angle meaning the physical and spiritual angle the Ying Yang represents pure evil. Evil in the physical and spiritual and the circle is the perfect containment unit because 360 hath no beginning or no ending – it is perfect. No one can find the beginning or ending of Life hence no one can find the beginning or ending of a circle.

Comprehend?

Yes

So with this comprehension how can we say we are different and that we hate each other?

Are we not hating ourselves?

Are we not telling God that we hate him?

From a different angle God is the circle that contains the Ying and the Yang. We are the center of it but he's the containment meaning he's the one to preserve and sustain - maintain life.

Do you overstand what I am saying to you?

BY NO MEANS IS THIS GOD IN HIS TRUEST FORM. THIS IS HOW WE AS HUMANS CAN EXPLAIN IT FOR YOU TO COMPREHEND. THE SCOPE AND KNOWLEDGE OF GOD GOES FAR BEYOND THIS.

What you have is knowledge of the physical and spiritual but you still do not have knowledge of the angelic realm nor the realm of God and this is where you, me and everyone must strive to be. We must strive to be in the realm of God.

Now you know so when man, woman, spirits, beasts or whatever comes to you to tell you about God do not be deceived.

Hey Paul, know that they will use anything for example you know that 1+1=2 right.

Yes

Four halves equal two and eight quarters equal two.

This you know infinitely to be two right?

Yes

This is 2 right?

Yes

Wrong

This is not two and could never be two

But 4 halves is 2

Yes but it is not two and never will be

Count how many halves and quarters you have
$\frac{1}{2} + \frac{1}{2} + \frac{1}{2} + \frac{1}{2} = 4$

$\frac{1}{4} + \frac{1}{4} + \frac{1}{4} + \frac{1}{4} + \frac{1}{4} + \frac{1}{4} + \frac{1}{4} + \frac{1}{4} = 8$

Put these pieces together

Are they whole?

Yes

How is it whole?

Did you not cut the puzzle up?

So how can it be whole?

They equal at the end

Equal what?

Add the top and the bottom and tell me what do you get?

4 over 8 and 8 over 32

So how can this be two (2)?

But we were taught in school

Stop right there

You said the key word

We were taught

Everything we were taught but infact do we know and knowing is the key.

This is how Eve got caught she was taught and shown another way and this man was not incorrect in what he said because God confirmed it by saying "man has become one of us knowing good and evil."

But was this the full truth

Yes and yes Jane this is the surface because it goes deeper than this.

Good you got it but you only have ½ the truth and this is why people will tell you black is not a colour and will go to any lengths to prove otherwise.

See this man did not tell her if she ate of the fruit and you all know what the fruit is and no baby it is no damned tree, no not an apple tree or a poppy seed go back up to the previous pages and look beside penis, got it.

No no no that could not be

Yes Yes Yes Yes Yes Yes it is

No

Stop. Yes Eve did the nasty. She got buck wild with this man-need I say more.

Now back to the

But but but

She did and afterwards she laid with her husband if you are going by biblical account but I've already told you that Adam was Satan. Cain was Satan's son but how I saw the children of Satan in the spiritual I saw them as triplets, three daughters and each had a 6 in their foreheads. They had the mark of their father in their foreheads. Some will tell you it is a cross but it was not a cross. They had the number six and did not the bible tell you God placed a mark on Cain so that anyone see him would not kill him.

Do not the Muslims tell you of the prayer mark you have to have in your forehead?

Do not Hindu's mark their child with a red dot in their foreheads?

Some of the women until this day wear a red dot in their forehead to represent the mark of the beast but in fact the dot does not represent the mark of the beast in true terms and when I confirm this I will advise you of the true meaning.

Read it

Think people what has an apple ever done to you.

If it was bad why are we still eating it – the fruit that is?

Why is the apple tree still around and why didn't God condemn it – make it a curse unto all of humanity?

Why would God put enmity between her seed and his seed?

Man now I've gone into my next book. Sorry my Peeps. No it's not and will not be controversial as this. *__I think this is the most controversial that my books will ever get.__*

Now back to the truth at hand. This man did not give Eve the full truth. She did die immediately SPIRITUALLY because God is not physical he is energy. You can feel him, feel energy but you cannot see energy in the fullest form but Eve could see him. Her eyes were open and as soon as she did what she did she could no longer see God. She was cast out of the garden never to return and eventually she died in the physical. Long after yes and this is what God is trying to protect us and shield us from.

Now look at the picture of the Ying and Yang. Are they not side by side?

Yes

Look in the middle. Remember I told you heaven and hell is side by side and you can see over to the next realm. This is what the Ying and Yang is showing you on another level.

Now back on board.

God is saying I am whole, you don't need this or that to come to me. I do not want you to run here and there to get to me. See me, I am protecting you, stay and don't listen to people that tell lies and telling you this and that to get to me. Stop listening to lies. If you want answers come to me clean and honest – true and I will give you the right answers.

Tell me something when you were being conceived did your parents need someone to speak on their behalf meaning intercede for them?

When we do good do we need anyone to intercede for us?

So when we do wrongs and commit wrongs why do we need someone to intercede for us?

We did wrong and we are guilty?

Wrong infinitely could never be right. When you are wrong you are wrong you cannot expect to get right and this is what God is trying to tell you and show you.

Instead of listening to God we listen to others that show us half and quarter ways to get to God and say in the end it is whole but look at the analogy above is it whole. Why put yourself in debt to get to God?

Why break God up in pieces to get to him when is giving you himself whole?

Do you understand what I am saying to you so let no one tell you black is not a colour because you of yourself know that it is. You are made up of it. Each and every one of us is made up of this. It is not melanin but ENERGY, Positive and Negative Energy.

Both dies meaning negative energy die in the physical and spiritual so let no one tell you otherwise because no one can intercede for you in death. Evil hath time – limited time to do its work but God hath no time – its time is unlimited because good cannot die it continues on to greater life.

Yes the body dies because it is our prison in the physical world but the beauty of life is in the spiritual. This is where God resides and if I could tell you about the inside of God's abode trust me infinitely I would. My eyes have not behold the beauty of God's kingdom apart from the Crystal City but know infinitely no one can tell you about God's abode if he has not given you person to do so. Trust me this is the highest honor and privilege anyone can get in the living.

Because we've accepted death and some have sealed their faiths and they must die in both realms meaning the physical and spiritual.

What you do meaning the life you live on earth determines the life you live in the hereafter.

Once your flesh dies and depending on the life you live on earth determines where you go in the spiritual and this is why you, me and everyone have to try and live our lives honestly and truthfully and yes clean.

Yes we make mistakes because honey I am still making them but I am learning. I cannot live your life for you and you can't live my life for me. Yes I can ask God to bless you but bless you how. If I am filthy, dirty meaning not living the life of God honestly how can I pray for you and my prayers be answered. You have to think. Do not put God in a human context because he is not. Even in the physical he is not. By no means am I putting God in a human context, I am using what you know which is the physical to explain God and show you God because this is what we know.

We are no longer spiritual but physical. We've closed the door to the spiritual by accepting evil and this is why our spirits cannot leave our bodies freely. The flesh and bones are our prisons like I've said. Remember our soft spot. We closed that off permanently.

Yes we are both spiritual and physical but we are no longer spiritual. Meaning we have lost the connection we had with God. Think of the garden when Adam and Eve were there. They were both physical and spiritual, they could see and talk to God but because of what they did and what we are doing today we no longer have that connection meaning we cannot see him and we have to pray, meditate and do so many different things to try and get him back. Do you comprehend what I am trying to say without losing you?

Yes

I hope so because I don't want to confuse you. Yes we pray but how do you pray?

Never pray bowing down to the ground as you want and need blessings from God.

We have two of everything and if we don't we have a left side and a right side. Please don't make me break this down for you people.

Jamaican's we have two hole I know you say we don't but we do.

Reg we do

But Granny say

Mi a tell yu wi ave

Get it now

Ooh

Zeen

Figet di nose ole inno count ya so but you have two.

Biagio I know you are ahead of the game and yes this is why Revelations said that Satan has come down to earth to make or wage war with the people of earth. But in truth Satan cannot wage war with people man just used the word Satan to give evil a human form. No I don't think I explained that right. Yes I think I did. We all have evil in us (black) and we all have good (white) and vise versa in us and this is true in the physical and in the spiritual realm. This evil, good and evil is ENERGY and one pulls more than the other IT CAN NEVER BE SKIN COLOUR BECAUSE WE KNOW THERE IS GOOD AND BAD IN EVERYONE. EVERY RACE, COLOUR AND CREED HAS EVIL IN THEM FOR THOSE WHO USE THIS ANALOGY.

So you are saying black energy as in the black hole is bad in the physical and this is where death comes from.

Yes

And you are saying white energy as in paper, the white clothes we wear is bad in the spiritual and this is where death comes from.

Yes

You are saying God is all this. Both black and white energy, black and white and if we look at God from a physical content he is both black and white and this is why you saw black and whites in the garden in your dream and this is why you saw the Jewish Man as white in your dream and the children as black. God was showing you the difference but he used people to show you because this is what you could see, this is what you know in the physical world and now we know.

Bingo by George I think you've got it. Now you have full overstanding as well as overstand the concept of the guilty blued eyed as the Muslims call those that have blue eyes. Note this is the physical analogy in the physical content but in the spiritual this is infinitely different.

So now you see God. Every one of us can see God. When you see me as well as others you see God.

Genesis: "let us make man in our own image, in the image of God created he him, male and female created he them."

Read it for yourself in Genesis.

Do you have full comprehension now?

No, no don't jump the gun let's leave that for another time sweetie. I am tired.

I know, I know you want more food but I truly have to go.

Now you over stand the concept of the Ying and the Yang which is Energy and that which we call God because of lack of terminology.

Stay Sweet.

But you have not taught us how to pray

I did above

Oh come on people I told you

Tell us again

Oh man look at the six pointed star people

But that represents the male and female

It represents God too and so many other things people. God is upright and please forget sex now. You are on a different level you are in the Sr. Kinder garden stage.

Oh Lord how do I connect with these people? Okay lets bring back the male and female when your mate is atop of you he`s giving to you the female who is upright. So we are giving to God if you comprehend what I mean. He`s giving and you are receiving. So you are upright when you are getting and receiving so when you pray you sit around the table or lay upright on the bed. No, no standing but sitting upright in the form of the upright triangle. Full over standing and comprehension. Do you have It? Yes you can stand and pray – talk to God. I do when I am washing the dishes, showering. Listen God is constantly on my mind. I consume myself with him daily.

Good so now I have to truly go but before I go I caught a nice video on the internet please check it out. It's called This is Love by Monsta ft. J. Boog.

Listen to the song and if you are apart of God's true family you will know the meaning of a true family and this song.

358

So to God - Allelujah I dedicate this song to you because you are our true family. When we fall we run to you and you pick us up and dry our tears. At times we don't have money to buy food, pay our rent and you provide for us in the right time. You are the truth, you are love and for all that you have done for me, my family and others around the earth-globe I give you thanks with true and pure love. I truly love you.

My Peeps and true loved ones, my family I dedicate this song to you as well because despite what I write and the feelings I stir inside of you we are still one family and I truly love you all. Never forget that because family does not condemn, a true family does not condemn but look live and love as a family and no matter what is said and done we are all apart of God`s family because Ja made us and out of many we are one people and this is what God needs you to know. This is why he left Jamaica there. Not the country but the name to show you and tell you we need to come home. We are all his people no matter race colour or creed. He made us all and we need to listen to him and not go around the corner to here there and everywhere to find him when he resides in you, me, everything we can think about he is it and resides in it.

Yes you can hate me for what I write and say all manner of things to disprove my words but no man can disprove God and will never disprove God.

No man can disprove that which is in them and that is God so no matter how we say this and that and go about this and that to disprove God will forever PROVE.

DO NOT TAKE MY WORD FOR IT GO TO GOD IN PRAYER AND ASK HIM TO SHOW YOU. ASK HIM TO SHOW YOU THE TRUTH HIS TRUTH AND NOT MANS.

FORGET MY WORDS AND ASK GOD, YOU OWE IT TO YOURSELF BECAUSE THIS IS YOUR LIFE NOT JUST IN THE PHYSICAL BUT IN THE SPIRITUAL AS WELL.

So stay safe and know that this is true Love which is what a true Family is. Listen to J. Boog and Manstra. Manstra told you his father told him this is about what? Family. J. Boog told you this is real love and it is the truth and not a trend.

True love and family could never be a trend.

God is not a trend, he's not religion, he's not makeup, he's not fake, he's not wars, he's not a business deal nor a way to make money to deceive and mistreat, he's not abuse and slavery, he does not enslave mentally, physically and spiritually, GOD IS TRUE LOVE.

God is showing you him. Over the centuries he's tried to show you but comprehension is not with you but now it is. It is up to you to listen and walk in God's true love. Yes we will make mistakes, like I've said I am still making mistakes but the beauty of God is knowing that he's with me and he has me. He's Love and he's calling me and I am listening because I want to return to him and how he showed me this was with these two songs. Love is Calling my Name and Return by Duane Stephenson. You may listen to the song and get a different meaning but I comprehend what he is trying to tell me because of what I was going through and what I told him.

In all he was telling me He is Love and Love is calling me, he is calling me and I am to return to him because he is always there for me.

Trust me he wore me out in my sleep because Love is Calling and Return was what I kept hearing, and yes he showed me Duane Stephenson so I had to play the songs and it is through hearing the songs I got full comprehension of what he is saying to me.

Yes people I did tell God that I divorced him and wanted him out of my life and this was his way of telling me to come back because I am his and he loved me. So know that God does not forsake, he loves us and when we leave his fold he hurts. He`s torn up by it.

People God never did us wrong we are the ones to do him wrong and when we do we do not realize that we are hurting him. So we need to think about what we are doing because if he truly leaves us we will be like Adam and Eve, the people of Noah`s time.

We are heading this way today and he is giving us another chance. Pull up Love is Calling and Return by Duane Stephenson. God told me this so I am telling you because these songs mean a lot.

Love is Calling	*Duane Stephenson*
Return	*Duane Stephenson*
Free Yourself	*Alborosie*
This is Love	*Monsta ft J. Boog*
New World Order	*Queen Ifrica ft Steele*

Like I said you don`t have to listen to me but LISTEN TO GOD. DO YOU HEAR ME PEOPLE LISTEN TO GOD AND WHAT HE IS TRYING TO TELL YOU.

I am going to add this one in the lot. Bone Thugs and Harmony Crossroads. Here what they said when they say "what are you going to do when judgment come for you?"

Listen each and every day we pray but yet we still die – judgment which is death comes for us – take our spirits. Take note and know that some people can see death. Some see death long before it happens and some actually see death himself. See the black well this is how death comes to the physical. Death is clothed in full black like the actor wears in this video. For some we see death descending or coming down from the heavens – sky descending atop us. Meaning they come atop you and suck the life out of your body. This song is the closest I can show you as to how death takes life in the physical.

No one can stop death if he or she does not have authority from God to do so but know that death can be stopped – shut down permanently.

As messengers of God you have certain authority in the spiritual realm to do certain things but it is only a selected few that has this authority.

<u>Death is the final stage in life for evil and although evil has a greater pull it is very destructive in the physical. Know that evil hath no authority in the spiritual realm. Evil cannot conquer the spiritual realm and this is why wicked and evil people - spirits linger in the physical. Evil has command of the physical but it does not have command of the spiritual. The reason why evil has command of the physical is due to our sins – the evils we commit on a daily basis.</u>

<u>Remember God's knowledge is greater and you have to ask him to clarify what he is trying to tell you because you will not comprehend or understand fully. I still don't and it does take time. So to hate one based on colour or religion, whatever, is wrong because God does not hate and could never hate. If he did he would hating himself, all that he created, including you and me.</u>

Michelle

P.S. I know that I have left a lot of unanswered questions and now I am editing this book over 1 year later and adding to it because some information in it were incorrect. I did not clearly clarify Adam because Adam is Satan. Yes I used biblical analogy which is false but the story of Adam and Eve is wrong – false because he was the one to cause Eve to lose her crown. He was a Nodite – from the land of Nod. He was Indian hence you have the Doogla race. Doogla's are a mixture of black and Indian hence they have a different texture hair. These people are of Sudanese, Somali, Ethiopian, and some are of Kenyan and West Indian descent. Yes I said Satan is white and he is. Death in its true form - state is white. Meaning in the spiritual realm death is white hence a white Jesus and a white god.

This is why I tell everyone to hate based on color of skin is unwarranted because all of us have the genes of sin within us.

The only way to eradicate this gene is before you have children you petition God to let your child or children be born with good genes. They must not be born with the genes of sin but the genes of good. They must be good and walk in the goodness of the True and Living God. They must walk in the integrity of God. They must infinitely never ever follow the ways of evil -sin. They must never, infinitely never walk in sin or desire to be with sin or lay with sin and sins people.

If I have confused you with Ying and Yang meaning black and white just look at your hair. When we are young its colour is different but when we are older it turns silver. This is also the Ying and the Yang.

For those that believe or know about 6th and 9th ether it is referring to spiritual death. You say 6th ether is 9th ether in death and I did explain this earlier. It just means when a evil black person dies in the spiritual realm he or she dies in white as a white person. White people you stay the same. Yes this is confusing for many but it is simple and this is why I stress to know your colors in this realm because it is significant.

Yes good people wear white as well but it is how you see them. They are just telling you that they are dead. That's the best way I can explain it.

To the real Jews I am going to clarify you. You can hate me all you want but you need to clean yourself up because you have all strayed from God and none of you will like what I say now.

Like I said you can all hate me but none of you can dispute the truth of God and yes I might swear at all of you.

Stop misleading the children of God because a true Jew is not just white they are black and a mixture of black and white.

Go back to my vision because all the children were female. None were males except for the Jewish man and the two Muslim men. They were all black females and his daughter was a mixture of black and white. His daughter was female and she was the one that was of mixed lineage.

Yes I know about the devil and the daughters of sin, but the devil and his children do not come into play here.

Even though he (the Jewish man) told me these two Muslim men can sit in the back I am going to go on record and say he was infinitely wrong to tell me this. I refuse to accept what he said because I know for a fact the devil uses the back door to get in and by him telling me they can sit in the back he is giving them (evil) a way in and I will never accept this.

Not even God can tell me to accept this. I refuse to accept it because I know what the devil is capable of. Once he's in we will have no peace in the spiritual realm.

I know people that God is forgiving but he cannot tell me one thing and go against it. He cannot show me evil coming in through the back door and have this man tell me that these people can sit in the back. Fuck that. I know he had the knowledge and the key to make them flee but I will never, infinitely never ever accept them because of what they stand for and what they do to God. I see and hear the lies, I see the massacre here on earth and I will never accept them or let them sit in the back of anything. I love and respect God too much to let evil sit with God's people so to this Jewish man in the spiritual realm that say Muslims can sit in the back I refuse you because you do not mean God any good nor do you represent God. I know and was shown the past and I will never disobey God and if God say Michelle no you have to change and forgive I would walk away from God and tell him God his abode is not clean enough for me. I will infinitely never forgive them for their barbaric ways and infinitely never ever forgive God if he said to allow these people in through the back or front door or any door for that matter. Millions have lost their lives because of their barbaric acts of sin and I'm to forgive them. Am to forgive the hate that they spread and the hate that they have for God and his people hell no? No peace lies in them and I refuse to be indoctrinated again by them because nothing that Satan and his race do or does is good. God's people are not fools and I respect God infinitely, so I will never, infinitely never allow any of them at the back or through the back of anything. Come on now. Why should I lose the respect of God? Come on now. My God the God of life, lose his respect for crap – shit hell no. God and I have come too far for me to turn against him. Never gonna happen that's all I've got to say.

Come on now these people bow down to the devil – Satan. ***Not one Muslim can or will respect or accept God. The day they accept God is the day Satan accepts defeat and trust me Satan and his people will infinitely never accept defeat.***

Why the fuck should I let them sit in the back shit I'm trying to close the back door not leave it open come on now.

A true child of God, a true Jew would never accept this because we know how cunning and devious evil and his people are.

Like I said even though this man had the key to let evil flee I will never accept his words because he was wrong. He did not truly love or respect God because God would infinitely never ever let evil sit with his children or his people and no matter how the devil try and come in the disguise of a Jew I am not biting. Like I said the devil can kiss my ass but no my ass is too clean for his lips so no he cannot kiss it because my ass is too good and holy – blessed for him and his people to kiss.

You see what God was trying to show me and tell me is that it is you the white Jews that let evil in through the back door because you are the ones sitting in your dens writing lies and bullshit about the True and Living God. You've all married evil hence you condone evil and tell us to practice evil by writing crap that leads humanity to hell. You sold out God as well. But guess what when it is all said and done you will all burn alongside your dirty pieces of silver because it will go down with all of you. How dare you. How fucking dare the lots of you say you are Jews and can't even respect or represent God. Let me get racist here and take it into the physical. Yes My Peeps and True Loved Ones this is wrong, infinitely wrong but I am going to go there just to put these people in their place and teach them what racism is truly all about because I can be more racist than their ass because I will give them the truth of them in the physical and spiritual.

Ya'll want to hog God and say God is yours then live for God and not spread lies nor write lies on God come on now. The beauty of God is truth and when you know truth the universe and all its goodness opens up to you.

To all you Jews that say you are Jews, KNOW that all the children of God that I saw in my dream were black with the exception of one child who was half caste meaning she was mixed.

The brides of heaven were all black I did not see one white in the lot.

My other dream that I had about the children of God the children were all black so how the hell can any of you say you are Jews when every child with the exception of one were black.

On the mountain I only saw 1 (one) white not many but one and I know people with me seeing one (1) white person means nothing because one (1) represents more than one I'm just being racist which is infinitely wrong. And no I am not gloating because like I said whether you are White, Chinese or Black and you do good you fall under the category of Black in God's world so please do not get it twisted or deviate from this because if you do woe be unto you and me. I will infinitely cuss you out. Are we clear on this?

Yes

Good

Onwards I go because I was just having it out with the Jews – the fake Jews that is.

Where the fuck is your history because Moses did not take your asses into the promised land? Moses took life out of Egypt and your asses came along for the ride. He left your asses wondering in the desert because none of you meant God any good. All that God told you to do you went against him so Moses left your asses there to wonder. So fuck the lot of you because none of you are Jewish because none of you know the truth about God hence you cannot comprehend the scope and language of God. You don't know it so you can't tell about it and this is why you sit and write lies each and every day so get the fuck off the Jewish train because none of you are children of God.

I'm not Eve and I'm certainly not gullible. She got cast out and could never return unto God's fold because she gave birth to evil and the first thing that evil did was shed blood. Cain according to your book of sin shed blood and this is why every child of sin must shed blood. They must wage war and make war to keep evil going – satisfied. Evil must be shut down in the physical and spiritual. All doors must be closed because in the end it is God that we serve meaning look to for life and true love – good food.

Listen if Eve could not get back into God's abode what say you the Jews because you did marry sin.

So tell me now how are any of you going to get back into God's abode or even see God?

Eve was locked out permanently and infinitely. What say you today that have done the same unto God and even worse because you took it further, you maliciously and blatantly tell lies on God. You have turned the entire globe meaning turn humanity from God with your lies. Lies conjured up by you and the Babylonians to deceive and mislead.

Woe man oh man I would love to see what Satan himself is going to do to the lot of you in his pit – Hell.

Woe Nelly I don't feel sorry for none of you because you took the lies and deceit too far.

You all claimed to be when each and every one of you knew and know that you are not.

Listen this is the way I feel and God knows this.

I do not hide anything from God and I refuse to now. Like I said God needs roots in his life he does not need leafs and branches that sway this way and that way when someone gives them the scrapings off their deceitful and sinful table.

Yes my conscience is clear. Evil has done too much, caused too much pain for me to easily forgive. I will never forget hence I will infinitely never trust evil or its people around me or around my family – the good seeds that God have given me. Trust me I don't love evil. Let evil stay with death because evil chose death and I chose Life so therefore we can infinitely never ever abide peacefully in any kingdom or the same kingdom.

Okay now here we go
If you are a Roman Catholic Jew *__you are not Jewish__* you are of the synagogue of Satan. You are walking in the way of abominations of sin.

If you are an Orthodox Jew *__you are not Jewish__* you are of the synagogue of Satan because you are walking in the way of sin and abominations. You are also the ones keeping the lies of sin alive with your pack of lies.

If you are a Christian Jew you are not Jewish you are of the synagogue of Satan. You are going against God and walking in the ways of sin. You are no different from the Orthodox Jew. You are one in the same.

If you are a converted Jew *you are not Jewish* you are of the synagogue of Satan because NO JEW ON THE FACE OF THIS PLANET WHETHER LIVING OR DEAD CAN BE CONVERTED.

If you are a Sephardic Jew, a Zionist Jew or any form of conversion *you are not Jewish* you are of the synagogue of Satan and you are walking in sin. You are an abomination of sin.

If you are black and say you are a converted Jew *you are not Jewish*. You are of the synagogue of Satan and you are walking in sin. You are an abomination of sin.

If you are White, Chinese or Indian and you say you are a converted Jew *you are not Jewish* you are of the synagogue of Satan and an abomination of sin.

I WILL REPEAT ANYONE THAT SAY THEY ARE A CONVERTED JEW OR REPRESENT ANY FORM OF RELIGION *IS NOT A JEW* THEY ARE OF THE SYNAGOGUE OF SATAN AND I NEED NOT FORWARD ALL OF YOU TO REVELATIONS.

We know Jesus never existed therefore he could never be Jewish.

Abraham you say is Jewish and many of you follow Abraham to a tee.

Well let me clarify things for you and like I said ***you cannot be converted and say you are a Jew***. So therefore Abram/Abraham was not Jewish and could never be Jewish because he was a Nodite. His ancestry belongs to the people of Nod and not God. Hence Abram/Abraham was from the synagogue of Satan. He walked in sin hence he was an abomination of sin.

Forget it because you cannot say you are a Muslim Jew this is an outright abomination of sin. ***You are not Jewish but a part of Satan's clan*** and woe be unto your ass when God is done with you. You're all a fucking condemnation of sin. You're all of the living dead.

How the fuck can a Jew say they are Christian or Muslim? Read Revelations you are not of God but a part of the synagogue of Satan because it said in part woe be unto the Jews that call themselves Jews because they are of the synagogue of Satan. Read it your damned self and get full comprehension.

Some of you are saying I am ¼ Jew.

Some of you are saying I am ½ Jew.

Bitch there is no such thing as ¼ or ½ Jew. You are full Jew.

Is God ½ or ¼? So how can any of you say you are ½ or ¼ Jew?

Why the hell don't you ½ and ¼ Jews just come out and say it. Tell the truth that you're all ashamed to be Jewish. You're all ashamed of God, ashamed to be God's children.

Let me tell you something. God is proud – damned proud of the bond that he has with his children and he protects them with his life hence we have life.

If you are ashamed of God and want to relinquish all rights to God then do so but do not insult the intelligence of God and his people – children.

Divorce God if you do not want him come on now.

Go before God and tell him truthfully that you divorce him – are divorcing him. This you can do in prayer then go to man – before man and tell them that you are divorcing God so that all records are clean – exact - clear. Tell God and man that you relinquish all rights to him God.

I wish I could say no givesy backsy but I am not God because we all leave his fold for some reason or another. Once you relinquish all rights to God in this way then your words will be absolute – final. I did tell God I did not want him but I did not go before man and relinquish my rights and this is where the difference between me and you come in. I was going through turmoil and wanted out and God told me to return and I did and trust me my life is getting better. If you do not want to relinquish God then do not go before man. If you are mad at him let him know because he is merciful and he does infinitely understand and overstand. You are the one that have to learn to trust him and I will tell you that it is not easily. Trusting God infinitely does not come overnight. It takes time. You will get upset at God and like I said this is okay. Take your frustrations out on God he God does not mind but know when you are done if you swear at God apologize and say sorry. If this is your anger let him know by saying you did not mean to swear at him.

Know that before you go into a relationship with God you cannot be fake with him. Like I said if you are fake with him it would mean that you were not true.

NO TRUE JEW AND YOU THE TRUE JEW KNOW WHO YOU ARE. NO TRUE JEW CAN SAY THEY FOLLOW JESUS OR ABRAHAM BECAUSE JESUS DID NOT EXIST NOR WAS ABRAHAM A JEW.

NO TRUE JEW CAN FOLLOW THEM OR GIVE ORDINANCE UNTO THEM.

Tell me something you the true Jews what makes Abraham a Jew. Forget the fact that the bible said he crossed over one land to the next but tell me what made him a Jew?
Tell me come on and tell me. Yes I am yelling. Have you forgotten Moses and what Moses did?

Have you forgotten God so loosely?

Who were the children of God?

Every child of God were female not male. In order for anyone to say they are a Jew they had to marry into the fold. One of the daughters of God had to marry you and this is how you can say you are Jewish – you are a Jew.

And no, Abraham did not marry one of the daughters of God.

To every Jewish nation on the face of this planet when did God give you idols to worship and make sacrifices unto?

Tell me something how come God changed Abrams name to Abraham and did not change Moses or Noah's?

Who the fuck do any of you think you are fooling. Abram was never Jewish and could never be Jewish because he was Hindu. Read your damned bibles correctly. Abram was a Muslim he changed his name from Singh to Mohammed but hey the bible will not tell you this. It is only in Islam that one have to give up their birth name and accept that of Mohammed.

Tell me something Mr. True Jew why would God tell someone to change their name?

Did God not give you his name meaning the name he has chosen for you so why go against God and accept something that does not belong to you?

When did God become sinful?

When did God tell you to follow abominations of sin?

Did God not give you everything so why have all of you turned against God?

Why are all of you condemning God and calling him a liar?

Abrams father was an idol worshipper and Abram himself was an idol worshipper. He practiced animal sacrifices and all of you say this is of God come on now. This is of the dead. Only Satanist, Voodoo Priest and Priestess use blood. Oh I forgot the church have you drinking blood and eating flesh and they too are of Satan. So fuck the lot of you with your lies. You've all converted and accepted Satan. No wonder Satan's clan hates your asses because none of you are loyal to the True and Living God. You're all a fucking joke. Look at the lot of you begging bread, the scrapings off Satan's table. You're all worthless because none of you can repent of your filthy and dirty ways. None of you are true to God.

Repent you heathens – repent of your sinful and deceitful ways. Repent.

When does the lies stop? Tell me when does the lies stop?
You can hate me all you want but I don't care. Like I said know the truth in the living and don't wait until you are dead to find out because that will be it for you.

All of you know God. All of you know that the life you live in the living determines where you go in the spiritual so why are the lot of you accepting Sin and participating in sin.

Why are you begging sin for his dirty food when you have the clean food of God? But wait you sold out God so you have to beg sin for his dirty food. Ain't that a bitch? You gave up God, sold him out now you too have to wallow in shit and kiss Satan's ass. You made the choice but guess what God is truly forgiving hence all you have to do is repent and cut the hair and walk in God's glory from now on.

Tell me something Mr. Jewish man what have God done to you for all of you to be disrespecting God and writing books of lies about God?

Can the truth lie?

So therefore, from the day you started to write lies about God – the True and Living God the entire globe know and knows that none of you are the truth. The globe – every nation on the face of this planet know that you are all liars and deceivers, backbiting heathens that make your God – Satan out to be truthful hence Revelations say and I quote "woe be unto the Jews that call themselves Jews because they are of the synagogue of Satan. Simply put your asses are all Satan's children because no child of God can get up and tell lie about God like that. None.

When we do that all we are telling the world is that we hate God and do not respect him.

You sold out God for a piece of dirty loaf – a piece of bread. And no the Jamaicans are no different because we too sold out God for a piece of dirty loaf, so all around God's people are selling him out piece by piece and handing everything God has given them over to the devil – Satan.

Tell me something are you happy?

Are you happy that you are kissing Satan's ass?

"No"

Then wake the fuck up and respect your heritage. If you are a true Jew you know what you have to do and I need not remind you of the hair.

Tell me something why would God give you a man that practiced animal and human sacrifices to redeem you?

Why would God – the True and Living God send a man that is a condemnation of sin to teach and preach to you? Come on tell me because I need to know and God need to know as well.

Abraham or Abram indulged in abominations of sin but yet you hold him in high esteem.

Go to your bible and read what skin color Abram was he certainly was not white and you know this because it said and don't quote me verse for verse or word for word. The bible said Abraham put his hand in his chest and it became leprous as snow and when he put his hand back it returned to the natural state. First of all God would never tell anyone to put their hand in their chest and turn them into a leper. This is infinitely impossible because like I've said and will forever tell you God do not deal in stink. God infinitely does not deal with evil and he would infinitely never ever commit sin like this. If you are clean why the hell would God want you to become dirty? Come on now and come again with your pack of lies. The man was a fucking leper. He was plagued with leprosy. He was a walking living, breathing curse and you're telling me God used him to teach you. Come on now. God infinitely do not go out of his race when it comes to educating his people. Come on now. Why the hell would God use sin to teach clean when sin know not cleanliness.

This man was a non Jew – not a child of God and God used him to teach his people. No a non-Jew, come on now who the fuck do you think you're fooling. Get real and start telling the truth. Wow it's amazing how we put evil and his race in high esteem then turn around and destroy all that God has given us and when things go sour we turn and cry to God for help.

Why the fuck should he help any of us? We don't care about him. We use him. We are all users and abusers because we use God and abuse him.

We all do and I need not remind you of the shoes in churches because this is our abuse. We trample God under foot and think we are doing something good. Well we are not and trust me we will pay for this blatant abuse – sin.

To all the Jewish nations when did God indulge in incest or tell you to follow the ways of incest.

Abraham married his half sister. He was banging his own sister (half sister) and to all of you this is correct and fine. Come on now. No wonder we are all screwed up in this world. No wonder some of think it's okay to inbreed – marry into your own family. This is what the bible taught. It tells us God us okay with inbreeding and marrying your own family member.

No, looking into it and beating myself up about this I know now that this is wrong. God would never condone this hence we have the different races that his children can marry into.

Come on now his own brother had sex with his own daughter and this is okay to all of you.

God condoned all this shit. Pleaseeeeeee!! I don't give a shit or a fuck what anyone says or how the bible word it. His family indulged in incest and we say this is of God come on now.

Cousins and cousins getting it on is not okay either. This is sin and sinful – hurtful – painful.

Yes family members are married to family members but this we can blame our nasty and disgusting mothers and fathers for.

Some of these parents are so fucking nasty that only hell can tell.

Fathers and mothers whoring and women giving another man jacket – another man's child. This is wrong because you are not thinking of the implications in the future. Nasty bitch. The men are no different because they too are nasty bitches. You cannot breed up and spread your germs from one woman to the next and have children in the east, west, north and south without telling your wife or baby mama – your children. You have so many kids that none of your children know who is who. When they grow up and find a mate and end up marrying your son or daughter meaning brother marrying sister and sister marrying brother what are you going to say? Who the fuck do they have to blame? Is it not you? They can't blame God and you can't blame God because God never told you to go and whore. Become a prostitute running from bed to bed, no not bed to bed but shed to shed.

Do you think God respects you or even look upon you when you have 25 different Baby Mama? Come on now. Solomon lost everything because he condone and participated in shit like that so what say you? Do you think God will accept you in his kingdom with whoredom such as this? Come on now. If it was sinful for Solomon it is sinful for you too hence Solomon told you. So I suggest all of you repent and do that which is right and just – pleasing in the sight of God if you want to keep your crown.

He Abraham practiced animal sacrifices and this is okay with all of you.

He Abraham caused his wife to wear a face covering not because she was beautiful but to hide his shame and disgrace in other lands. Sarah was his sister and wife. Wow can you imagine the shame and disgrace in other lands, come on now. He had to make her hide her face because they would be scorned.

Tell me when did God become a heathen?

When did God become an abomination unto man?

When did God become disgusting in your sight and in the eyes of man?

No the women of the past our ancestors did not wear a face covering.

Tell me what face covering did Eve wear?

When did God tell Eve to wear a face covering?
Tell me. Come on and tell me.

Tell me something all of you Jews when did Islam become a part of your life and practice?

Stop telling people you are Jewish because you are not. All of you practice the Islamic way. Not one of you practice God's way.

We have all sinned and trust me we are more than short of the glory of God. No I will not take myself out of this because I too have sinned and there is but one thing that I have to do to redeem myself but I need God to make this way right for me.

Yes it has to do with my hair.

Why are we indulging in sinful things and saying it is of God.

Have all of you forgotten the truth and what we were taught?

We were enslaved and forced to accept the Babylonian way.

This is the song we were taught as taken from one of my visions.......

A new day is dawn
A new day has come when Mutuyaahu will come down

I cannot remember the entire song but this was the song every Jewish child was taught. In the vision the children were young black males and females. They were taught to hate the Jews nor did they acknowledge that they were Jewish.

I said to the little boy I'm a Jew and you're a Jew and it's not so bad but the little boy cried because he believed he was not Jewish nor did he want to be referred to as Jewish. I said to him I am sorry as I continued to rub his skin with cream – lotion from head to toe. I was putting lotion on the children's skin but with this particular boy the lotion burned him as if the lotion got in his eye and was burning him. Yes people all the children were black and this time they were males and females and young. They were also laying on their backs facing upwards. People in the dream with this particular young boy the cream was turning his skin blue. Like I said the children were taught that they were not Jewish and the song that they were taught is mentioned in part above.

We were taught about Mutuyaahu. I am not versed in Hebrew nor do I know who Mutuyaahu is. The spelling is my spelling so if someone knows who

Mutuyaahu is please let me know because I don't know.

As children of God, what I have found is that God has given us all the goodness of his world and this world and we have turned the goodness that God have given us into something dirty – evil and for this we must pay.

We cannot take up what other cultures have beaten into us and say it is of God. We have to teach our children the truth when the enemy is around as well as when the enemy is not around. Truth be known too, if we were true to God none of us would be living this way. God has never deceived us nor did he turn from us so why are we turning from him.

None of the things that we do is from our history or from God but yet we say it is and this is wrong. No look into it. The bible teaches us how to sin because when we engage in these practices we've committed sin and God walks away from us meaning move further away from us in time and the farther he gets is the farther it is to reach him.

How can God come back in our lives if we live in sin on a daily basis?

The bible does not tell you how to maintain and attain God it tells you how to repel God – keep him out of our lives so how is this book holy?

How is this book from God?

We know it is the book of sin so therefore this book – the bible can only be from sin because it is sinful and deceitful people writing and maintaining it hence they are from the house of Satan meaning these writers are from the house of Satan. These pastors and preaches that preach from it on a daily basis and say the bible is divine is also from the synagogue of Satan because God never told any of them to preach or teach from books of lies. God infinitely never game them any authority to.

The bible is Satan's book. It could infinitely never ever be the book of God - Good because in God's book no sin is written. No sin is condoned because like I've said before God has nothing to do with sin - filth.

Yes his goodness is left on earth but it is not for the sake of evil that his goodness still resides on earth it is for the sake of his people – children because some of us are still here on this planet.

Like I've said evil seek to destroy and do destroy because we let evil do this. In days gone by evil could never infinitely never ever destroy but because the lies of sin were so truthful we believed and we married evil and it did cost us our crown – glory.

Today there is no difference in what evil is doing. Evil just got a little more sophisticated. They use books, diseases created by men, wars, economic despair, political agendas, hate, racial injustice, prejudice, rape, you name it evil has done it and is still doing it.

My son said to me the other day. Mama with all the money people have given into finding cures for diseases you would think they would come up with a cure by now and I looked into what he said and came to the conclusion that he is infinitely correct. If man – these corporations wanted to cure people they would a long time ago. But because of sin – greed none will stand up and give the cures for these diseases that they created because many of these diseases were created in laboratories to kill the masses but yet we think these companies and people are doing something great for us. If they wanted to cure cancer, all cancers they would cure them but because the money is great and their agenda has nothing to do with human life or dignity but money we will never have cures. To cure people would mean less profit and to have less profit would mean their companies would become obsolete. But shortly given the next 19 years their companies and money will mean nothing. They will become obsolete in the global starvation market. Their money will not be able to save them given the global weather trend – the lack of rain – deforestation, global warming.

I will forever say it. Human life has no value because it comes down to a damned dollar bill – sin – evil. Hence I will forever tell you that God has nothing to do with evil because evil and wicked people value not life they value death.

No one can see that in all evil has promised them they are going to die because evil cannot maintain or sustain life it can only take it – kill it.

Let me tell you something if there was no more of God's children on the face of this planet do you think God would be around?

He would never be. He would have taken the remainder of him, his goodness and leave. Leave evil to its own demise but because his children still reside on the planet he cannot abandon them or take away his goodness because we depend on him for so much and that so much is LIFE.

As children of God yes Jews we do not walk right nor do we praise right. We have the truth but yet turn from the truth to follow and wallow in lies - shit.

As Jews yes you the white Jews I am now talking to you because you were to protect the children of Israel but you have failed them. You failed God. You failed his people – your people.

Tell me something when did God tell you to stand before a wailing wall and pray?

Tell me the difference with you doing this and the difference with you going to Mecca and walking around the Kaaba. What Muslims excluded you so you had to find a wall to show support? You love Islam that much that you had to mimic them?

Tell me and yes I am yelling.

Was this the way Moses prayed?

Did Moses teach you this?

Is this the way of God?

Tell me and tell me how Moses failed God? Tell me how the fuck did Moses fail God because Moses did not fail God you all failed God. Every one of you failed God.

How dare you?

How dare every one of you that said Moses killed.

Moses killed no one. He was not a murderous Babylonian like all of you.

Moses could never have killed anyone and carry forth life out of Egypt.

Who the hell are you to lie on Moses like this?

Who the fuck are you?

Go back to David.

No blood was on Moses hand so how dare the lot of you believe and say this. What gaul – nerve. You know not of Moses hence you write lies about Moses then have the audacity to say Moses took you out of Egypt. You came along for the ride and he left your asses in the desert to wonder because like I said none of you were true and faithful to God and your books of lies are proof until this day.

Know that God would never send a murderer send a murderer to take his people and life out of Egypt.

Tell me how did Moses break the laws of God? Tell me bitches tell me, because I am off now.

Tell me how did Moses displease God?

The laws that Moses received none of you can read the language. If you are not chosen by God you cannot read it because this language is not just a language it is everything in the sight of God because this language is of God.

If Moses got the commandments of God which is more than ten – read them yourself in God's language and he did get it no one on the face of this planet can or could read it. You have to be chosen by God to read it and yes write this language. Like I've said this language heals, cures, can trap the devil, untie all manner of evil. All that is good this language is but yet some that have it use it for evil. This language is that powerful – that strong.

Stop telling people that Moses never saw the Promised Land. Moses saw the Promised Land and is living in the Promised Land. Moses went up to the mountain. He was on the mountain but none of you know the significance of the mountain and until this day none of you know.

Stop telling people that Moses spoke to a burning bush on Mount of Sinai or whatever mountain it was. Moses could never infinitely never ever have spoken to a burning bush because God does not infinitely never ever does not deal in FIRE. God, the True and Living God deal and deals in WATER.

Water is the staff of life. It is pure – pure energy - TRUE.

Water is what cleans ALL.

Fire kills but water heals – cure.

Fire destroy but water Saves.

Fire is HELL – Death.

Water is of God. It is Life – True life – the true blessings of God.

Water is abundant on earth as well as in the spiritual realm. No fire is found in goodness.

Evil deals with fire – smokeless fire. Meaning when true evil – demons come around you, you see smoke first and then fire.

You may see them in a ball of fire.

You may see them smoking cigarettes.

So when you say Moses was talking to a burning bush, Moses could not have been talking to God because that fire represented evil. What you are telling me is that Moses was speaking to evil therefore, the commandments that Moses received could infinitely never ever have been from God they were from evil – given to him by evil.

You say thou shalt not kill but yet we kill

You say thou shalt not steal but yet we steal

You that thou shalt not covet thy neighbor's wife but yet we covet thy neighbor's wife

You say thou shalt not commit adultery but yet we commit adultery

You say thou shalt not take the name of the Lord thy God's name in vain but yet each and every day we take God's name in vain because we destroy his goodness, destroy his teachings, destroy his people, destroy his land, destroy his heritage, destroy the waterways therefore destroying self – Life.

Anyone that asks God to bless them – rain down his blessings on them will receive their blessing in the form of water. So if your book of lies had said Moses went up the mount and spoke to the water or even saw green grass and fruit trees then I would know that you were correct because like I said water is pure – pure energy. The greenness of the mountain also represent the Life – the Life of God – Nature but because you said fire I infinitely know you are lying because none of you know the truth about Moses and what he was put on the earth to do.

Know this the land that God's messengers see is not the same land you see nor is it the same land that you will dwell in. The top level is reserved for God's messengers and true people but the first and second level is reserved for man.

Enough is enough. Come on now do you truly think God would let Moses reside with you. You turned from God and did everything to displease God. Moses was faithful to God and could never live with any of you.

Moses was successful because he brought the Ying and the Yang (Life) into China where it rests until this day.

Why do you think many of you were left wondering the desert for well over 40 thousand years and you are still wondering because many of you are still in the desert?

You were never God's people. There's a big difference between a fake Jew and a true Jew. A true Jew cannot lie and spread lies about God and his messengers.

Every true Jew know that Moses did not speak to no damned burning bush because Moses did not go into hell he went to see Life on the Mountain and Life which is God told him what he needed him to do.

Like I said God don't deal in fire he deals in water both in the spiritual and physical realm. If you were true Jews you would know this.

Now you are all crying and saying you were in the desert for 40 years. Well fuck the lot of you because you were all pagans that was along for the ride so God got rid of your asses. He kicked the lots of you off his coat tail because you're all wanna be but could never be. You all mean God no good that is why you keep the lies of your father who is Satan going until this day.

A true Jew stands for God – Life and lives for God – Truth.

The lot of you should be ashamed of yourself because you're all a disgrace and an abomination unto life – God. You're all a condemnation.

Oh yea, stop misusing the 40 years and 40 days because the 40 represents the square the number 4. Evil does not have 40 days to roam the earth once they have passed away or passed on. This is an infinite lie. Evil wonder the earth and create havoc on the earth long after 40 days. As long as there is evil on this planet evil will roam it. Good does not roam the planet because good move on to a higher life.

Once the 24000 years of evil has expired that's it for all evil life.

Between now and 2032 God's people have to – they must separate themselves from all evil because the earth must be cleansed. If God's people do not prepare for this they will go down with evil and this is why I tell them they can no longer enjoy the delicacies of evil anymore.

We can no longer buy the clothes or food of evil.

Nor can we shop in the same places that evil shop.

We can no longer go the doctors and pharmacies of evil anymore.

We can no longer listen to the music of people that glorify and pay homage to the devil – evil.

We can no longer marry wicked and evil people.

All that is evil we must separate ourselves from.

We can no longer give evil our blessings and if we continue to do so then we will go down with them therefore disrespecting God and giving evil the victory over God.

W have to shop in clean places and go to clean hospitals that do not house evil people because evils agenda is not to cure or give you the best care it's to kill. Evil must continue to kill and by them killing they are destroying life hence destroying you.

No there is no blood to put on your door because God does not deal in nastiness. He does not deal in blood.

Trust me God know if your house is clean.

He will shield and protect you from evil. Remember even though you are clean you and your children have unclean friends and by us having unclean friends in our household our homes become dirty – unclean. I have to tell you this because you might be saying my house is clean but yet things are not right, I can't seem to get ahead well now you know.

You can be clean but the people around are not. Our children are unclean too trust me on that and the reason for this is because we did not ask God before hand for good and clean children. Hence we have to drill cleanliness in them. Drill choosing the right friend into them.

Any friend that tells you to smoke, drink, take drugs, do wrongs is not a true and good friend. Any friend that tells you to cheat on your mate is not a good or true friend.

With God we cannot live wrong and expect to get right this will infinitely never happen hence all I write I do not write for evil I write for God and his people.

I don't care – infinitely do not care what evil does or do to his people because they are not of God.

BUT I INFINITELY CARE WHAT EVIL DO AND DOES TO GOD'S PEOPLE – MY PEOPLE BECAUSE THEY – WE ARE OF GOD.

I do not represent evil, I represent God so therefore, I have to teach God's people correctly. I have to teach them the truth. If God's people refuse my words they are refusing God in many ways and I have to leave them alone because they too have made their choice and I cannot go against the choice that they have made. I have to respect their decision.

Onwards I go.

You the Jews accepted idol worship and practiced all manner of sin and today you are still doing it. You cannot accept God because God is in none of you.

It wasn't all God's people that Moses took out of Egypt. A lot of other nations came with Moses but they could not journey onward with Moses because they were not God's people. All of you know this but yet turned from the truth to accept lies.

Stop it. Stop telling lies on Moses. None of you told lies on Abram but yet you all tell lies on Moses and have accepted this lie. Who the fuck do you think you are? He was not a viper or leper nor was he an abomination of sin. Moses was not an idol worshipper like many of you. He did not accept idols. He was in Egypt and never once did he bow down to the idols of Pharaoh so tell me how did Moses displease God?

How did Moses not reach the Promised Land?

What laws of God did Moses break?

Tell me you lying and deceitful demons. Yes you the writers of the Bible. This book that is so divinely inspired.

Inspired from what Satan's library?

Inspired from what Greek Mythology?

No book that is from God teaches you how to sin. It tells you of sin and what sin does.

Tell me would God give anyone messengers that bask in incest and murder to save them?

Come on is God that low and filthy that he would send a man that practiced idol worship and animal sacrifices to you to save you?

Do we put God this low that we would believe these vile things of God? Come on tell me?

We put Satan and his agents of sin in high esteem and when it comes to God we let him down. Give him pork – unclean meat to eat. Tell me when you do this where are you going to go? Where are all of you truly going to go?

Where are you going to call home?

Do you think you are going to go to God's abode?

If you think you are you had better think again.

Certain things God has and have made provision for but this one takes the cake of lowliness.

We have made God out to be this vile and disgusting God that I don't know.

Enough is enough. Nothing that we do is fair to God but yet we stand and proclaim our love for him. None of us truly love God nor do we love him. We are spiteful and disgusting because none of us can be man or woman enough to stand up and tell God that we hate his ass. Come on now. Who are we fooling?

Certainly not God.

When someone accuse you of lying or stealing do you not go to any lengths to prove them wrong?

When someone bullies and hurt your child do you not do all you can to let people know that the person or child is a bully?

When someone murders your child and do all manner of evil against your child or even onto you do you not go to every and any lengths to prove your innocence but yet when it comes to God we all condemn him and crucify him. We go to every length to displease him and prove him wrong and disgusting.

We believe that he would send unclean men and women to teach and preach to us.

Each and every day we murder God and bask in the offerings of the devil and say yes it is from God.

Don't you think if the churches start telling humanity the truth this world and the people within this world would be better?

Don't you think if the churches start telling people that all that they know is false – wrong this world and the people within this world would be better?

Don't you think if the churches start telling people that they are serving Satan and not the True and Living God that this world and the people within this world would be better?

No come on now. The church would not lose anything apart from a few people but people would still go to church because they believe and some know the devil meaning they have made the devil – evil their God.

Tell me when did God become Satan?

Tell me something Israel when did God tell you to wage war against the Palestinians?

Are you not a part of the whoring clan?

Are you not the same as the Palestinians?

Do you not worship the way they do?

Do you not dress the way they do?
All of you accepted Abraham and some of you accepted Abraham and Jesus so what justifies you to say that Palestine or the Palestinians do not have a say in Israel?

Tell me because you did accept Mutuyaahu which is their God.

Because of your actions they have all rights and claim to Israel.

You accepted Abraham as a prophet of God and because of this you cannot deny them their right because you are the ones saying Abraham is Jewish when you know he was Muslim and he Abraham practiced the Islamic way. He was an idol worshipper and he practiced this way – his way of life. The Babylonian and Pagan way of life.

You accepted their God, so therefore because of this, your acceptance of their God they are justified in their claim to Israel and you cannot deny them this. If you did not accept their God then they would have no right or claim but you did and no one in the Jewish kingdom whether false or true can deny this because you have made it law and it is law meaning it is so.

You married evil because the Mogen David – Star of David is interlocked. You went against God – the laws of God because Jews and Muslims are forbidden to co-habitate – live together.

To you the people of Palestine and Israel let me clear the record and give it to you straight because the true Jews are not doing it. They are hiding behind their Rabbi's and whatever segment of lies they want to hide behind and like I said I do not care if the Jewish world hate me because you cannot say you are a Jew and hide behind lies nor can you condone lies. This is wrong and it is an abomination unto God and every Jew upon the face of this planet know it. There is no such thing as ¼ Jew. There is no such thing as a Catholic Jew. There is no such thing as a converted Jew. There is no such thing as a half Jew and to say that you are these things is blasphemy and yes it is an abomination unto to God. No Jew can say they are a Jew and live a sinful life. There are laws that every Jew must adhere to regardless if you leave the fold or not. If you chose to relinquish your Jewish rights that is your choice but know this after a time an allotted time you cannot come back so know what you are doing because God is keeping tabs. If you know you do not want to be Jewish you have to go before God and the council of man and relinquish those rights and you know it. There is no half way or in between. Onwards I go.

To the Palestinian and Jewish nations Abraham was not a Jew. Read it and get it through your mother fucking thick skull ABRAHAM WAS NOT A JEW HE WAS AND STILL IS HINDU and nothing that you do or say entitles you to the land of Israel.

Absolutely nothing do you hear me. None of you are from the tribe of Israel or of the tribe of Judah because the Children of Israel were and still are black and a mixture of white. They are also white. We are Africans – God's children that are spread across the globe. We have mixed with different races and it is not all of us that have mixed with the races can call ourselves Jews because when you mix with the wrong race you are locked out of God's kingdom infinitely.

Isaac and Ishmael entitle you to nothing. If you want a home go back to Nod and all the other lands in-between.

Like I said Abraham entitles you to nothing because God did not give Abraham this land. God's people were there meaning resided there long before Abraham resided there.

You cannot massacre and steal peoples land and say it is yours it is wrong and you the Israeli's are wrong as well. Remember Israel and Judah went a whoring and committed abominable acts of sin before God and it repented God meaning you hurt God dearly. You know the wrongs that you did in the past and the wrongs you are doing now. You cannot continue to marry evil and think God is going to continue to shield and protect you. You must do right in the sight of God and one of those rights is coming clean to humanity with the truth. ***Like I've said and will forever say the devil cannot come in unless you let the devil in***. You know this is true so why are you giving evil access to destroy God. If you truly love God you would be protecting him and doing that which is right and good in his sight. No one on the face of this planet can say they are holy when they know they are doing wrong and you are doing wrong. This is not fair nor is it right. God is not hurting you nor is he telling lies on you so why are you disgracing God as well as telling people that God is a liar. Enough is enough and don't you dare say I am not a Jew I should not be saying these things. Do not say I know nothing of your ways and culture because baby I know a hell of a lot more than all of you. You claim to be God's chosen people so do better and represent God truthfully and not with lies because you know and the world know that not every race on the face of this planet can say they are from God. All I have to say is go back to Genesis and read what it said. You cannot be the truth and the light and do wrong all that makes you is sinful and of the devils clan-seed.

It's not an eye for an eye or a tooth for a tooth.

What are you showing the world? Are you saying Jews are murders?

How much more blood must you shed?

Tell me how can you say Israel is a holy land when you are siding with the devil. You are keeping the devil alive in your books of lies?

You are making God out to be this vile monster when you know you are the snake the true snake in the grass.

A true Jew would never defile God and cast him so lowly and vile but yet this is what you are telling the people of this world. You are the ones editing

and writing bibles and saying they are divinely inspired when you know this is wrong.

Tell me what have God done to you for you to hate God so much?

I need to know why the lot of you hate God because it is only a sinful and deceitful yes hateful person and people could do this to God.

You were sworn to protect the children of God but yet you spit in God's face and have the Gaul to say you are God's children and people.

Did God ever give you piss to drink or shit to eat?

Tell me truly tell me the reason why you hate God so much that you would go to any lengths to deceive the world with your pack of lies.

Tell me what makes Israel so holy?

What makes Israel holier than other lands?

Was it not the Jews that sold their own people into slavery?

Is it not you the Jews white Jews that taught the black Jews to say they are not Jewish?

Was it not you that taught them to displease God as well as taught them of Mutuyaahu.

You made us sing songs unto false Gods because you of yourself sold out God

You accepted the Pagan way of doing things and cast the blacks aside because you accepted the colour superiority bullshit.

Take a good look at your flag what does it represent? Now take a good look at God's flag the Jamaican Flag and tell me now which nation God favors? Yes here you can call me racist because I was being racist.

Just as how I get nasty and foul with my people I am going to get nasty and foul with you because you are my people and you too have brought shame and disgrace to God.

If you do not know about Moses do not talk about him, say you do not know.

Yes there are rights and customs that we must adhere to and trust me I don't know them all. I am just learning but as God's people you have to stop the lies.

You cannot keep writing lies about God nor can you go on living the Pagan way. You know it is wrong so why are you doing it?

Each Jew know who Mutuyaahu is and I will not correlate the name to the living because you of yourself can do it

No Jew upon the face of the earth is true to God and to say Jews are whites only is a grave injustice to the blacks because the daughters of God are blacks and whites. I know what I said in the dreams above in relation to seeing the children of Israel as black but it does not mean they were not white as well. Go back to what I said in the spiritual realm. ***Goodness is represented as black people meaning if you are white and good you are black***.

If you are Chinese and good you are black

If you are white and good you are black

If you are Indian and good you are black

If you are pink purple whatever color so long as you are good you are black

The color of skin is not important in the physical world it only becomes important in the spiritual because this color distinguishes where you go. Do not get it confused with the black clothing because I know many of you will.

If you see a black person dressed in white then you are okay – the skin colour is what matters and a prime example of this are the trees. Look at the bark or trunk of the tree. Do you see the color?

It is charcoal or black right?

Yes

Well this is what I meant.

If you see a black person or white person dressed in full suit of black or full black clothing run like hell because this is physical death. When death or evil comes down to the physical they wear full black clothing. And even though I said death dies in white as a white person you infinitely have to know how you see the person. Do not change from what I've told you about spiritual death. This cannot change. If God sends you a white person clothed in full white this is death, run like hell. Know that God will never send you a white person clothed in full white. The person must be wearing another color like a red sash or band around his or her waist. When you see this you know that this person is here to warn you. You are doing something wrong or about to do something wrong. Red is used to warn you meaning that person that is dressed in red and white is there to warn you. If you see a person holding up red that means that person is hiding something. I truly hope I have not confused you again. Like I said it is hard to explain and many things is left for face to face conversation where I can show you.

Remember there is a physical death and spiritual a death and both are on earth meaning both come to earth. Physical deaths are those clothed in black clothing and spiritual deaths are those clothed in white clothing.

Black moves on to the abode of God but white does not, it dies.

Yes you can say this is a lie but it is not. Look at the Ying and Yang more importantly look at your hair in old age. It turns silver – white. White is death and black is life. It is that simple.

As humanity we need to stop the madness and stop basing things off color the colour of skin in this realm. Knowing the colors and the significance of colors does not mean hate. No one should hate each other based on skin colour but we made it so.

We tell lies on God and expect God to forgive us of our lies.

Like I've said God does not hate anyone based on the color of skin. It's not to say he can't hate you. He can but for the sins and lies you tell and commit.

Trust me infinitely God does not hate because if he did evil would not be living right now. Yes evil must die and will die but it is evil that will kill himself and herself.

The reality is no one trust God anymore

No one knows God anymore

No one can communicate with God properly anymore.

Tell me did God deserve this?

Look and me and tell me if God deserved this?

Tell me how can a nation say they are of God and have sold God out to the highest bidder?

Tell me how can any of us say God is a good God but yet enslave and poison the hearts of man when it comes to God?

What right do we have to do this?

What right do you have to do this?

Why do we mock God and cause him to hold his head down in shame and disgrace each and every day?

How can we say we love when all we have is hate?

God has done us nothing. He has given us everything to sustain and maintain our lives but instead of listening to God we listen to man and destroy it all.

How the fuck can any of us say we are of God and living in our cesspool of sin each and every day?

No people, I am not taking myself out of this because like I've told you I have sinned against God and no matter how much I repent it still does not make it right nor does it justify my actions. Yes I know God has forgiven me but it does hurt and we have hurt God big time.

Because of my sins it does not make me better than you or anyone. I am just as guilty as the next man or woman. We have all sinned and recognizing the errors of our ways and yes admitting them and asking for forgiveness makes me the better person because I went to God in truth and truly asked him for forgiveness and yes I told him I was sorry. Many of us still do not know or can do this meaning go to God in truth and honesty.

You know the sad part of this is and what truly hurts me now is that despite the knowledge of truth and the good food that God is giving everyone we will, my people will stand against God and yes stand against me.

No one will remember the song by the rivers of Babylon.

Our forefathers did cry

They did weep

They had to endure many hardships

They had to endure slavery but with all that they endured none of us will listen. We will continue to displease and go on doing our own thing.

Yes it's sad but what can I do.

God is not there to rob anyone of their soul. All God is saying separate from evil and live a clean life.

Do not do the will of evil.

You have a choice so chose right and live right.

Like I've told God this time around once you have given everyone the truth if they don't accept it walk away. Leave humanity alone and let us suffer our own faiths because we did not choose him we chose death over him.

We cannot hold God hostage anymore by giving him unclean food to eat.

Tell me would you knowingly give your children dirty water to drink and rotten meat to eat?

None of you would but yet we give this to God each time we pray. We do not have a conscience when it comes to God. We don't care but yet say we care.

Tell me how many of you go to evil to get a job?

Tell me how many of you burn incense in your office?

How many of you spray your office with those stinking oils in the workplace to keep your jobs?

How many of you rub yourselves up with oil a get job

Oil a keep job

Oil a fire the boss so I can have his position

Oil a stay in job

Dear God some of those offices are so stink of witchcraft that a child of God can never stay in the workplace.

Dear God some of these people rub these oils over themselves and no matter how the boss tries to fire them they cannot. Trust me some of these bosses get fired themselves.

Tell me with all that we do how can our environment be clean.

How can any of us say we have God knowing that we are filthy and unclean?

You cannot rob another man of his land and say it is yours it is not right.

You cannot murder another man and take his land and say it is yours it is not right.

You cannot go into another man's land and say it is yours when you know fully it is not yours.

What God has given to his people you cannot destroy it nor can you destroy them and change the record books to include you. You have your own history use it. Don't take mine and claim it as yours because you know it is not yours. This is wrong.

God is not a thief and the children of God are not thieves so why are you in our lands stealing what rightfully belongs to us?

This is what God has given to us and not you. You have no right to it nor do you have any claim to it. We do not go into your homelands and steal your land because we know it's not right so why are you stealing ours.

Why are you fighting us for our own?

Right is right and wrong is wrong and no one can do wrong and get right in the sight of God not even his messengers. Not even me.

Do not take the name of God and shorten it and say God is Allah when you know God is Allelujah. You all hate Jews so much leave our God alone he is not yours he is ours. Do not shorten his name to suit you. God's children are the only one to do so and God does not tell us to do it.

How the fuck can you hate us when you know Allah is not yours but ours. You can't even cry out Allelujah but you want to say Allah. Come on now be real. You don't represent God nor can you represent God because evil resides in all of you.

Like I've said Mr. Muslim man I don't hate you I truly love you but trust me I refuse to have anyone class me and take my God and heritage away from me.

You know nothing of God because if you did Islam would not be in turmoil. It would not be an abomination unto the true Jews. Nor would it be an abomination unto God.

Let me educate you and the world a little bit more. The female angels or guides whichever word you want to use do not wear face veils. None of God's angels hide their face. Evil hides hence when evil kills evil run and hide just like Cain. When a man commit sin – murder or even steal they run and hide and tell lies to get a Bly. God's angels dress appropriate but none wear a face veil. When you wear a face veil it means you are hiding something, and this is what Abraham taught. He was hiding his own sister from other men because he knew the wrong he committed. He was hiding his shame and disgrace. It was not because she was beautiful he hid her. He married his own sister was banging her. He committed incest his entire family practiced incest and this is how incest came about. Incest is a known practice in his circle, the Nodite lifestyle and it is so until this day. He was a pagan and he did things the Pagan-Babylonian way. No Christian, No Jew, No Muslim no one on the face of the earth can say this is a lie because the bible that you so hold holy and clean tells you this. It is in there.

This is what we learnt. We learnt that nastiness like this is condoned by God because it is condoned in the bible but it is not okay. And yes this is why we think that it is okay to marry cousins, brothers and sisters. It does not matter the gene pool meaning if you have the same mother but different father. The blood is strong and this I learnt recently. You cannot be a quarter or half of anything because blood is blood and it does run through our veins.

Yes he married an Egyptian but it does not mean Hagar was black. Egypt had to be conquered just like Ethiopia like I've told you.

Ethiopia, man no one knows the truth of Ethiopia well read the bible and see why they fell from grace trust me not even they the Ethiopians know about their true history.

Africans you don't know because you have walked away from the truth to accept the Pagan way of life.

When I say Africans you are included in this white people because your ass is black but refuse to admit it. Do not look at it from a physical standpoint look at it from a spiritual standpoint.

Trust me infinitely God cannot hate you based on color of skin he would be wrong

God cannot judge you based on the color of skin he would be wrong and infinitely remember I tell you this GOD DOES NOT JUDGE ANYONE.

What did I say?

I said God does not judge anyone

We all have WILL meaning we have a choice to choose good or evil.

Good lives on forever

Evil dies

Also remember I tell you this and will forever tell you this NO ONE CAN SPEAK FOR GOD BECAUSE GOD CAN AND DOES SPEAK FOR HIMSELF.

Come on now. God is not mute he can speak so tell me humanity why are you speaking for God?

Why are we speaking for God?

Did God tell any of you to speak for him?

Did God tell any of you to act on his behalf?

No I am no exception to the rule. God told me to write a book and he has shown me certain things and it is those certain things he has shown me that I am writing about.

I cannot come to you with lies because God never gave me lies to tell you nor did he give me lies to write.

Yes the way I write may sound racist in the undertone but by no means do I intend it to be and this is why I am depending on God to shield you from any racial or racist undertone.

Like I said I am just putting this man in his place and telling him about his history and mine.

God did not tell me to write hate and if I sound hateful I truly and wholeheartedly apologize because God does not hate anyone but he can hate you for your sins and lies.

Listen to what I said ***he can*** hate you for your sins and lies. I did not say he hates I said he can.

A Jew cannot say God favors them over you because I am Jewish. He cannot say that because not all Jews are Jews and refer to Revelations.

I cannot say well God favors blacks over whites because not all blacks are black and not all whites are white meaning some whites are black and some blacks are white and this go by their spiritual accord.

So black people when some blacks say they are not blacks but white leave them the hell alone. They are just telling you that they are of the spiritually wicked.

When some whites say they are black leave them alone because they are of the spiritual GOOD. They too are a child of God meaning they do good in the sight of God and they fall under God's banner because they too are the children of God. God's people.

To hate any race on the face of this planet is to hate self because we are all made up of good and evil and the representation of this is the Ying and the Yang yes black and white. For some it is Blue and White the Blue and the White Nile the land of good and evil to put it perfectly. Yes the Blue and White that the Jews use and yes the blond and blue eyed white people. Yes the blue eyed black people, no, not them because some their eye colour changes after birth so no not them.

Tell me something people God gave everything life and he God is life but yet he was born in the living as a man. How do I put this – he was born in a manger a stable with all the animals. Come on now people think no wonder humanity say black people come from animals.

Come on we put God so low that it is beyond me. This is God you people are saying and you are telling him God that he is no better than an animal. He belongs with the animals because his son and for some he God is nothing but an animal because he was born amongst animals in a stable. Man I can't remember the story where animals raised a child and a woman bruk him out. But the story of Jesus draws from this. I want to say the Melchesidic or Melchezidic but I cannot.

Tell me who among you were born in a barn or a manger – stable with the animals.

Jesus was his son and he made him be born in a manger wow God really hated his son didn't he?

Everything that is associated with lies and hate you make God out to be but everything that is associated with good you make them prophets - holy.

When did God become the liar and the hated?

I am going to ask this again.

When did God ever lie or told a lies on you?

Look at your life and history and tell me what lies did God ever tell on you or your ancestors?

Name one lie that God has ever told you or on you?

So why are you lying and telling lies on God?

Yes we want God to be this this and this but God cannot be who he isn't. God cannot be a liar, he can only be the truth and this is why I say live for God meaning live in God's truth and live. Live for Life.

Live by the honesty and truth of God. That which is true love – truth.

Every race on the face of this planet can live with God but none of us can live with God if we lie to each other and kill each other.

No Jew can say they are going to go to heaven and live with God because they are Jewish and is entitled to God. None can say this because being Jewish cannot get you in. You have to be clean and truthful. You cannot base your life on lies nor can you live in lies.

Yes once upon a time we were entitled to God's kingdom but not anymore because we followed unto sin and did everything that was sinful and abominable in the sight of God and we lost this right.

We gave away our rights to the Pagans and this is why we were enslaved. We too sold our own into slavery. We too have blood on our hands.

As children of God we have forgotten that we are married to God meaning we have a bond with God. Man we have forgotten how beautiful and wonderful this bond is. It is so perfect and pure that you do not want to let go of that goodness.

With God you are special. I can't even describe it because the feeling inside of you want to escape and touch God himself but it is trapped. Your spirit is dying to escape this trap but can't.

This energy goes up to the centre of your head and if you are not careful you get this massive headache.

Yes it's hard to describe and this is way I say sometimes I need someone to touch me and feel that energy – that goodness flowing through me. This feeling is so beautiful that you don't want it to end you want it to say every second of the day with you for all eternity. It is that beautiful and loving.

So for all that say I am spiteful and hateful I will not change you nor do I want to change you. No one not even God can change you.

Let's put it this way God cannot and will never change evil. If he did he would be going against Will, the Ying and the Yang, he would be going against his laws of creation.

You as a person must want change meaning you must want and need positive changes for you and you must live by your goodness, your truth which is the truth of God.

No man can tell you what God's abode looks like not even me.

Know that God's abode is not heaven.

Remember good is God and evil is Nod. Now put it together on your own because you now have knowledge of the garden of Eden.

If you can't use the Blue and White Nile

No

Use heaven and hell

Psalms 1 then people

Heaven and hell is side by side and good must separate from evil. This is how it was in the beginning and this is how it must be in the end. Now you can figure out Genesis and know for a fact and this is infinitely true God did not I repeat God did not put enmity between His seed and Satan's seed. Enmity was always there because the two races were separated. Just as heaven and hell is separated so were God's people separated from evil's people.

Yes God told Eve not to lay with the man outside the garden not because he was of a different race or colour to put it in human or physical context for you to comprehend but because he was not clean. He was not a good person and all that God showed Eve she did not comprehend. She did not listen she was stubborn as a mule and this is why the bible call us stiff necked. It means we do not listen we want to do our own thing even when it causes us pain and heartache.

Eve did not listen and it cost us and it is still costing us because when God speaks no one listens. No one wants to listen and when we end up in the gutter meaning feeling so much pain and heartache we cry to him.

How dare the lot of you. You walk in abominations of sin and say it is of God.

You the Jews were the ones to turn from God and sold your own and you have the gaul to say your race is holy. What makes you holy?

Did the bible not say the children of Israel – all the children of Israel were destroyed, so if they were destroyed why are you claiming to be Jewish,

Israelite? None of you are Jewish then so stop claiming to be because this is what the bible says and this is what many believe.

Like I said you sold out God and destroyed the tribe of Israel so what tribe are you all from? Tell me what tribe are you all from and do not bring Ishmael and Isaac into this nor bring Abraham into this because none belong to the tribe of Israel. You know they belong to the land of Nod meaning they are of that bloodline.

You have caused your own as well as other nations to commit abominable acts of sin unto God so tell me how are you the Jewish nations going to pay?

How are you going to get to God's abode?

Tell the world the truth. You sold your own people out and then lied about it. Enough is enough. Herald you claim killed all the male children of Israel because he feared the King of the Jews would rise them up but what Herald did not know nor did you know was that it was not the males that would bring back the truth to God's people it was the females. Just as I saw them in my vision and just as I saw them in heaven. The brides of heaven are females therefore the children of God are females in the spiritual realm and the physical realm. Goodness cannot change and will never change in either realm.

Females are the spiritual leaders – they are the chosen ones but the earth does not know this. Satan knew this and this is why he deceived Eve. He had to produce a child with her and he did. Herald did not know that God's lineage passed through the females hence he killed the males. He killed the wrong people.

You say and others say the children of Israel is no more but God would not let his own die that is why they are scattered in different lands. You tried to kill all the blacks but God one upped all of you. HE TOOK THE RIGHT FEMALE OUT OF YOUR CLUTCHES and that is why you say and put it in your book of lies that all the children of Israel were wiped off the face of the planet. ***I know it's a lie and you know it's a lie. God cannot kill that which he loves and adore.*** Many of you accept Islam and this is why you have the interlocking triangles. Look at my flag do you see an interlocking triangle. We do not disrespect God in that way. We honor him. We know the importance of life meaning God's true people know the importance of life. We show God the respect and honor he deserves by separating from evil.

Look at the colors of your flag it represents death on one level. You married death to life and this is part and parcel why Islam wants to marry you as well as why I had the vision. Some of you are married to death but yet say otherwise.

Tell me do you truly think you are hurting God? None of you are hurting God because you are the ones to die.

Tell me how the hell can you say God is dead and God has died when you tell the world each and every day that GOD IS REAL. LOOK AT THE NAME OF YOUR COUNTRY. Yes you say Israel

move the a and put the e there. Stop telling people God is dead in your books of the dead and evil because your name say otherwise.

Tell me something Isreal when you go into Ethiopia and take out black people and bring them back to Isreal and say they are black Jews what does that prove?

Tell me because I am yelling.

Tell me.

Fuck the lot of you that's all I have to say because none of you are a Jew. Fuck ya, fuck ya, fuck ya and any black person that come up to me and say I am racist fuck the lot of you and know your mother fucking history.

Ethiopia had to be conquered like I've stated. Yes Ethiopia was a blessed land and trust me they are hated by God because like the Jews they committed abominable acts of sin in the eyes of God. I say hate because this is the best word I can find. No displeased is better. God is displeased with them.

Moses respected God when God told him to take off his shoes because the ground he was standing on was holy ground but the Ethiopians didn't. They also mixed their seed with the people of Nod. You the Greeks need to start telling the truth because you know who the horse Pegasus represent. What race of people Pegasus represents so start telling the truth or I will do it for you and trust me you will not like the way I do. You cannot hide the truth anymore so come infinitely clean because Pegasus represented a specific race of people. You have the truth as well as know the truth but refuse to disclose it. Come on now do better and maybe your land could recover.

All of you telling a pack of lies and none of you know the truth nor the significance of the MOON.

Isreal what are you trying to prove? Did God tell you to go to Ethiopia and take the people out of the land and bring them to Isreal? Did God tell you to do it? Yes I am yelling.

You are not proving anything and by doing this you are wrong because you of yourself know that they are not of the tribe of Isreal. They are not Jewish. They have no right to Isreal. So why are you taking non Jews into Jewish land?

Are you going to train them in the ways of Mutayahu?

Bitch you can't train them because they are just like you. Pagans that have displeased God to the point where they are known in the spiritual realm for the grave wrong they did.

No one wants to be like them because they were the first nation to disgrace and disrespect God hence like I've said they are mentioned in the book of sin and at the very beginning too.

God's children have a name but none of you know it and it is not all that have the name can say they are of God because the land you are born in plays an important role and none of you look at me because ***the one to save the world must be clean meaning she must live a clean and pure life.*** You the true Jews know this. You cannot walk in the ways of sin and say you are of God.

You cannot accept false teachings and beliefs and say it is of God.

Stop interlocking the triangles because you know the triangles represent life and death and by you interlocking it you are telling God that you are married to death and have accepted death. Heaven and Hell, good and evil is side by side this is the way it was and this is the way it must be in the end. Good must separate from evil and by you interlocking the triangle in your flag you are telling God you do not want to separate or leave evil. You are telling God you are fine with what Eve did. Eve married Evil and you know this. God showed her what her life would be like and she did not listen she forged ahead because she loved him. She did not truly love God nor did she respect God because if she did she would have listen. She would not have accepted the offerings of sin. She loved Satan more than God hence she gave up her life for him. She had children for him.

You know that God's people could not die. Evil is the one to die. Good could never die they lived forever because God did tell Eve the day you eat the fruit according to the bible you will die and she did die. She did not listen to God. She allowed evil in because God was trying to protect her. Much the same today. God is trying to protect his people but his people are telling him they don't want him nor are they going to listen to him.

Each and every one of you have sinned including me but the beauty of being blessed by God is knowing that he does forgive.

There are no sin offerings there is just a wall a shame. This is what I call it. I call it the wall of shame and disgrace and no it is not the wailing wall.

I will not remind you of the cutting of the hair because this is our shame and disgrace. The cutting of hair is not significant in death it is significant in the living it is our sin and shame. When you cut your hair you are admitting shame and disgrace in the eyes of God because we have committed abominable acts of sin unto God.

Cutting our hair is one of the hardest things to do for a true Jew but we must do it. This is our sin offering. Shedding of blood is not God's way. Sacrificing animals and humans is the pagan's way but the true Jewish way is the cutting of the hair. You know this. Trust me this is so hard to do but it must be done.

Like I said every Jew on the face of this planet can hate me. You can kill me even set me up to kill me but the flesh means nothing in the end.

I will repeat like Bob Marley said you can kill us but we will keep resurfacing.

You can kill the flesh but you cannot kill the spirit. None of you can kill the spirit trust me I know how the spirit/soul dies and none of you can kill it not even God and yes God knows what I mean when I say not even him and I am going off what he has shown me in the spiritual.

Like I said we pick up evil ways and say it is of God when we know it is not. Tell me something how many of you use the Psalms to work black magic, voodoo, witchcraft and many other abominable acts of sin?

You want to get a man use Psalms so and so burn this candle, write the person's name on parchment paper and wear this. Come on is this of God. I've seen the books and read them so I know. Like I've said we've all walked in the ways of sin and I am no exception because I too have walked in the ways of sin and trust me I did learn. I know what evil can and will do to stay alive in man but man refuse to listen to God.

We live for the flesh but none live for the spirit/soul. None of us live to live we all live to die and that's the sad part of life.
None of us on the face of this planet can say we live for life because we have all accepted death in one way or the other.

All of you can petition to ban my books but none of you can ban God because whether you learn the truth in earth or in the grave you will know the truth somehow because there is no belief in God's world only knowledge. I've told you it is better to know the truth in the living rather than in the grave. In the living you can change your way of doing things but in the grave you cannot. There is no repeats and this is why I say if you are for God be for God and if you are for evil be for evil. You

cannot have or be both. Your bible also tells you this. If you are for evil stay being for evil, if you are for good stay doing good.

Evil kills but life lives and it is up to you to live a good life so that your spirit/soul can move on to a better and higher life. If you do not live a good and clean life in the physical your spirit/soul cannot move forward in life.

I will tell everyone if God is protecting you let him continue to protect you. What you cannot see he God sees because he is further ahead in time.

If God say Brian your house is dirty clean your house. Clean every corner every room in that house including you. Yes you. You as a person are a part of that house. Trust me clean the outside too. Yes clean your thoughts too.

How do you clean yourself – bathing and drinking more water and thinking of God in a positive way. No do not go down on your knees and pray. I know some of you truly love this form of prayer and if this is what you truly love tell God. Say God this is how I truly love to communicate with you by going on my knee. Trust me infinitely God will not hold it against you but make sure the spot you chose is clean and yes you can buy a cushion and use it to kneel on. Make sure that cushion is designated for prayer only and do not use it for sex. In many ways going on your keys is a way of shame and disgrace meaning going on your keys and bowing down to the filth in the ground is your shame. You are saying you accept the filth of the earth and you are like the filth of the earth – the dead. You are saying you are everything that is disgusting and abominable.

If you dedicate an area for God let it be for God. Respect, respect, respect !!!!!!!!!!!!!!!!!!!!!!!!!

If you think I am hateful and racist go to God and say God this racist so and so and yes you can call me a nigger hey you can call me the anti-christ too because this is how you feel. Tell God this is the way you feel every negative word in the book if this is the way you feel about me call me those name and tell God this is the way you feel. God cannot hold you guilty nor can he charge you for sin because you did go to him truthfully and tell him this is the way you truly feel about me.

Where this becomes wrong is when you want to pick up arms against the person. This is wrong because God does not pick up arms against you.

I will not hate you based on race – fuck that because we are all made the same way.

We were all given a choice including evil and it is us to disrespect and hate each other.

Trust me the time spend hating you is time spent hating God and I refuse to hate anyone but don't tell lies on me or on my race or you will feel the wrong side of me and I don't care who you are.

Trust me do not tell lies on God because when I am through you will hold your head down in shame and disgrace. I will too because I will use languages worse than the ones I've used above. When it comes to me and God don't mess around.

If you don't want God stay the hell away from him. Don't pray to him or use his name.

Don't tell me God favors one race over the next when it is he who created all the races – everything. Yes people I know the environment plays a factor in the different races but guess what everything is in our genes.

Like I've told you there are no sections in heaven nor are there sections in God's abode for this religion and that religion.

There is no section in heaven or in God's abode for this race and that race. No this is incorrect because I did see 3 races on the mountain so this statement is incorrect.

Anyone that says they hate based on color of skin cannot and will never get into heaven or God's abode.

No man woman or child and yes no spirit can get you into heaven or God's abode. You are the only one that can get yourself in and that is through the goodness that you do upon the face of the earth as well as within earth.

Forget it to those that are now going to say I am going to do all the good that I can to get into heaven. Trust me you will never get in. The goodness that you do must be truthful and honest. You cannot do to get, you have to do because it is truthfully in you to do. Do good without wanting anything in return this is what God is looking for. You already know that goodness begets blessings from God so don't do to get, do for the true love of you and God. Let's hope I explained that right.

Also giving does not have to do with materialistic giving. Suppose your next door neighbor is out of a job and you know this. You get the paper everyday cut jobs out of the classified and give it to him that is your blessing because you see his or her need and you are trying to help them.

You're always complaining that you don't have time for yourself. Grandma is willing to take the kids send them to grandma's house for a couple of hours and don't take advantage or disadvantage of Grandma.

Grandma is in a nursing home well let them spend time in the nursing home with grandma for a couple of hours.

Grandma eats certain foods and you don't so tell grandma

Grandma is a evil person she practices witchcraft. No don't send your child to grandma's house. Evil is evil and it is not condoned. Keep your children away from evil.

Their father and I are separated and he's a wicked man. Keep your children with you do not bring them into an evil environment because evil pulls. Trust me infinitely evil pulls.

Evil will look innocent and good to you and sometimes not even a good person can tell so in this case rely on God to show you and this is why I say know your colors in the spiritual realm because God shows you evil in their colour. This is significant. No it is not the colour of skin but the colour that they wear and how it is being used because good wear full white but it is how you see the person and what you see on the person. This is extremely hard to explain. Basically know your colors because like I said it is vital to your existence on earth and significant infinitely significant in the spiritual realm.

Like I've told you all of humanity renewable energy is the way to go. Listen to God and start using more renewable energy.

There is so much that we can do to save us and our future. Listen to what God is telling you because God knows about tomorrow you don't.

Don't listen to others and follow hate or sin. Listen to God.

Live for life and live. Do not live for death and die because life was what was given to all of us. We are the ones to pollute it and not God. So live for life.

Yes everyone can hate me and want to kill me because of what I have said but at the end of the day your soul is yours. I do not have a right to take it or cause you to sin meaning kill to maintain it. No one can sin and maintain his or her soul. You are going to die.

Life is what maintains humanity and all the universes so like I said we have to live for life and we must live life clean and be clean.

I cannot tell you how to live your life only God can and he does tell you how to. It is up to you to listen because no one can go to God with hate. Trust me he will just shut you down meaning turn from you.

No race including the Jews can say this race enslaved us and they were wrong.

If you do not let the devil in the devil cannot harm you nor will he be able to get in.

I repeat if you do not let the devil in the devil cannot harm you nor will he be able to get in.

Evil cannot come into your home just like that. I don't know if you have ever watched some of the old vampire movies. There is one in particular that showed you the true Dracula. He could not go into the woman's house. He had to stand at the door. I can't remember the movie fully but he said he could not come in because she did not invite him in. I cannot quote the movie word for word but it was something along these lines he said. This is evil. If you do not invite evil into your abode evil cannot come into your abode.

Bombs and ammunition you say. Well you are not listening to me nor are you hearing what I said. I said if you do not invite evil into your abode evil cannot come into your abode. It does not matter if the country has amassed infinite weapons of mass destruction they cannot use it against you. All that they try to do to you will befall them. They will never be able to hurt you. Never and do not bring the garden of Eden into this because Eve did let evil in she refused God meaning she did not listen to him and she allowed evil in this is why evil was able to infiltrate the garden and lead everyone astray. Yes it only takes one this is why unity has been echoed throughout the centuries. If you do not have unity meaning if everyone is not living under one accord meaning the same banner evil can and will get in because there is no unity and yes this is why we have many branches in religion. There is no unity only disloyalty and disunity.

We are the ones to allow the devil to get in. We are the ones to displease God by going against God so what God has done is that he has given you over to what you want. He has lift his hand of protection from you so now you have to live with the consequences.

If God said Rabbi Stein Michelle is evil do not go to her home don't go to her home. Never go to her home and never send your children there. If they ask why tell them the truth that she is evil. She practices the way of the Pagan, she does things that is not of the true and living God which is Allelujah – God – Jah.

Don't just say don't go to the person house tell them the reason why. If you can show that child our evils or evil then show them. This is how we learn. God did show Eve but even with God showing her she still did not listen and the reason for this is that she did not truly love God. If you truly love God you cannot hurt God meaning you do not want to do things to displease him.

This is why I keep saying a person that truly loves another cannot hurt them because all that he or she does it is done in truth and honesty.

Like I said I truly love God but I will not use guns and ammunition against you. My truth, the truth that God has given me is my guns and ammunition.

I do not live to please man I live to please me and God. I cannot just live for God I also have to live for me and by me doing so I am living for God.

My ways are not fully straight because I still make mistakes but I refuse to covert to anyone's religion and say this is of God when I know it is not of God.

God never told any of us to convert to anything so why are we doing it? You know that conversion is a sin, so don't convert to anything. I did not know but now I know and have since asked God forgiveness. You must ask God for forgiveness of this sin.

God never said he is a religion so why are we bringing religion in the realm of God.

If you have devoted a sanctuary to God let it be about God and for God. Show and give God the respect. Take off your shoes and take idols out of the church. Take pictures of men out of the church because God is both male and female. He is the energy- life in everything.

Beautify your church with flowers and water and make it serene and peaceful. None of us know the beauty of God not even me and trust me God is that beautiful and more.

Respect God. Talk about life and what God wants. Yes you have man's book of lies and it is not God's book. Use it to teach people what not to be like if you want but you are duly warned. Because it is the book of sin it is unlawful. Never stray from God or stray from the truth. Tell them the truth about God , the pure and good love that God has for his children – people.

Tell them the truth that God does not kill nor does he steal.

Tell them that God would not send them into another man's land to kill them.

All those things of the bible is what evil does.

Evil kill and imprison and when we sin we are killing ourselves.

We sinned and this is why our spirit/soul is trapped in this body. I don't know how to explain it to you but as you move along meaning as you become true and honest with God you will know what I am talking about. At times your spirit/soul will want to escape and leave the body behind because to the spirit the body is a prison and it is a prison meaning your spirit is not free to roam freely and connect to God and your guides.

Know that the sin and evil that we do makes us grow old and wrinkly but life never grows old nor can it grow old.

The wrinkles of your skin have nothing to do with God it has to do with sin and the harmful chemicals we put in the environment.

Like I've said God is not partial nor is God a lie. We need to fix ourselves before we can fix others and if that person does not want to fix himself leave them alone. You live for God because when it is all said and done you have to account for your own soul – your own sins.

I cannot comprehend how any person can say they love God but yet turn around and hate him. I am not saying this to put anyone down because I never belonged to any religion. Trust me I never fit in and all I saw disgusted me until this day.

I cannot for the life of me comprehend a person that say they are of God but yet massacre another person – murder them.

Someone explain to me why are we fighting to get to hell because it's not heaven you're going to go to.

Did God tell any of you to fight for heaven?

Did God say fight for my abode and the winner gets in?

Blood is on your hands people you will never get in and no amount of penance or sin offering or animal sacrifices will get you into God's abode.

Yes repentance of sin is there but how many of us can repent of your sins or even know what repentance of sin is.

Remember not every Jew is a Jew and it is not all Jew reside with God because they too have sold God out for dirty pieces of silver and trust me hell is waiting for a lot of them unless they repent.

God has laws that we have to adhere to and if we constantly break those laws there are no forgiveness. We will not be forgiven no matter how much good we do. You need to tell the people this because this is the truth.

Yes God is merciful but it is not every sin that God forgives. If you blatantly go against the Ying and the Yang which is life and dead there is absolutely no forgiveness for this. Come clean and tell the people the truth because as it is man is dead meaning we are purposely going against God and all of humanity is going to go to hell.

Evil causes man to die and not God

Evil is the one to pit humanity against humanity and not God. No one on the face of the planet can say God has not tried to protect man because God has been doing it from the conception of time meaning when man knew about time.

Evil does not care about life and he will tell you anything for you to displease God and he is doing it because many of us think and even say God kills which is wrong and to say this you are lying on God and this is why I ask what lies or lie has God ever told on any of you so why do it to God. We left God and we were the ones to stop holding his hand. We told him we could chose for ourselves so in doing this we should not seek his help. We should not ask him for anything. We should be able to maintain and sustain ourselves without his help.

We are the ones to tell God that he is nothing but shit. We are the ones to tell God that he is garbage and all he deserves to eat and drink is piss and shit and no one on the face of the planet can dispute this. Anyone of you dispute this I can say you are a damned liar and you all should burn in hell because all I have to do is point on the shoes on your feet in temples – shrines, synagogues and churches dedicated unto God.

Muslims you are excluded because I know you take off your shoes. At least you give your God respect in this term and I will not be hypocritical in this term. I have to give you credit where credit is do. You respect your God in your holy temples all other religions don't. And people Buddhism is not a religion in my eyes because of certain characteristics and I will not get into it. At the end of the day God deserves respect and our true love. We cannot say God is compassionate when we of ourselves are not compassionate nor do we represent God on any level.

There are rules that we need to adhere to just like God and like I've said God cannot change himself to please any religion or anyone. This universe as well as humanity – man were created on the fundamental laws of the Ying and the Yang and they must be adhered to by everyone. As humans we change to please ourselves but we do not look at the implications or the cost of our changes. Each change that we make has a negative impact on the universe and time itself. For example, the more we drain the earth it's the quicker we die.

The more chemicals we put in the air as well as our food chain is the more we die, animals die, the trees and air we breathe die.

The more we bask and commit sin is the more we die meaning the quicker we die and the further time moves away from us causing us to die – die in time.

Like I said everyone knows the wages of sin is death so why are we living for death. We are we not living for life. Evil has a job to do and it is going to do it until it's time is up when he evil must die at his own hands.

Evil does not care who he kill or who he hurts this is his job and he has to be true to it. He has to be true to death because he is death.

He will give you everything but in the end he will take it all and he does take it all because we were the ones to give him that right. We gave evil access so if he has to make his lie look like the truth to get to you, evil will do so and that is what he is doing. In all that evil does like I've said evil must stay true to death. Evil must stay true to himself. God did tell us about evil and what evil do but like I've said we are the ones that are not listening.

Each individual have a birth and death certificate. Everything in life has a birth certificate but not everything or everyone has a death certificate. Like I've said as humans what we do affect life and it is our actions that cause the environment, animals, the air we breathe, the universe itself to die. Put it this way for every negative reaction there is a negative effect. Sometimes we don't see it until years even centuries later.

As living beings we affect life whether in a good or bad way but the one thing we cannot do is go against the Ying and the Yang which is life.

I've told you certain sins God does not forgive and will never forgive no matter the goodness that you do. This is automatic death and one such sin is knowingly changing you.

I am telling you this and know this. Anyone that willingly changes themselves there is no remission of sin nor is there any repentance for this. You are a walking abomination unto God meaning you are worse than Satan – evil in the eyes of God. You will never be forgiven by God because you are looked upon as being lower than Satan himself.

Anyone that goes against life, consider yourself dead in the eyes of God because you have not life in the eyes of God. This is one act like I said that is not forgiven. You are willingly doing something wrong by saying you are someone else when you know that you are the same person. You cannot lie to people like this. This is infinitely wrong.

What you are saying is that God made a mistake with you and God makes not mistakes. God cannot make mistakes because his law is right and just – good. God made everything good but it is us humans that gave sin life and this did not start with Adam and Eve it started long before this.

Remember heaven and hell is side by side. It was side by side on earth but one gave Satan an all access pass to destroy.

As parents we cannot say we are going to leave our children's birth certificate blank and let them choose. A child sex was chosen by you and your mate and this is how it must stay until their appointed time on the face of the planet.

A man cannot change his sex and become a female he is still a male and any law that say otherwise is going against God and is committing a carnal and grave sin. No law can change God's laws because the laws of God is absolute and you cannot change your birth certificate to say transgender nor can you change your birth certificate to reflect female this is infinitely wrong.

A woman that changes her sex to male is still a female and the above law still applies. She cannot change her birth certificate to say male or transgender. This is infinitely wrong.

There is no forgiveness for this sin. You are a male and she is a female. You cannot go against God to suit your pleasures. It is sinful and wrong.

You cannot alter your body and say God is going to bless you because he will not. It is not to say if you are in an accident and you need reconstructive face surgery God will be against you he will not be because he sees the need. He is compassionate I am talking about those that blatantly change their sex to please themselves. This is not of God and it is wrong and trust me infinitely when I tell you God does not condone this. Any law and/or practice that condone this is against God and goes beyond disrespecting God. This is beyond sinful and when God gives me the right word to tell you what he calls this I will let you know because sinful is mild compared to the real word that I am to use.

No one not even evil can go against the laws outlined by God and anyone that say evil does not call and cry out to God think again. Need I remind you of Allelujah. Good and evil must cry out to Allelujah – yes to All.

Like I've said it does not matter if you don't like me at the end of the day as long as God truly loves me that is all I care about. I have to care about my soul and where it ends up. If you don't want to preserve your soul that is your business because despite what I write no one can say they did not know. We all know we've just turned a blind eye to it. We cannot say God this this and this because you did have your book of lies to show you what you should not become or be. Your book of lies well ¼ lies did tell you some truth.

I will repeat no one can save you but you. I cannot save you because I am not her. God told me to do something and I have to do what he told me to do no matter how harsh my spirit gets. Once God has given me truthful people to teach my job will be to maintain and sustain those people to the best of my ability with the true help and grace of God himself. I am also depending on God to maintain and sustain those people and not let them go because he God is more than important to you and me. He is life and I do want and need to live for life. I need and want all of humanity to live for life. In all honesty I need every one to live a good peaceful and honest life with God. I don't want anyone to die I want and need all of humanity to live but it's not all of us that can live and that is the disheartening and hurtful part.

Everyone need to know the truth. For those of you that have sold your soul know this too there is no repentance for you. Once your soul is gone it is gone you cannot get it back. There are no givesy backsey when it comes to the devil and God. Once you have sold your soul to the devil he has you. You willingly gave Satan or the devil all rights to your life. And Christians stop saying God is a compassionate God he has mercy on everyone because God does not have mercy on everyone. Like I've told you not everyone belongs to God. Just as God has his race of people the devil has his and good and evil was separated long before man walked the earth. Man was the one to join with sin and do all that is sinful in the eyes of God.

I am going to tell you again a person that truly loves cannot hurt nor can they deceive.

I will state this until the day my breath leaves my body and I will repeat it like a broken record. Anyone can say they love but it is not many that can say they truly love you. True love cannot rob you of anything. True love cannot take another man's life. True love is humble and peaceful. True love is honest and kind. It is the truth, it is true love. True love is God because God does protect the good and the bad meaning he does not kill and you know this because good and evil breathe air, drink water, eat food and so much more. This is God and we do not know the extent of his mercy and love. Listen I don't want evil to go to hell but it is a choice evil and wicked people have and has made. It is their choice so they have to die because the wages of sin is death. There is no getting around this. Like I've said we have to live clean and do things that is right in the sight of God. God does not stop anyone from making money or living a lavish lifestyle but do it clean and honest. Be true to you and the planet that he has given to you. If you cut down a tree plant another one or two in its place. If you cut down the forest replant the trees that you cut down because the trees help to clean the air we breathe and it also help with generating water for us to drink.

We are all everyone's keeper and if we cannot be good keepers here on earth how are we going to be good keepers with God.

If we cannot keep ourselves and the earth clean how can we keep God's abode clean?

How can we keep God clean?

Like I've said if the head is dirty how can the body be clean?

So, if you are dirty how can you or anyone say that they are going to reside and live with God?

God does not deal in sin, evil does. Evil and wicked people deal in sin and for anyone to say they are going to God's abode and do evil and wicked acts you are fooling yourself because you will never get in.

God don't deal in stink. God infinitely deal in clean so clean yourself up and live.

Like I said and will repeat again and again, the life you live in the physical determines where you go in the spiritual so live for life and not live for death.

Satan infinitely does not care about you because at the end of the day Satan will go down in flames with his children – people.

You alone can make the right decision. I can only write, I cannot make the choice for you. Not even God can, because like I said if he did he would be committing sin and going against the Ying and the Yang.

Michelle

Other Books by Michelle J. Lyons

Jamaican Tsunami

Bodaciously You

Blind Obsession

A Thin Line Between Love and Hate

The Dark Side of Love

A Collection of Three Book – Book One

A Little Talk With God

Coming Soon

Between Heaven and Hell
Prince and Sable